A BRIEF HISTORY OF
GOD'S LOVE

Also by Jack J. Blanco

The Clear Word

Savior: Four Gospels, One Story

Visions and Dreams

Witness

Chosen

Warriors

Rulers

Survivors

The Devotional Clear Word

Words to Live By

A BRIEF HISTORY OF GOD'S LOVE

FROM EDEN LOST TO EDEN RESTORED

JACK BLANCO

Pacific Press® Publishing Association

Nampa, Idaho | www.pacificpress.com

Cover design by Gerald Monks
Cover design resources from Galaxy: iStockphoto | alex-mit; Earth: iStockphoto | loops7
Inside design by Aaron Troia
Edited by Alicia Adams

Copyright © 2019 by Pacific Press® Publishing Association
Printed in the United States of America
All rights reserved

The author assumes full responsibility for the accuracy of all facts and quotations as cited in this book.

Unless otherwise noted, all Scripture quotations are paraphrased by the author.

Scripture quotations marked ASV are from the American Standard Version.

Additional copies of this book may be purchased by calling toll-free 1-800-765-6955 or by visiting AdventistBookCenter.com.

Library of Congress Cataloging-in-Publication Data

Names: Blanco, Jack J., 1929- author.
Title: A brief history of God's love : from Eden lost to Eden restored / Jack J. Blanco.
Description: Nampa : Pacific Press Publishing Association, 2019.
Identifiers: LCCN 2018052361 | ISBN 9780816364787 (pbk. : alk. paper)
Subjects: LCSH: God (Christianity)—Love—Biblical teaching.
Classification: LCC BT140 .B53 2019 | DDC 220.9—dc23 LC record available at https://lccn.loc.gov/2018052361

May 2019

Contents

Preface	7
The Patriarchs	8
The Kings	62
The Savior	102
The Disciples	170
The Great War	212

Preface

As a religion professor, I regularly witnessed young people struggling with hectic schedules. I also saw working adults, especially those with children, who were no less harried. They often did not have enough time for adequate rest or nutritious meals. How in the world could they possibly squeeze in leisure reading, especially works as long and thoughtful as *The Desire of Ages* or *The Great Controversy*? Yet these magnificent books by Ellen G. White contain profound spiritual messages that benefit and transform the daily lives of young and old alike.

To make sure readers clearly see the full picture of God's great love for us, I decided to take the key thoughts from each chapter of White's Conflict of the Ages series, paraphrase them in easy-to-read language, and reduce them to bite-sized chunks that even the busiest person can digest.

Throughout this book, you will find direct quotes pulled from the five original books—*Patriarchs and Prophets* (1890), *Prophets and Kings* (1917), *The Desire of Ages* (1898), *The Acts of the Apostles* (1911), and *The Great Controversy* (1858). These will give you a taste of White's beautiful writing.

If you decide to make time in your schedule to read her five original books, which contain so much more fascinating information than I have space for here, you can find them online at www.whiteestate.org or you can buy the printed books at www.adventistbookcenter.com.

Blessings.

THE
PATRIARCHS

Insights From
Patriarchs and Prophets

Why Was Sin Permitted?
The Bible says that God is love, yet history is full of good *and* evil. How can these two things coexist? It began in heaven when Lucifer, the leading angel, wanted to be like God. Lucifer rebelled against God and Christ, the Son of God. God the Father and His Son had created all beings in the universe, including us.

Lucifer was especially jealous of the Son of God and was determined to take His place. It wasn't enough that God had given Lucifer a high position in charge of all the other angels. There was no sense of gratitude in his heart. He thought himself the smartest, most beautiful, most important being in heaven. He began to plant seeds of discord among the angels. Some of them believed his lies, and they were ready to accept Lucifer as their leader instead of God.

As a result, God the Father had to remind them about Christ's true position, which had always been by God's side. He was one with God before anything was created. The Father was very patient with Lucifer and his bad attitude; if he had humbled himself and apologized, the Father would have given him back his position, but since he refused, he had to be sent out of heaven.

The Creation
After Lucifer was gone, God and His Son decided to create this earth with its animals and then human beings. The first human created was Adam and then Eve as his companion. God brought them together and performed the first marriage. Both were to reflect God's character.

God saw that the Sabbath was essential to help them stay close to Him, so He set it aside as a day of worship and fellowship with their Father.

God loved them and wanted them to love Him. He put Adam and Eve in charge of the Garden and all the animals. In return, God asked that they listen to and obey Him. Their commitment to their Father had to be tested. There was one tree in the Garden of Eden from which God told them not to eat.

The Temptation and Fall

Satan was jealous of Adam and Eve's happiness, so he decided to get even with God. He would attack those who were created in His image. The angels warned Adam and Eve about the danger they faced and told them to stay together to safeguard against Lucifer's attacks. Sadly, Eve didn't listen and went wandering around the Garden of Eden by herself. Soon she found herself next to the forbidden tree. Nestled in its branches was a beautiful talking serpent.

The serpent told Eve the tree had magical powers; he had eaten its fruit and received the ability to speak. Then he urged her to do the same so that she, too, would become wise and know as much as God. Eve believed what the serpent said rather than believing what God had said, and she took the fruit from the serpent and ate it. When she did, she felt invigorated and powerful.

She then took more fruit, ran with it to her husband, told him what had happened, and offered the fruit to him. He immediately knew that Satan had used this beautiful serpent to trick Eve into eating from the forbidden tree. He believed she would die. He couldn't bear the thought of being without her, so he took the fruit she offered him and ate it, knowing he, too, would die. Satan was thrilled that his plan had worked.

> After the plan of salvation had been devised, God, as we have seen, could still, through the ministry of His Son and the holy angels, communicate with men across the gulf which sin had made. Sometimes He spoke face to face with them, as in the case of Moses, but more frequently by dreams and visions.
> —*Patriarchs and Prophets*, 21

When God came to see Adam and Eve, they both ran and hid. God said, "Why are you hiding from Me? Have you done something wrong?" They couldn't deny it. Adam blamed Eve, and Eve blamed God for creating the serpent. Then God decided to discipline the serpent by making it crawl on the ground rather than fly. He then told Adam and Eve the troubles they would have because of their sin and said that they could no longer stay in the Garden of Eden. An angel would see to it that they left.

The Plan of Redemption

All heaven felt sick over what had happened. God and His Son were deeply hurt, and their hearts went out to Adam and Eve. Still, God knew that disobedience could not be allowed in any part of the universe and that lawbreakers would have to experience consequences. So Christ pleaded with the Father that they enact a plan of salvation for Adam and Eve and their children. The Father and the Son talked about this and about when and how to do it. The Father loved the human race so much that He was willing to sacrifice His Son for it.

When the angels learned about the plan, they were terribly sad. Not one of them could redeem man; only the Creator had the power to redeem creation. But the angels were told that they could be God's helpers in this. They were overjoyed.

When God told Satan that He would put a hatred of him in the heart of every human being and that his power over them would finally be broken, the universe heard the first whisper of the plan of redemption. The Son of God would come, and Satan, like a poisonous, snake would strike at Him, but Christ would crush his head. It was a marvel to the universe that the Son of God would humble Himself and willingly be crucified to save humankind and to defend the character of His Father.

> The history of the great conflict between good and evil, from the time it first began in heaven to the final overthrow of rebellion and the total eradication of sin, is also a demonstration of God's unchanging love.
> —*Patriarchs and Prophets,* 33

Cain and Abel Tested

Adam's two sons, Cain and Abel, were very different. They both worshiped the Creator, but in not the same way. Abel believed that God and the plan of redemption were just. He sacrificed a lamb, as God had asked, to point to the death of Christ for sin. Cain resented the curse of sin. Instead of a lamb, Cain brought some grain that he had grown just to show his faith in God. Lightning flashed from heaven and burned up Abel's lamb but not Cain's grain offering. This made Cain angry, and he decided to kill his brother.

So Cain was the first murderer. God could have taken Cain's life for doing this, but He didn't. He hoped that Cain would change his mind and do what was right, but Cain didn't. So his rebellious spirit spread to his descendants, and Satan rejoiced and did all he could to deepen their spirit against God.

Seth and Enoch

Adam had another son. His name was Seth, and he reflected his father's and his older brother Abel's commitment to God. Before the entrance of sin, Adam and Eve kept the Sabbath as God told them to do. Even after they left the Garden of Eden, they remained loyal to God and kept the Sabbath.

As the number of people on earth increased, some continued to follow Cain's example, and soon there were two groups of people. One group was loyal to God and the other did their own thing and disobeyed God. Cain and his descendants continued to disobey God, and soon there were murders, men taking many wives, and other evils.

Unfortunately, when the descendants of Seth saw that the girls of Cain's clan were very beautiful, they began to marry them, and the wickedness of Cain's descendants spread into the villages of the good people. Adam lived for hundreds of years, and when he saw all this, he realized he was the cause of all this brokenness. He bowed down in anguish and pain, confessing his sin over and over again.

In spite of all the evil, there was a group who continued to obey God and be faithful to Him. One such man was Enoch, who lived for hundreds of years and always kept God's commandments. His love for God grew stronger as the years went by. Evil was everywhere, so he withdrew from the wickedness to spend time in meditation and prayer. However, he was passionate about telling people about God's love and never tired of begging them to repent and return to Him.

The world had gotten so wicked that God had to take action. He revealed to Enoch the coming of the Flood and beyond that to the coming of Christ, His crucifixion, death, resurrection, ascension, and eventual return. All Enoch's life he shared his faith with the people and lived so close to God that God decided to take him to directly heaven at the end of his life so Enoch would be with Him rather than dying and awaiting the Second Coming.

> The King of the universe summoned the heavenly hosts before Him, that in their presence He might set forth the true position of His Son and show the relation He sustained to all created beings. The Son of God shared the Father's throne, and the glory of the eternal, self-existent One encircled both.
> —*Patriarchs and Prophets*, 36

The Flood
In the days of Noah, the earth was still beautiful, and men lived hundreds of years. The people were giants and had exceptional powers of wisdom and skill. But they gave in to their sinful nature and did things that weren't right in spite of their wisdom and power. They built beautiful houses for themselves and tried to outdo one another. They ended up worshiping what they could do and put God out of their thinking.

Their wickedness was open and defiant, criminal in nature. In addition, they had many wives, contrary to God's original plan. Iniquity had become so widespread that God as Judge had to do what He could to bring order back into society.

For 120 years Noah and others tried their best to keep the love of God and the call to obedience in front of the people. But it wasn't working. God told Noah to build a huge boat and get ready for a powerful flood. Up to that time it had never rained, because the earth was watered by a mist every night. When Noah told the people water would be coming down from heaven, they laughed at him. Noah believed God and, with the help of others, began building the huge ship called the ark. People laughed and made fun of him, but God had given Noah the exact dimensions so they kept right on building. The ark would be three stories high with only one huge door. Light would come into the boat from the top. Over and over, Noah invited people to repent of their sins, get on the boat, and be saved from the water.

The ark was finally finished and filled with food. Suddenly the laughing crowd was silent because they saw all kinds of animals, carefully selected by God, coming from everywhere, making their way to the ark. Then God invited Noah and his family into the ark, and the massive door was shut by unseen hands. For a whole week, nothing happened. On the eighth day, dark clouds appeared and it started to rain, and then it poured. As the storm increased, the terror of the people increased and they were frantic, trying to grab on to the ark to get in, but it was too late. The huge flood swept them away. Only eight people believed what Noah had told them for more than 120 years.

> A compassionate Creator, in yearning pity for Lucifer and his followers, was seeking to draw them back from the abyss of ruin into which they were about to plunge.
> —*Patriarchs and Prophets*, 39

After the Flood

The water rose up and up, more than twenty-two feet higher than the highest mountain peak. Noah's family rode the waves in the ark for five months. Finally, the rain stopped and the floodwater began to subside, and the Lord sent a strong wind to help dry things up, but oceans remained. Then God placed a brilliant rainbow in the sky and promised to never again destroy the whole world with a flood.

The flood changed earth forever. God covered all the bodies of dead people and animals with earth and trees. Whole forests were buried. The ground groaned with earthquakes and volcanoes, and these things will become even more frequent as the Second Coming draws near.

The Literal Week

Today geologists claim to find evidence in the earth that it is much older than the Bible says and that people were much larger and more powerful than we think. It is true that in the days of Noah, people, animals, and trees were much larger. God intended that this evidence would be uncovered to confirm the faith of those who believe the Bible.

Some suggest that creation was the result of natural causes and that the planet and the human race evolved from nothing; even some Christians believe this. This approach makes the Bible seem unreliable and contradicts Scripture. Others go a step further and deny the existence of God and become atheists or agnostics. They believe there are fixed laws of nature that even God can't interfere with.

However, God created everything, and true science will eventually be in harmony with what the Bible says. No matter how intelligent men are, they are unable to solve all the mysteries of nature, and they certainly cannot understand everything that God does. The intricacies of nature testify that things did not just happen by chance but that God created everything.

> The schemes of the Babel builders ended in shame and defeat. The monument to their pride became the memorial of their folly. Yet men are continually pursuing the same course—depending upon self, and rejecting God's law. It is the principle that Satan tried to carry out in heaven; the same that governed Cain in presenting his offering.
> —*Patriarchs and Prophets*, 123

The Tower of Babel

During the flood, God had preserved Noah and his three sons, Shem, Ham, and Japheth, and their families. They were the founders of the human race as we know it today. By divine inspiration, Noah foretold the history of the descendants of his three sons. The evil traits in Ham were carried on by his son Canaan and his descendants. On the other hand, Shem and Japheth demonstrated respect for their father through their love for God.

For a time, the descendants of Noah lived by the mountain on which the ark had come to rest after the Flood. Eventually, some decided to move away and to build a city with a tower so big and tall that people could live there and not be in danger of drowning in a flood again. They didn't believe God when He said there would never be a worldwide flood again.

The builders were making good progress and were determined to set up a government apart from God. God decided to stop the building process. Until then, all of humanity spoke a single language. God rewired their vocabulary, so that the various

The Call of Abraham

With the earth's inhabitants now scattered around the world, God decided to keep his covenant alive through the family of Abraham, a descendant of Shem. He promised Abraham that from his descendants a Redeemer would come. Then He told Abraham to get away from his relatives and move to another country, which Abraham and his wife, Sarah, did. Their nephew Lot went with them. With their flocks they stopped at different places and Abraham learned some important lessons of submission, faith, and trust as he followed God's leading.

Along their journey, they stopped in Egypt. Sarah was very beautiful. The king of Egypt wanted to take Sarah as one of his wives. Abraham thought the king might kill him in order to have her, so he lied and said that Sarah was his sister. Pharaoh took her to his palace, but the Lord protected Sarah, and when the king learned that she was Abraham's wife, he told Abraham to take his wife and his flocks and leave Egypt, which he did.

Abraham in Canaan

Abraham had large flocks and herds, and so did Lot. It was hard for them to stay in the same place, so they decided to separate. Abraham said, "You choose first; if you go one way, I'll go the other way." Out of courtesy, Lot should have let Abraham, who was his older relative, choose first. But Abraham insisted that Lot choose first, and he chose to move toward Sodom and Gomorrah.

Abraham didn't leave right away; he wanted to witness for God to the local people. They respected him greatly. Abraham was righteous, and he was not a coward. When the local king of Salem was attacked, Abraham and his men helped defend him, for which the king was grateful.

> When to Isaac's question, "Where is the lamb for a burnt offering?" Abraham made answer, "God will provide Himself a lamb;" and when the father's hand was stayed as he was about to slay his son, and the ram which God had provided was offered in the place of Isaac—then light was shed upon the mystery of redemption, and even the angels understood more clearly the wonderful provision that God had made for man's salvation.
> —*Patriarchs and Prophets*, 155

16 A BRIEF HISTORY OF GOD'S LOVE

Abraham was concerned about the future and his descendants. He asked God to show him more clearly what to do. Abraham sacrificed a cow, a goat, and a ram. He stayed there, protecting the sacrifices from wild animals, but soon got tired and fell asleep. Then he heard the voice of God explain the plan of redemption, reveal that Christ would give His life for people so that the promise of a new heaven and a new earth would be fulfilled. That made a big impression on Abraham.

One day when Abraham was sitting in front of his tent, three strangers came by. He invited them to stop, wash up, and rest, and he served them water and food. That's when Abraham realized that one was the Son of God. The other two were angels who had taken on the appearance of men. He was told that the inhabitants of Sodom and Gomorrah were irreversibly wicked and that something had to be done about it. Abraham asked, "What about Lot and his family?" He was told that they would be rescued, which they were.

The Test of Faith

Abraham had been promised a son. Instead of waiting for God to bring a child into his family with Sarah, he took Sarah's servant as his second wife and had a baby with her. This created jealousy and drama. Sarah got tired of Hagar trying to exalt herself and insisted she and her son, Ishmael, leave their camp.

When Abraham was almost one hundred years old and still did not have an heir, God repeated his promise. Then Sarah got pregnant and had a baby boy, and they named him Isaac. Abraham was the ancestor of God's people and the father of the faithful, but his own faith had to be tested. So when Abraham was 120 years old and Isaac was a young man, God told Abraham to go to Mt. Moriah to offer Isaac as a sacrifice. This would be a three-day journey, so he told Sarah that he was going to offer a sacrifice, but he didn't tell her it was to be their son. Then he and Isaac took some servants and donkeys to carry what was needed.

When they got to the mountain, Abraham told the servants to stay at the bottom as he and Isaac went to the top of the mountain to offer the sacrifice. When they got to the top, they gathered some stones to build an altar and put wood on it. That's when Abraham told his son that God wanted him to be the sacrifice. Isaac was a young man and had grown up loving God. He was ready to do whatever God wanted him to do, even giving his life for God.

Obediently, he climbed onto the altar. Abraham tied Isaac's hands together and, with grieved and trembling hands, raised his knife. Suddenly, an angel of God called to him, "Stop! Don't touch the young man! Now I know that you love Me and have not withheld your only son from Me." What Abraham and Isaac did was symbolic of God giving His only Son to die to save us. Then Abraham saw a ram caught by its horns in a thorn bush nearby, and he killed it and offered it instead. God had provided, just as Abraham believed He would.

Destruction of Sodom

Even though the people of Sodom and Gomorrah were hopelessly wicked and were constantly ridiculing God, their wickedness had not spread everywhere. To prevent that from happening, the two cities had to be destroyed. The last day was like all the other days; people were enjoying themselves and having fun being wicked.

In the early evening, two strangers came into town looking for a place to stay. Lot invited them to stay with him. They said, "Thank you, but we'll just stay out here for the night." Lot knew what could happen to them in that dangerous town, so he insisted. They agreed to spend the night at his house. The people of the city had seen the visitors and knew they had been asking about the city's problems. They came to Lot's house in an angry mob and were ready to break the door down, come in, and force the visitors to come with them. Fortunately, the two visitors were angels who had come to rescue Lot. They struck the men and youth with partial blindness to make them turn away and grope their way back home.

Then they told Lot to talk to his larger family and relatives and urge them to quickly leave, because the cities would soon be destroyed. They laughed at him, because they were not ready to leave their fancy houses and luxurious living. Finally, the angels took Lot, his wife, and their two daughters by the hand and led them out of the city. Sadly, Lot's wife's heart was still with her other children and friends in the city, and she couldn't stand leaving them. Though she had been told not to look back, she turned around and gazed at her former home. When the city was destroyed, she died too.

Lot went to the little town of Zoar and planned to stay there for a while, but the wickedness there was like Sodom and Gomorrah, so he decided to go live in the nearby mountains.

The Marriage of Isaac

Time went on, and Abraham was getting older and would soon die, but he was worried about Isaac's future. In those days parents arranged marriages for their children, and Isaac trusted his father and God to direct matters. Abraham decided to ask Eliezer, his most trusted servant, to go to his relatives back in Mesopotamia to find a wife for Isaac. The servant got ready, took a couple of camels, and was on his way. When he got there, he stopped by the city well where the young women would come to draw water. There was one young woman who captured his attention; she was kind and even offered to draw water for him and his camels.

He thanked her and gave her some gifts for her kindness. Then he asked about her family. Rebekah told him that she was the daughter of Bethuel, Abraham's nephew, so he bowed his head and thanked the Lord. Eliezer told her that he was the servant of Abraham and wondered if he could spend the night with her family. Rebekah ran home, told her brother Laban about what had happened, and he rushed to the well to meet the stranger and invite him home.

When they got there, Eliezer refused to sit down and eat until he told Laban why he had come—to find a wife for Abraham's son Isaac. Laban said, "My sister Rebekah is right here; ask her if she is willing to go with you and be Isaac's wife." Rebekah said, "Yes, I'm willing to go." Eliezer could hardly believe it. He praised the Lord for helping him find a good wife for Isaac.

Eliezer and Rebekah got ready to go, said goodbye to the family, and set out for home. Abraham and Isaac prayed the whole time Eliezer was gone. One evening as Isaac went out in the field to pray, he saw them coming. Rebekah covered her face with a veil, and Eliezer introduced her to Isaac and told his master how the Lord had led. Isaac was thrilled, marriage arrangements were made, and she became Isaac's wife.

Jacob and Esau

A short time later, Isaac and Rebekah had twin boys, Jacob and Esau. The two of them couldn't be more different. Esau was self-centered, loved to do his own thing, and became a hunter. He would kill an animal, carry it home, prepare a meal, and tell his father about the exciting time he had hunting. Jacob was different. He was gentler and loved to take care of the flocks and herds. Rebekah felt closer to Jacob than to Esau. Isaac had made it clear that since Esau came out of the womb ahead of Jacob, he was the firstborn and was entitled to inherit a double portion of the family's material wealth and the spiritual leadership role, but the father had not considered Esau's character. Rebekah talked to Isaac about it, but Isaac wouldn't listen.

Jacob loved God, but his heart wasn't really converted. He wanted to be the firstborn and inherit the spiritual birthright. So one day when Esau came home very tired and hungry from hunting, he stopped to see Jacob. Jacob prepared some food for him, and asked Esau if he would let him have the birthright. Esau didn't want it anyway; he just wanted something eat. So he took an oath to give Jacob the birthright.

Years went by and everything seemed to be fine until Isaac got old and blind and

> How many, even of professed Christians, cling to indulgences that are injurious to health and that benumb the sensibilities of the soul. When the duty is presented of cleansing themselves from all filthiness of the flesh and spirit, perfecting holiness in the fear of God, they are offended. They see that they cannot retain these hurtful gratifications and yet secure heaven, and they conclude that since the way to eternal life is so strait, they will no longer walk therein.
>
> —*Patriarchs and Prophets*, 182

decided that before he died he needed to bless Esau officially. Isaac told his son to go hunting, bring an animal home, and prepare a meal to eat together. Then he would officially transfer the spiritual leadership role and give him control of the family's estate.

Rebekah learned about this plan and decided that while Esau was out hunting she would send Jacob in to trick his father into giving him the blessing. Jacob hesitated to deceive his father, but Rebekah insisted. She dressed Jacob in Esau's clothes and made him smell like he'd been out hunting. Then Jacob, pretending to be Esau, went to see Isaac and asked for the family blessing. Isaac hesitated because Jacob didn't sound like Esau, but Jacob lied and insisted that he was Esau. So Isaac blessed him and gave him the family holdings that belonged to the firstborn. Jacob felt so guilty that his soul never had real peace. Isaac was distraught over the deception, and when Esau returned from hunting and heard what had transpired, he was filled with rage.

Jacob's Flight and Exile

Esau was ready to kill Jacob because he had taken the birthright through deception, even though Esau had carelessly given it to him in exchange for a meal some years before. Jacob had to leave in a hurry to save his own life. His mother suggested that he go to her brother Laban, Jacob's uncle, who lived hundreds of miles away, for safety.

As he was slowly making his way to his uncle's, he thought about how he was responsible for all that had happened. He lost all confidence in himself. Toward evening on the second day, he felt a strong need of God in his life. He knelt down, confessed his sin with deep humility, and asked for evidence that God still loved him. Then he took a stone to use as a pillow and went to sleep. During the night, he dreamed about a glorious ladder that reached from the earth to heaven. Angels walked up and down on it. The Lord stood at the top and said, "I am the Lord, the God of Abraham. The promise I gave to him belongs also to you. I will never leave you."

Jacob woke up and said to himself, "Wow! The Lord is in this place." He took the stone he had used for a pillow, added more stones to it, and built an altar to God. He named the spot Bethel. Then he promised the Lord that he would be faithful to Him and would give the Lord one-tenth of all he earned.

With renewed faith in God, he continued on his way and finally arrived near his uncle's place. At the same well outside of town where his grandfather's servant had met Rebekah, Jacob met his cousin Rachel, who was also there waiting her turn for water. She invited him home, and his uncle Laban was glad to see him. He invited Jacob to stay and work for him.

While there, Jacob fell in love with Rachel and asked her to marry him. She agreed, but her dad wanted to know if Jacob would be able to support a wife and family. If not, Jacob could work for him for seven years to earn enough to take care of a family. Jacob loved Rachel so much that he gladly accepted the terms of marriage.

Jacob had to work hard as a shepherd, watching the sheep day and night. Laban paid him by giving him a few sheep as his own. Over time the sheep multiplied, and Jacob had quite a large flock. Laban didn't want to lose his good worker, so he tricked Jacob into marrying his other daughter, Leah, and forced Jacob to work another seven years to marry Rachel.

Jacob continued to work for Laban a while longer because he was afraid to go back home. Finally, he decided it was time. So while Laban was away for a few days, Jacob left. When they learned Jacob had gone, Laban and his men went after him to force him to come back. But God spoke to Laban and told him to leave Jacob alone and let him go back home. Laban did so, and Jacob and Rachel and Leah went on their way in peace.

The Night of Wrestling

As Jacob got close to home, he remembered Esau's threats and got scared for himself and his family. Then Jacob felt courage as he remembered the dream he had had at Bethel. Jacob sent some of his men with words of reconciliation to his brother, but they returned with news that Esau was coming with four hundred soldiers. Jacob got scared and knew he needed God to help him. Jacob sent his family to a safe place and stayed behind to be alone with God and pray.

It got dark, and as he was praying, Jacob he felt a hand grab him and he thought he was being attacked. He fought and wrestled with this Man off and on all night and was getting nowhere. Suddenly the Man touched Jacob's leg, which crippled him instantly. That's when Jacob realized he was wrestling with the Son of God. Jacob held onto Him and would not let go unless He first blessed him. Then the Lord said, "By faith you have won, so I am changing your name from Jacob to Israel." Jacob learned that trusting in human power does no good.

Meanwhile, God sent Esau a dream in which he saw all that Jacob had gone through for the past twenty years. Esau told his men about it and asked them not to hurt Jacob or his family. When Esau saw Jacob walking toward him, battered and limping because of the pain in his leg, his heart went out to him. He ran to meet him, gave him a brotherly hug, kissed him on both cheeks, and they wept together for a long while. At the end of time, humankind will also wrestle in darkness and pain, but God will have mercy and deliver them.

The Return to Canaan

Jacob was glad to get back home and decided to buy a piece of property close to the city of Shechem. Years before, this was where Abraham had lived for a while. Jacob built a little altar beside his tent where he and his family could have worship every morning and evening. Dinah, one of Jacob's daughters by Leah, was a very beautiful young woman. She wanted to meet some other young women, so she went into the city to look around. Hamor, the prince in charge of the city, had a son named Shechem. When Shechem saw Dinah, he fell in love with her, raped her, and decided to marry her. Hamor sent a message to Jacob and Dinah's brothers asking their permission. Her brothers said Jewish girls could not marry non-Jewish men unless they were circumcised. Hamor and Shechem agreed that all the men in their city should be circumcised in case other men wanted to marry Jewish girls, because the two groups were getting along very well.

This gave Jacob's sons the opportunity to avenge their sister, whom they believed had been wronged. When all the men in Shechem were in pain after being circumcised, Simeon and Levi went in and killed all the men, including Shechem and his father. Then they took Dinah and brought her back home. When Jacob learned what had happened, he was filled with horror at his sons' outright cruelty.

The Lord told Jacob to move to Bethel, which Jacob and his family did. Rachel, Jacob's beloved wife, died in childbirth; Jacob named their son Benjamin. From there it was two days travel to Hebron where his father Isaac lived. Isaac was 180 years old, sick, and blind but was glad to have Jacob comfort him in his last days. While he was there, Esau also came, and they both comforted their father until he passed away.

Jacob had twelve sons, but he loved Joseph, Rachel's oldest boy, the most. Jacob would often ask Joseph to go find his brothers to see how they were doing in the fields with the flocks and to bring back a report. The brothers hated Joseph because their father showed preference for Joseph; he'd even given him a colorful coat that was usually worn only by very important people. They especially hated him after Joseph told them about the dreams he had where they had bowed down to him.

Joseph's brothers decided that the next time Joseph came to see them in the field, they would get rid of him, once and for all. They would have killed him on the spot

> There are few who realize the influence of the little things of life upon the development of character. Nothing with which we have to do is really small. The varied circumstances that we meet day by day are designed to test our faithfulness and to qualify us for greater trusts. By adherence to principle in the transactions of ordinary life, the mind becomes accustomed to hold the claims of duty above those of pleasure and inclination.
> —*Patriarchs and Prophets*, 222, 223

if Reuben had not spoken up. He said, "Let's not kill our brother. Let's throw him in this pit for now until we decide what to do with him." So that's what they did. Reuben had decided that he would pull him out of the pit during the night and send him back home. However, the next day, while Reuben was not around, the brothers saw a caravan of merchants passing by on their way to Egypt. The brothers decided to sell Joseph to them, so the merchants took Joseph with them and planned to sell him on the slave market when they got to Egypt.

When Reuben came back, and he found Joseph gone. When the brothers told him what they did, he was shocked. What would they tell their father? They talked it over and decided to take Joseph's colorful robe, which they had taken, dip it in the blood of an animal, show it to their father, and tell him that some wild animal killed Joseph. The depth of Jacob's grief was unfathomable, and the brothers had tremendous guilt.

Joseph in Egypt
As he traveled toward Egypt, Joseph decided that no matter what happened to him, he would be faithful to God. When the caravan got to Egypt, Joseph was put up for sale. Potiphar, the captain of Pharaoh's guards, bought him to be his personal slave. He was pleased with Joseph's work and eventually put him in charge of everything he had. Joseph's faithfulness was such that soon Potiphar thought of him as his son rather than his slave.

Joseph's loyalty to God was to be tested. Potiphar's wife liked young Joseph and tried to seduce him, but Joseph refused. This really upset her, so one time when no one else was in the house, she grabbed Joseph by the coat and pulled him toward her. Joseph twisted out of the coat and ran. She called the guards, showed them the coat, and told them that Joseph had tried to rape her. They believed her, arrested Joseph, and threw him in prison. When Potiphar heard about this, he didn't believe the accusations, but to avoid shaming his household, he allowed Joseph to be arrested and jailed.

Joseph's good behavior in prison soon gained the confidence of the man in charge, and he made Joseph his assistant. One day Pharaoh's chief baker and the chief butler, the one in charge of the king's household, were both put in prison for some minor offense. While there they both had dreams that bothered them. Joseph prayed for help, and God gave him the interpretations. The baker told Joseph that he dreamed he was carrying three baskets of bread on his head and the birds came and ate the bread. The butler said that he dreamed he was squeezing grapes from three vines to make the king some wine. Joseph told the baker that in three days he would be executed and told the butler that in three days he would be released to serve the king again. And that's exactly what happened.

One night Pharaoh had two bothersome dreams. He asked his wise men for the interpretation, but they couldn't help him. Then the butler remembered Joseph and told the king about Joseph's ability to interpret dreams. So Pharaoh called for Joseph and told him about the two dreams. In one dream he saw seven skinny cows eat seven fat ones, and in the other dream he saw seven thin ears of corn eat seven good ears. Joseph told the king that he was not the one who could interpret dreams, but that interpretations come from God. Then he told the king that there would be seven years of great harvests for Egypt followed by seven of famine. He suggested to Pharaoh that during the seven good years, preparations should be made for the seven bad years.

When Pharaoh heard this, he knew that it was too much for him to do and that he needed to give the job to someone else. "Since God has helped you interpret dreams, you are the man to handle the job," he told Joseph. "I appoint you as the head of Pharaoh's house, and you will have authority over everything except me and my responsibilities." Pharaoh had Joseph ride in the royal chariot with him and had the chariot drivers shout to the people, "Bow to the pharaoh and to our new governor!" Joseph's dedication to God and his life of self-discipline down to the smallest detail had created an unmistakably noble character and great wisdom.

Joseph and His Brothers

During the seven years of prosperity, Joseph had huge storehouses built to hold the overflow harvest. There they gathered plenty of grain to see them through the lean years. Then the seven years of famine came. The famine not only included Egypt but also spread all the way to Canaan where Jacob and his family lived. When they heard about the stored grain in Egypt, Jacob told his sons to go there and buy what they needed. So they went and, like others, were directed to Joseph, the governor of Egypt. When they saw him wearing a royal robe, they bowed before him. Joseph recognized his brothers, and when he saw them bow, he thought of the dreams that he had had years before.

He looked at his brothers, asked where they were from, and added, "I think you're spies who've come to find out what you can about the strength of Egypt."

They said, "No, sir, we have come here to buy food." Joseph said, "How do I know you're telling the truth?"

They answered, "Sir, we are twelve brothers; one is no more and the youngest is still at home."

Joseph wondered if they were lying and thought they may have done something bad to Benjamin as they had done to him. Joseph held Simeon in prison and sent the others back home to get Benjamin. He gave them the grain they had purchased but also secretly returned their money to their bags.

Jacob was eager for his sons to come back. When they did, the whole family came together to hear how things went in Egypt. Jacob was distraught that he'd lost Joseph, Simeon was in an Egyptian prison, and now the governor wanted Benjamin too.

When it was time to buy more grain, the brothers left for Egypt. They had persuaded Jacob to let them take Benjamin along. When they got there and Joseph saw his younger brother, he could hardly keep from crying. He told his servant to get Simeon out of prison and prepare a meal for his brothers. When the meal was ready and they were told where to sit, they were surprised that they were arranged to sit according to their ages. Joseph sat by himself, because as governor he was not allowed to sit with them. The brothers didn't know that Joseph could speak their language, so, as they talked with one another, Joseph listened undetected.

Then Joseph decided to test the attitude of his brothers toward Benjamin. While they were eating, Joseph told his servant to put his silver drinking cup in Benjamin's sack, and the servant did. The brothers finished eating, thanked the governor for his hospitality, and left for home. They had barely gotten out of the city when Joseph sent his personal steward after them. The steward and some guards galloped after them and accused them of stealing.

The brothers denied it and said, "If that's true, the one who stole from the governor's table should be executed, and we are willing be the governor's slaves."

The steward said, "Not so, just the one who stole from the governor's table will be his slave."

They all opened their sacks, and there was the governor's silver cup in Benjamin's sack. The brothers couldn't believe it. They went back to the city and Judah asked to speak to the governor. He quietly told the governor how much their father loved Benjamin and that he had promised to protect Benjamin with his life, and he offered to be the governor's slave in place of Benjamin.

From this Joseph could see that the brothers had changed and were not the same as they used to be. He looked at them and told them that he was Joseph, whom they had sold as a slave twenty years before. The brothers stood there in shock with their mouths agape. He hugged all of them and then told them that he had forgiven them and that God had worked things out to save them from the famine. He told them to go home, get Jacob and their families, and come and live in Egypt, because the famine would continue for five more years.

When Pharaoh heard about this, out of gratitude to Joseph, he personally invited Joseph's whole family to live in Egypt. The brothers returned home, told the good news to their father that Joseph was alive and governor of Egypt. Jacob could hardly believe it. Then they told him that the Pharaoh himself had invited them to come live in Egypt and to bring their flocks and herds along. After they came, Joseph took his father and introduced him to Pharaoh, who looked at him and ask him how old he was. He told him that he was 130 years old but his ancestors had lived a lot longer than that. Pharaoh could hardly believe it. Jacob thanked Pharaoh for his kindness, raised his hands, and blessed him.

The next seventeen years were very peaceful and happy for Jacob and his family. When Jacob was 147 years old, he sensed that he wouldn't live much longer, so he called his sons together to give them a final blessing. He told each one what he thought their future would be like and said, "After I die, don't bury me here in Egypt, but take my body back to Canaan and bury me by my ancestors." Then he blessed them and died, and they took his body back to Canaan as he asked them to do.

Joseph lived for another fifty-four years; when he sensed that the end was near, he called the families together and told them that one day they would return to Canaan and when they did, they should take his bones with them. Joseph died at 110 years old, having lived to see his grandchildren and great-grandchildren. They embalmed his body and kept it in an Egyptian coffin to be taken with them when they went back to Canaan.

Joseph, who was sold into slavery and eventually became a savior to those who wronged him, represents Christ, who was betrayed by His own disciples and went on to redeem them and all humankind.

Moses

As the years passed a new pharaoh came to the throne who didn't care about all the good Joseph had done for Egypt. He was also concerned about the Israelites, who had become very numerous. He was afraid that they might side with the enemies of Egypt if a war broke out. So he made them slaves and forced them to work harder and harder building things for Egypt, hoping the toil would slow the growth of their community. That didn't work, so he ordered the Israelite midwives to kill all baby boys as soon as they were born. They refused, so Pharaoh ordered that the babies be thrown into the Nile River.

A Levite woman named Jochebed had a baby boy, and she decided to hide him from Pharaoh's soldiers. She did that for three months, but he eventually got too big and loud. Then she made a little basket, made it watertight with pitch, put her baby in it, and set it in the river. Miriam, the baby's sister, hid nearby to watch the little basket. About that time, Pharaoh's daughter came by to bathe herself. She noticed the little basket and told her servant to fetch it. When the princess opened it, the baby started to cry. Her love went out to the baby and she decided to adopt him. Miriam approached cautiously and said, "I can get a Hebrew woman to nurse the baby and raise him for you." The princess agreed, so Miriam ran home to get Jochebed. Jochebed agreed to nurse and raise the baby but was careful not to let the princess know that he was her own son. Jochebed taught Moses about God as he grew. When he was twelve years old, the princess officially adopted Moses, a name that means "saved from the water."

Moses lived at Pharaoh's palace and received the highest education and military training available. Then Pharaoh adopted him as his grandson and possible successor to the throne. Moses was such a good military leader that all the troops respected him.

All the members of royal family had to take part in the national religion, but Moses held on to his Hebrew faith. The princess warned him that if he did not change she would have to disown him and he would not inherit the treasures of Egypt, but Moses stood firm and continued to be loyal to God.

Often Moses visited his people and saw how they were mistreated to get them to do more work, especially since they rested on the Sabbath. One day he saw an Egyptian taskmaster severely beating one of the Hebrews. Moses went up and told the man to stop, but the man told Moses that he had no right to tell him what to do. In a rage, Moses killed him and buried his body in the sand. He thought no one would know, but word got back to Pharaoh, who decided Moses must die to pay for his crime and to prevent him from leading the Hebrews in an attack on Egypt.

Moses fled Egypt and crossed the border heading for Arabia. On the way, he stayed with Jethro, a priest and prince of Midian, who also worshiped the God of Israel. Moses fell in love with and married one of Jethro's daughters. Then Jethro asked Moses to stay and work for him taking care of his herds and flocks, which he did for forty years. During this time, Moses kept thinking about his people in Egypt and wished he could have an army to deliver them. But that was not God's plan. God used those years to refine Moses' character, developing patience and humility.

One day as Moses was taking care of Jethro's sheep near Mt. Horeb, he noticed a large bush on fire near the top, but it didn't burn up. That was strange. A voice within the flames called him by name and told him the ground was holy. From this we learn that, though God invites us to come to Him, we must do so with reverence and humility.

God told Moses to go back to Egypt and free His people. God said, "I'll be going with you and will deliver My people." Moses said, "Who should I say will be delivering them?" The Lord said, "Tell them, 'I AM THAT I AM' has sent you to save them." Moses wasn't sure it would work, so God demonstrated some of the supernatural signs

> By obedience the people were to give evidence of their faith. So all who hope to be saved by the merits of the blood of Christ should realize that they themselves have something to do in securing their salvation. While it is Christ only that can redeem us from the penalty of transgression, we are to turn from sin to obedience. Man is to be saved by faith, not by works; yet his faith must be shown by his works.
> —*Patriarchs and Prophets*, 279

Moses was to use to prove to the Hebrew people and the Egyptians that God had really sent him. God also sent Moses' brother, Aaron, to help speak for him, because Moses had forgotten much of the Egyptian language.

Moses told Jethro, his father-in-law, that he wanted to go back to Egypt to visit his people. Jethro gave him permission, so Moses took his wife, Zipporah, and their children and headed for Egypt. When they were almost there, he decided the risk to their safety was too great, so he sent them back to Jethro.

The Plagues of Egypt

After the two brothers got to Egypt and told the Hebrews about God's plan, they went to ask Pharaoh to let the Hebrews go for a couple of days to worship God. Pharaoh said, "Who is your God? I don't know Him, so why should I let you go? And why is this Sabbath business so important to you? Just for that, you'll have to do twice as much work, and if you don't do it, you'll be whipped."

Moses and Aaron left the palace and prayed, "Lord, we went to talk to Pharaoh as you asked us to, but he didn't listen and only made things worse for our people." The Hebrews didn't realize their faith would be tested on the road to freedom. They wondered why God didn't step in and do something. Their elders continued to point them back to Joseph and how God had worked for them in the past. In the meantime, the Egyptians kept making fun of their God, and in spite of the miraculous signs Moses and Aaron presented to Pharaoh, he kept refusing to let God's people go.

Finally, Moses and Aaron told Pharaoh that God would send plagues on Egypt to force Pharaoh to let the Hebrews go. But even though the plagues hurt the economy of Egypt, Pharaoh wouldn't budge.

The Passover

The Lord decided to do something that would grip Pharaoh's attention. Pharaoh had warned Moses not to come and see him again or he would have him killed. Nevertheless, Moses went to give Pharaoh one last message: "At midnight, all the firstborn of Egypt will die, both of men and cattle, including the firstborn of Pharaoh. But not one firstborn among the Hebrews will die. This will be done by the Lord to let everyone know that He makes a difference between His people who love and worship Him and those who worship and serve gods of their own making."

Then Moses told the Israelites to sacrifice a lamb and to put some of its blood on the doorposts of their houses so that when the destroying angel passed over, he would see the blood on the doorposts and skip those houses. They followed his instructions and made preparations to leave Egypt.

At midnight, all the firstborn Egyptians and livestock died. Shrieks and wails were heard everywhere. Pharaoh was humbled; his pride was gone. He called for Moses and

Aaron and told them to take their people, along with their families and flocks, and herds and leave Egypt.

The Exodus
The Hebrews, approximately six hundred thousand men plus women and children, and all their livestock, left Egypt. Instead of just going out to worship the Lord for a few days and then going back to Egypt, they continued south toward the Red Sea. The Lord led them by a pillar of cloud during the day and a pillar of fire by night.

When Pharaoh heard that the Israelites were actually leaving Egypt, he took his army and went after them. The Israelites didn't know what to do. The Red Sea was in front of them and Pharaoh's army behind them. God asked Moses to command the Red Sea to open up and make a dry path for the Israelites to cross over. When Pharaoh saw this, he commanded his army to follow them, but when the Israelites were across, the sea closed on Pharaoh and the Egyptian army, and they all drowned.

The exodus experience is a lesson for all generations. Even when problems seem insurmountable and solutions unattainable, God will make a way for His people in His time. We must keep the faith, even when things seem dark.

From the Red Sea to Sinai
The Israelites continued on their way, and as they did, they struggled to find water and food. They complained nonstop and even got angry at Moses for bringing them out of Egypt, where they had had plenty food and water even though they were slaves there. Moses cried out to the Lord: "What should I do?" He was told to stand on a huge rock and to strike it with his shepherd's rod, and water would come out. He did so, and enough water flowed to quench all the people and animals. Then the Lord also rained down food from heaven called manna, which was a small white grain that could be cooked and baked.

> Ten precepts, brief, comprehensive, and authoritative, cover the duty of man to God and to his fellow man; and all based upon the great fundamental principle of love. "Thou shalt love the Lord thy God with all thy heart, and with all thy soul, and with all thy strength, and with all thy mind; and thy neighbor as thyself." Luke 10:27. . . . In the Ten Commandments these principles are carried out in detail, and made applicable to the condition and circumstances of man.
> —*Patriarchs and Prophets*, 305

Because the Israelites kept complaining about God, even though He had provided all they needed, God allowed the Amalekites to attack them. Moses sent Joshua and his soldiers to fight them off. Moses stood on a hill overlooking the battlefield. He raised his hands to God and prayed that Joshua and his men would defeat their enemies. As he prayed and held up his arms toward heaven, Joshua began winning. When Moses lowered his arms, Joshua started losing. When Moses got too tired to hold his arms up, Aaron and Hur, Miriam's husband, supported his arms until the sun went down and Joshua finally won. By this we see that we have no power on our own; only by God's mercy do we succeed in our endeavors.

The Israelites continued to follow the pillar of cloud, and soon they reached a place not far from where Moses' father-in-law, Jethro, lived. Jethro heard they were nearby, so he brought Moses' wife and two sons to him for a joyful reunion. Jethro spent a few days observing how much work Moses had to do each day in helping people solve their personal problems in addition to leading the nation. Jethro saw that it was too much and that Moses should get some assistants to handle the smaller issues. Moses agreed, and the system worked much better.

Then the Israelites continued on to Mt. Sinai, where they settled for almost a year. The beautiful scene helped inspire the people with awe for God and their minds were elevated.

The Law Given to Israel

After the people had set up camp, God asked Moses to come up to the top of the mountain to talk. God told him that now that the people were out of Egypt, He wanted them to accept God not only as Lord but also as their King. So Moses went back down and told the elders everything that God had said. They responded, "God is our King and everything He tells us to do, we will do."

Then God asked Moses to come back up the mountain so He could explain to Moses how He would reveal His law. God said He would first read it aloud to the people, then He would give Moses a written copy, which He had engraved with His finger on two slabs of granite stone. Moses went back down to get the people ready for this event. They needed to consecrate themselves to God, confess their sins, make things right between one another, and pledge their love and loyalty to God. This took a couple of days before everyone was ready.

In the morning on the third day, dark clouds swept in, God's glory engulfed the top of the mountain like fire, thunder rolled, and a trumpet sounded louder and louder. The people all fell on their faces in fear and awe. The Lord said, "I am the one who brought you out of Egypt, because I love you." Then He read the Ten Commandments to them.

1. There is only one God, and I am He.
2. Don't worship an image that represents Me or anything else.

3. Respect My name; don't misuse it, literally or figuratively.
4. Keep the Sabbath, rest, and worship.
5. Respect your parents.
6. Don't kill anyone.
7. Don't commit adultery.
8. Don't steal.
9. Don't lie.
10. Don't be selfish.

> And when in later times the Jews were scattered as captives in distant lands, they still at the appointed hour turned their faces toward Jerusalem and offered up their petitions to the God of Israel. In this custom Christians have an example for morning and evening prayer. While God condemns a mere round of ceremonies, without the spirit of worship, He looks with great pleasure upon those who love Him, bowing morning and evening to seek pardon for sins committed and to present their requests for needed blessings.
> —*Patriarchs and Prophets*, 354

After He read the Ten Commandments to the people, He gave Moses the two slabs of granite on which He had written them. There were other instructions that God gave to Moses that outlined the broader picture of what He would do for His people and what He expected of them in return. This was called the covenant. Moses presented it to the people, they accepted the agreement, and the nation built an altar at the bottom of the mountain.

Again Moses was summoned up the mountain, this time with Joshua. Aaron and Hur were in charge during their absence. Moses and Joshua spent six days preparing to meet God. Then Moses went into His holy presence, and remained there forty days, receiving plans for building the tabernacle.

Idolatry at Sinai

In the weeks that Moses and Joshua were gone, the people wondered what had happened to them. They grew restless without a leader. They wanted something tangible to represent God, and they were so determined that Aaron feared for his life and gave in to the people. He told them to bring their golden earrings and ornaments; then he melted them and made a small golden calf, built an altar in front of it, and announced, "Tomorrow we will hold a feast to the Lord!" Had he stood firm regardless of the possible outcome, this wouldn't have happened. The feast turned into a huge, godless party.

God knew what the people were doing, so he told Moses to go back down and deal with them. God was very angry and told Moses the people had voided their covenant with Him. Moses begged God to forgive them and returned with Joshua to the camp down the mountain. However, when Moses saw the massive heathen-like party in front of a small golden calf, he got so angry and overwhelmed that he threw down the granite slabs with the Ten Commandments written on them so hard that they broke into pieces. This illustrated that God's people were breaking the law and their covenant with God. Then Moses threw the golden calf into the fire, ground it to powder, and dumped the worthless dust into the stream for the people to drink. Then, per God's command, those who remained faithful killed about three thousand of the unrepentant Israelites who had instigated the treasonous rebellion.

Moses again pleaded with God for mercy on those who remained. He even offered to give up his own eternal life in exchange for the Israelites. God said, "The Lord is kind, gracious, forgiving of sins but will not clear those who are determined to keep on sinning." He agreed to forgive the people and renew His covenant with them but determined that He would no longer journey with them in the pillar of cloud.

Whenever Moses spent time with God, his face shone so brightly that people were awestruck and afraid and had to look away. On such occasions, Moses covered his face with a veil for their sake. If people could hardly look at the face of Moses, what will happen when Jesus comes back to take His people home? Do our faces shine with His glory and love when we commune with Him now?

Satan's Enmity Against the Law

When Lucifer was still in heaven, he had stubbornly set himself against the law of God. As a result, he had to be dismissed from heaven. Then he tempted Adam and Eve to sin and turned them against the law of God. Today, thousands of years later, people still disobey and distrust God and His law.

Satan hates God's law and is determined to get people to break it. The moment Moses carried the law from Sinai, Satan was already plotting to lead the people astray. He especially wants us to forget the Sabbath, a holy day to remember our Creator. When Lucifer turned against God's law, it changed his whole personality. He will be annihilated because of his stubbornness. The same thing that will happen to humans who listen to him and stubbornly continue to do what they want to do rather than obey God.

God's people don't need to be afraid if they love God, obey Him, and are faithful and loyal to Him. The Lord says to them, "I, even I, am with you. I will never leave you."

The Tabernacle and Its Services

During one of his visits on Mt. Sinai, God had given Moses detailed instructions on how to build a tabernacle for Him. He also gave certain men the skills and knowledge to do it. The people, humbled by God's greatness and mercy, responded to Moses' announcement by bringing all the building materials, gold, gems, and fine fabrics needed to build the sanctuary. The men worked on the wood and the women on the curtains. The tabernacle was essentially a portable church that they could take with them wherever they went.

When it was all done, it had a large courtyard for the people, a small area with an altar on which animals could be sacrificed, and a Holy Place and a Most Holy Place where the priests ministered. It also had a seven-branched golden candlestick, a small table with twelve loaves of bread representing the twelve tribes, and a small altar on which to offer incense. The Most Holy Place, where the high priest ministered, had the golden chest with the Ten Commandments in it. The priests wore special garments, and the high priest wore a very distinct one.

It took about a year and a half to do the building. Moses examined everything to make sure it was done right. Then the glory of the Lord's presence filled the sanctuary so that even Moses couldn't go in.

Every morning and evening a lamb was sacrificed to point forward to the time when Jesus would be crucified. God does not like ceremonies with no meaning. He prefers simple services where congregations worship Him with their whole hearts.

The Sin of Nadab and Abihu

Not long after the sanctuary was dedicated, Aaron's sons, Nadab and Abihu, were to offer incense to the Lord at the regular time of worship. They were supposed to use fire from the sanctuary to do this, but they took ordinary fire. They knew better, but they were drunk on wine and were careless. God sent a holy fire down and burned them to ash in front of all the people.

God wants His people to come to church and worship Him with respect, doing things right. Aaron had not trained his sons well when they were young. Nadab and Abihu didn't think the particulars really mattered, so they did things the way they wanted to and not the way God told them to. Their intemperance and lack of

> Success can only attend order and harmonious action. God requires order and system in His work now no less than in the days of Israel. All who are working for Him are to labor intelligently, not in a careless, haphazard manner. He would have his work done with faith and exactness, that He may place the seal of His approval upon it. —*Patriarchs and Prophets*, 376

THE PATRIARCHS

self-control should have disqualified them to serve in the sanctuary to begin with.

The Law and the Covenants
God had given Adam and Eve an understanding of His law at creation and had written it on their hearts. After they sinned, they were given the promise of a Savior and were instructed to offer sacrifices to represent Him. Had they not sinned, the system would have been unnecessary. The knowledge of God's law was passed down from generation to generation. To make sure that His people would remember His law and take it seriously, God ultimately wrote it down on granite slabs.

God also instructed Moses regarding the ceremonial law and the sanctuary. The Ten Commandment law and the ceremonial law are two different things. The ceremonial law and sacrifices pointed forward to Christ and ended when Christ came. The Ten Commandment law never ended; it is still in force today. Some people believe that both sets of laws were eliminated when Christ came and died. They preach that we must only live good lives and need not be concerned about the specifics of the Ten Commandments. However, the Ten Commandments have not changed, because God has not changed and never will. He's the same yesterday, today, and forever. Aren't you glad that God doesn't change? If He was always changing His mind, we would never know from one day to the next what He expects us to do.

From Sinai to Kadesh
The government in Israel was very carefully set up and organized. God was the center of authority, and Moses was His representative. Under Moses was the "council of seventy" governing the twelve tribes; then each of those had several levels of leaders. Each tribe had its assigned camping space around the sanctuary. Perfect order and cleanliness were required.

As the Israelites got to the Promised Land, they wondered how the people there would welcome them. God had been leading them by a cloud during the day and by a pillar of fire as it got dark. He had provided manna for food, but because they whined and complained about not having meat and fancy foods, He also sent birds they could catch and roast.

Zipporah, Moses' wife, saw the burdens he carried and how hard he worked. Worried, she suggested he get some helpers. Miriam, Moses' sister, didn't like Zipporah because she was not an Israelite. She was a darker-skinned Midianite. Miriam was jealous of her influence with the great leader. Miriam's complaining and disloyalty caused more problems for Moses, and God punished her by covering her with leprosy. Moses prayed for her healing, and God healed her but not before she was sent out of the camp for a week. She and Aaron both repented of their envy.

The Twelve Spies

Moses and the leaders of Israel decided to send twelve men, including Joshua, as spies into the country of Canaan to find out what kind of people lived there. They went in from the south, traveled all the way to the north, and got a good look at the country. They were gone for forty days; the people could hardly wait for their return to hear what they had to say. They told the people that the land was beautiful and fertile but also that the people living there were big and powerful, like giants, and that taking possession of it was a hopeless dream.

When the people heard this, they got scared and were ready to turn around and go back. They totally forgot what God can do. One of the twelve, Caleb, said, "We can take the land. Let's go in and do it." But the other ten spies exaggerated all the difficulties they would have to face.

The people really got upset and cursed Moses and Aaron for bringing them out of Egypt. They wished they had died in Egypt or along the way and didn't have to face the challenge ahead. They even thought about choosing another leader who would take them back to Egypt. Caleb and Joshua tried as hard as they could to calm the people down, but got nowhere. They would have killed Caleb and Joshua had God not intervened. The people were on the edge of the Promised Land, but because of their unfaithfulness, God killed the ten lying spies and told Moses to take the people back into the wilderness.

That night was spent in sadness, but when morning came, the people changed their minds and decided to make up for their cowardice by going into Canaan to fight. However, it was God's intention that they take the land by faith in His promise, not by warfare. Moses warned the people not to be hasty and disobey God, but they wouldn't listen. They marched in and got soundly defeated; many of their men were killed in battle. Out of options, the people went back and had Moses lead them into the wilderness for a generation.

> The strongest temptation cannot excuse sin. However great the pressure brought to bear upon the soul, transgression is our own act. It is not in the power of earth or hell to compel anyone to do evil. Satan attacks us at our weak points, but we need not be overcome. However severe or unexpected the assault, God has provided help for us, and in His strength we may conquer.
> —*Patriarchs and Prophets*, 421

The Rebellion of Korah

Korah was a Levite cousin of Moses. He started a movement to get rid of Moses and other leaders and install new ones. Two-hundred fifty men of influence supported him, and together they persuaded the people to rebel and blame Moses and Aaron for everything. They forgot that the Son of God was their invisible Leader.

At first, this undermining work was carried on secretly, but as soon as Korah gained prominence, he and his associates went to see Moses. They accused him of putting on a front as if God were leading him when it was not so. Moses said nothing to defend himself but appealed to God as a witness of his motives. Suddenly, a cloud of divine glory appeared above the sanctuary and a voice said to Moses and Aaron, "Get out of My way so I can discipline these rebellious men." The ground split open and swallowed Korah, Dathan, and Abiram. Then fire flashed from heaven and burned the 250 rebellious princes, as well. This action by God confirmed the fact that He had chosen Moses and Aaron to be Israel's leaders.

In the Wilderness

During all the years in the wilderness, the people didn't appreciate their freedom from slavery and all that God had done for them. That is why God waited to fulfill His promises to them. Even so, the sanctuary and God's presence there showed that God had not forsaken them. The years in the wilderness were a time for the people to discipline themselves and prepare for entrance into the Promised Land.

One sign of rebellion of the people against God was when they decided to work on the Sabbath instead of going to the sanctuary and worshiping Him. By breaking the Sabbath commandment, it only confirmed that they had forgotten who He was and what He had done for them.

The Smitten Rock

Earlier in their wanderings, the Son of God had stood on a huge rock and told Moses to strike it with his shepherd's rod to give the people water. In a spiritual sense, Christ

> Everyone who seeks to follow the path of duty will at times be assailed by doubt and unbelief. The way will sometimes be so barred by obstacles, apparently insurmountable, as to dishearten those who will yield to discouragement; but God is saying to such, Go forward. Do your duty at any cost. The difficulties that seem so formidable, that fill your soul with dread, will vanish as you move forward in the path of obedience, humbly trusting in God.
> —*Patriarchs and Prophets*, 437

is our Rock still today, giving us spiritual water to drink. Before God could take the Israelites into Canaan, they had to show that they believed His promise to do so. Yet the people kept complaining about Moses and Aaron bringing them out of Egypt. By now Moses was an old man. He had put up with the complaints of the people for so long that he was weary and running out of patience.

God decided to work another miracle to give the people evidence of His power to do what He promised. When they complained about needing water again, God told Moses not to hit the rock with his shepherd's rod as he had before but to just speak to the huge rock in front of the people and ask for water. However, because he let his emotions get the best of him, Moses walked up to the huge rock and said to the people, "You rebels, do I have to make water come out of this rock for you?" Then in anger, he struck the rock twice. Water did come out, but because Moses was rash and had taken the credit for himself, he was not allowed to enter Canaan years later when the people got to the border.

The Journey Around Edom

As the people were making their way toward Canaan, they hoped to take a shortcut through Edom, the land God had promised to Esau. They promised not to cause any trouble or do any damage to the little country. Yet the Edomite king said, "No, we will not let you pass through our country." So the Israelites had to take the long way around to get to the Promised Land.

On their way around Edom, they came across a small mountain range. It was on top of one of these mountains that Aaron died and was buried. For years Moses and Aaron had worked side by side in unselfish labor for God and had faced many problems together. Now they were old men. With deep sorrow, Moses took Aaron's priestly garments and put them on Eleazar, Aaron's son. The people mourned for Aaron, their high priest, but no one sorrowed more than his brother, Moses. After thirty days of mourning, the people moved on toward Canaan.

Through the desert, they came across an area that had lots of deadly snakes. Because of their continued complaining, God withdrew His protection from the poisonous serpents, and many were bitten and died. The people begged Moses to pray for them, which he did. God told Moses to make a brass snake and put it on a high pole so that those who were bitten could look up to God in faith and be healed. This was a symbol of the Son of God who would come, die on the cross, defeat the devil, and heal people of their sin. He alone could protect, heal, and save.

The Conquest of Bashan

After going south around Edom, the Israelites headed north. Now they had to go through the country of the Amorites, who were a fierce people and had a large army.

Moses politely asked their king for permission to pass through his country. When the king refused, that was their final defiance of God. The Israelites prepared for battle, crossed the river, fought the Amorites, and won.

Filled with courage, the Israelites moved north toward the country of Bashan. The country was well protected with walls and huge houses made of stone; the people there were giants. Og, their king, came against the Israelites with a large army. This time, Moses inspired the people with courage and faith in God, and the Israelites defeated the king and his men. Then one of the Israelite tribes occupied the territory.

Balaam
Next the Israelites came to the borders of Moab, and the people there were worried, because they had heard how the Israelites defeated nations that had previously taken Moabite territory in Canaan. They didn't want to risk an attack. So Balak, the king of the Moabites, sent for Balaam, who was once a prophet of God and claimed to worship Him but had since become involved in witchcraft and turned against God. The king wanted Balaam to curse Israel. Balaam knew that it wouldn't work, but the king offered to pay him a lot of money for doing so.

It was quite a distance to Balaam's house in another country. Balaam knew it was wrong to curse Israel, but as he thought about the reward, he finally gave in and decided to go. During the night, God told him not to go, so in the morning he told the messengers what God had said and sent them back. Then the king sent a second group of messengers to talk to Balaam. When he hesitated, they gave up and went back home. During the night, the Lord said to Balaam, "If you really want to go to Moab, go ahead." So in the morning, Balaam got on his donkey and headed for Moab.

On the way, an angel of the Lord stood in the road. The donkey saw him, got scared, and went out in the field to get around him. Balaam got mad at the donkey and beat her unmercifully until she got back on the road. Later they came to a very narrow place in the road where it was impossible for the donkey to get around the angel, so it crushed Balaam's foot on the wall and fell to the ground with Balaam on top. Balaam was furious and said to the donkey, "If I had a sword, I'd kill you."

> Yet we have a work to do to resist temptation. Those who would not fall a prey to Satan's devices must guard well the avenues of the soul; they must avoid reading, seeing, or hearing that which will suggest impure thoughts. The mind should not be left to wander at random upon every subject that the adversary of souls may suggest.
> —*Patriarchs and Prophets*, 460

38 A BRIEF HISTORY OF GOD'S LOVE

Then God spoke through the donkey, "What have I done to you for you to beat me three times?" Balaam didn't even realize that his donkey was talking to him and answered, "Because you've disobeyed me and made a fool of me." Then Balaam's eyes were opened and he saw the angel standing there with a sword in his hand ready to kill him. Balaam bowed and threw himself on the ground. The angel said, "You have beaten your innocent donkey three times because she tried to get around me. She saved your life." Balaam said, "I admit that I did wrong; may God forgive me. I didn't know you were blocking the road." Even today, many people become angry at roadblocks intended to save them from harm.

Then the Lord let Balaam continue to Moab. When the king heard that Balaam was on his way, he took some dignitaries and went out to welcome him. Balaam explained his delay and then said, "I can only say what God tells me to say." Balaam knew about the sacrificial system of the Hebrews, so he asked for seven altars to be set up on a high place and sacrificed on each one, promising God that he would say what He wanted him to say.

The king and his nobles gathered to hear what Balaam would say. They expected Balaam to curse Israel, thus stopping their advance. Instead, Balaam blessed the Hebrews. Balak the king was angry about this. To please the king, Balaam came up with another idea. Balaam would lead the Hebrews into idolatry and sin, which would displease God and separate them from His blessings. He suggested to the king that he hold a big festival near the border with music and dancing and invite the Hebrews to take part. Many of them did. Then the king sent Moabite women among the Hebrews to tempt their men to have sex with them.

> As the glow of the descending sun lights up the mountain peaks long after the sun itself has sunk behind the hills, so the works of the pure, the holy, and the good shed light upon the world long after the actors themselves have passed away. Their works, their words, their example, will forever live.
> —*Patriarchs and Prophets*, 481

The Israelites who could not be defeated in warfare were overcome by taking part in Moabite feastings and having sex with their prostitutes. Satan was the one behind all this. God had to discipline the Israelites for their disobedience and the Moabites for what they did to Israel. God's people must not let a single cherished sin, such as lust or love of riches, ruin their characters and cause our final destruction.

Apostasy at the Jordan

The Israelites moved ahead and settled in a beautiful valley so close to the Promised Land that only the river Jordan was between them. The people who lived there were vile idolaters who worshiped Baal. They were a terrible influence on the Israelites. The vile rituals were so disgraceful that thousands in the camp became ill and died. It got so bad that Zimri, one of the nobles in Israel, brought a royal Midianite princess into his tent in the Israelite camp to have sex with her. Zimri was drunk and boasted boldly about his fornication. When Phinehas, the son of the high priest, saw this, he took a spear, went into Zimri's tent, and killed him and the woman. Finally, Israel saw their sin for what it was and repented.

For someone who follows God to become as bold in sin as Zimri takes time. Gradually, the mind can be educated to think there's nothing wrong with sin as long as no one is being hurt. That is why God's people must guard their hearts and minds from giving in to even the smallest temptations.

The Law Repeated

The Lord told Moses that is was time for Israel to take possession of Canaan. As Moses stood on a small mountain overlooking the Promised Land, he wondered if God might change His mind and allow Moses to enter with his people, even though he had hit the rock to get water rather than speaking to it as God had commanded. He talked to God about it, but the Lord said, "Let's not keep talking about that. Look to the west, north, south, and east and take a good look at the land of Canaan, because you will not cross the Jordan River with the people." Moses submitted to the Lord's will, but was worried about who would take the leadership role. The Lord said, "Take Joshua, who has been your assistant for some time now, and go to the sanctuary. In front of the people lay your hands on him as a sign that you are transferring the leadership role to him."

Moses then reminded the people about what they had been through together, beginning with the deliverance from Egypt. Then he repeated God's law, told them how much God loved them, and encouraged them to continue to love Him, obey Him, and be faithful to Him. Finally, he reminded them that God does keep His promises.

The Death of Moses

Moses knew that he would soon die. God told him to leave the camp and go up Mt. Nebo. Moses had often left the camp to go there and pray, but this time he knew it would be the last time. Before he left, he stood before the people and blessed them, like a closing benediction to his life and leadership.

On the way up to Mt. Nebo, he thought about his life, beginning with his time in Egypt and the miraculous deliverance of the people. He thought of all the responsibilities and troubles he had as leader and how God had sustained him. Then God gave him an advanced view of the coming of Christ from the time He was a babe in Bethlehem to the time He was betrayed, crucified, and resurrected. He saw the whole journey of spiritual Israel through the end of time and into heaven.

Then Moses, the servant of the Lord, lay down like an old, tired warrior and died. The Lord had the angels bury him so that no one would try to come worship his burial spot. Satan rejoiced and claimed that all those who died belonged to him because they had sinned. Not long after, the Son of God came down personally to resurrect Moses. He did not argue with Satan about who Moses belonged to but rebuked him and his evil angels, raised Moses from the dead, and took him straight to heaven.

Crossing the Jordan

For thirty days the Israelites deeply mourned their departed leader. The memories of his unselfish life and powerful leadership never left them, and his influence did not die out. They remembered what he said and did. In addition, the signs of God's leadership were still visible, the pillar of cloud by day and the pillar of fire at night.

Joshua took over the leadership but not with self-confidence. He thought about the heavy responsibilities involved and the burdens he would have to carry. The first thing God told him to do was to take the Israelites across the Jordan River and into the Promised Land. However, just across the river was the fortified city of Jericho. Would the people there resist the Israelites or let them pass? Joshua sent two young men to spy out the city. Rahab, a woman of the city, saw that the men were in danger from the suspicious citizens and, at her own peril, took them in overnight.

The spies came back and told Joshua that the people were scared to death because they had heard what God had done for the Israelites and wondered what He would do next. Confident, Joshua decided to advance. When they got to the Jordan River, the priests carrying the ark and the holy things from the sanctuary led the way. As they stepped into the edge of the river, the water pulled away and made a dry path for the people to walk across, just as it had the Red Sea some forty years before. It stayed dry until the people were across and the priests stepped onto the bank. One representative from each of the twelve tribes had picked up a stone from the riverbed, and they used the stones to build a memorial of

> It is the will of God that union and brotherly love should exist among His people. The prayer of Christ just before His crucifixion was that His disciples might be one as He is one with the Father, that the world might believe that God had sent Him. This most touching and wonderful prayer reaches down the ages, even to our day; for His words were, "Neither pray I for these alone, but for them also which shall believe on Me through their word." John 17:20.
>
> —*Patriarchs and Prophets*, 520

what God had done. They camped on the plains of Jericho and celebrated Passover.

The Fall of Jericho
The city of Jericho was the center of worship of the goddess Ashtaroth, the goddess of the moon, and was heavily fortified. Joshua prayed and, in obedience to the Lord's command, prepared to move ahead. He marched his men around the city with the priests, carrying the holy things from the sanctuary, leading the way. Next came the trumpeters and the army. Per God's instructions, they marched around the city once a day for six days. On the seventh day they marched around the city seven times. Then Joshua ordered the trumpets to blow long and hard, and the walls around the city collapsed. The Israelite army stormed in, killed everyone and everything except Rahab and her family, and took possession of the territory. God can do great things when we just believe in and obey Him!

The Blessings and the Curses
Before the Israelites could finish driving out the people who lived in Canaan, they needed to re-dedicate themselves to God. Military operations were suspended, and with God's protection, Israel stopped to thank Him for everything He had done. Every seventh year, they were to hear the law of God and the statutes read aloud.

Over the years, it was the responsibility of the priests, teachers, and parents to make sure that the children understood the love and holiness of God and the meaning of the Ten Commandments. Years later, when the Bible was written, it was to help everyone, including the children, understand the history of God's people.

> The Lord would place a check upon the inordinate love of property and power. Great evils would result from the continued accumulation of wealth by one class, and the poverty and degradation of another. Without some restraint the power of the wealthy would become a monopoly, and the poor, though in every respect fully as worthy in God's sight, would be regarded and treated as inferior to their more prosperous brethren.
> —*Patriarchs and Prophets*, 534

League With the Gibeonites
As the Israelites were camped at Gilgal, a group of people who wanted to make a peace treaty with Joshua visited them. They claimed to be from a faraway country and had heard

about Israel from their neighbors. When Joshua asked them again who they were and what country they came from, they pointed to their dirty clothes and shoes to show that they came a long way. Joshua and the people didn't ask the Lord about it, so they made a peace treaty with these people. Three days later the Israelites found out that the people, the Gibeonites, had lied. They did not live very far away; in fact, they were almost neighbors. Joshua was angry that they had used deceit to form a treaty, but he honored it and let them stay and work for the Israelites doing whatever needed to be done.

The Gibeonites had four large cities in their territory governed by elders instead of a king. Their willingness to surrender to the Israelites without a fight made the neighboring kings angry. Five Canaanite kings banded together to attack the Gibeonites. The Gibeonites weren't prepared for battle, so they asked Joshua for help. Joshua immediately responded, took his forces, and marched all night to get there. The battle against the attacking Amorites lasted all day, and God fulfilled His promise to help Joshua defeat them by keeping the sun from going down at the usual time and letting the moon shine brighter. There has been no day like it since. Clearly, God is in control of all creation.

The Division of Canaan
Battles for the Promised Land territory continued for several more years, but eventually Joshua won all of Canaan and the land was at rest. However, many Canaanites still lived within its borders. Before Joshua, the high priest, could turn the command of Israel over to someone else, the land had to be divided among the tribes. Joshua and the tribal leaders met to decide where each tribe would settle. If there were any hostile Canaanites left in the chosen territories, each tribe would have to decide what to do with them.

Caleb, one of the men who had gone with Joshua to spy out the land years before and who had been helping Joshua all these years, was now an old man, more than eighty years old. He wanted to settle in a certain area that God had promised him long ago, and it was granted him.

As the tribes settled in their tribal areas, they made laws for their part of the country on how to deal with criminals. For instance, if someone committed murder, he was arrested and had to go to court. But a sentence could not be imposed on the basis of one witness; there had to be at least two witnesses. Also if the one who was accused of committing the murder was found innocent, he was allowed to escape to one of six cities of refuge that had been set up for those who had been accused of murder to protect them from anyone who might want to get even while they awaited judgment. If they didn't stay in that city, they could not be guaranteed protection.

The Last Words of Joshua

When the wars had ended and the people had settled down, Joshua retired. But as his age began to show, he was concerned about the future of Israel. He called the people together and, like a loving father, said to them, "You have seen all that the Lord has done for you. Now that you have peace, don't get so comfortable that you forget to obey the Lord and keep His commandments. Make up your mind once and for all. If God is God, and He is, then serve Him. As for me and my family, we will continue to serve the Lord."

Then he reminded them that they could not serve the Lord and obey Him in their own strength, no matter how hard they might try. They would need God's help; they just had to ask Him. Then he dismissed the people; his work was finished. The people had served the Lord all the days of Joshua, and they continued to serve God all the years of the elders who outlived Joshua.

Tithes and Offerings

To keep the economy of the country going, God's system of tithes and offerings continued as it had been for years. The Lord had said to the people, "The tithe is mine, which includes one-tenth of your income and from whatever you get from your flocks and herds. It is for the support of the priests, while the freewill offerings support the sanctuary and help those in need."

God also reminded the people that each person was a steward of the Lord's property because everything belonged to Him. In that sense we are laborers together with Him, advancing His kingdom, and He wants us to tangibly and sacrificially express our gratitude to Him. In return, he pours out blessings from heaven on the faithful.

God's Care for the Poor

God is very concerned about the poor and asks us to do all we can to help them. To do so blesses the giver and the receiver. In the days of Moses, every third year the people were asked to use their second tithe to feed and help the poor and needy in their own homes. Also, the poor were allowed to glean any produce leftover in the fields after

> The very ones whom God purposes to use as His instruments for a special work, Satan employs his utmost power to lead astray. He attacks us at our weak points, working through defects in the character to gain control of the whole man; and he knows that if these defects are cherished, he will succeed. But none need be overcome. Man is not left alone to conquer the power of evil by his own feeble efforts.
> —*Patriarchs and Prophets*, 568

the harvest. The people were told never to look down on the poor, for they, too, are God's children.

Every seventh year the land would be left to rest; no sowing or harvesting would be done. This practice would rejuvenate the land. Any crops that sprang up voluntarily were free for the poor to harvest. God said, "The land is Mine. I will give it rain in its season, and it will give you the grain, fruit, and the produce that you need."

The Annual Feasts

Three times a year all the people, young and old, came from everywhere in Israel for a special worship. But what would protect their homes from the hostile tribes nearby while they were gone? God had promised to do so. The first festival of the year was to celebrate the Passover, their freedom from Egypt. The second festival, Pentecost, was to celebrate the new harvest, and the third festival, Feast of Tabernacles, was a spiritual festival of thanksgiving.

At these festivals the people were encouraged to continue to be loyal to God. They would praise God for His love, His forgiveness of their sins, and His promise to continue to be with them.

The Earlier Judges

After the Israelites had taken a part of Canaan, they settled down and made agreements with the Canaanites in the rest of the country. This is not what God had in mind, because the Canaanites, with their idolatry and immoral practices, would influence the Israelites. All of this, together with feastings and uncontrolled appetite, lessened the strength of the Israelites and affected their health. Their enemies would try to steal their harvests, and the Midianites were always ready to attack them.

The Lord asked Gideon to get an army together to defeat the Midianites. Gideon wanted to make sure that this was what God was asking him to do. He decided to take a piece of wool outside to see if it would get wet when everything around it was dry. In the morning the wool was wet and the ground was still dry. But as Gideon thought about it, he realized that this was natural because wool naturally absorbs moisture. So he did the opposite and prayed that if the ground was wet and the wool was dry, that would be a miracle, and that's what happened.

Gideon called for men to fight the Midianites with him. Ten thousand volunteered. Then God told Gideon that he had too many men; if they won, they would take the credit for themselves. God told him to release those who had things to take care of back home. Those who were determined to stay should be tested. Gideon was to watch them as they approached a brook: those who drank leisurely with their face in the water were dismissed, but those who drank water from their cupped hand while looking around for the enemy were accepted.

Gideon took the three hundred remaining men and moved closer to the Midianite camp. Gideon went in the dark and stood quietly near the enemy camp. There he heard one Midianite soldier tell another about a dream he had in which he saw a huge loaf of bread come rolling down the hill, destroying their camp. The other soldier answered that only Gideon could defeat them. When Gideon heard that, he knew it was time to attack. In the middle of the night, he divided his troops, told them to light their torches and blow their trumpets, and commanded them to attack the Midianite camp from different sides. God's army of 300 Israelites killed 120,000 Midianites, forever eliminating them as a threat to Israel.

When the army got home, the people proposed that Gideon become their king. He refused and reminded them that God was their only King.

Samson
The Israelites continued to be troubled by their enemies, particularly the Philistines. One day an angel appeared to Manoah's wife, who had no children, and told her that she would have a baby boy through whom God would deliver Israel from the Philistines. She and Manoah thanked the Lord and prayed that God would help them know how to raise this child. The angel appeared again and said, "Your wife should not drink any wine or strong drink and should eat only healthful food. And when he's born and you raise him, don't give in to him and give him everything he wants." Parents have an enormous responsibility to seek God's wisdom and to stay as close as possible to God's ideals for humankind, because everything they do, good *and* bad, will affect their children and their children's children.

When the baby was born, they named him Samson. As he grew, Samson's parents told him that God had chosen him to do something special for Israel, and as a sign of this promise, he was to let his hair grow long and never cut it. When he was a young man, Samson often visited the Philistines to visit friends. One time while he was there, he fell in love with a beautiful Philistine woman and decided to marry her. His parents did not approve of the marriage, because she was not an Israelite. However, he insisted that she was the only one who made him happy, and he decided to marry her in spite of their objections.

During the marriage feast, Samson's bride made him angry, so he decided to go home to visit his parents awhile. When he came back his father-in-law said, "Because you were gone so long, I thought you didn't care for my daughter anymore, so I gave her to someone else. Why don't you marry her younger sister?" Samson was furious and ruined all their crops in revenge. This made the Philistines so angry that they killed the wife, and this, in turn, so enraged Samson that he slaughtered thousands of them. At this victory, the Israelites decided to make Samson a judge, and he served in that role for twenty years.

Samson fell in love with a woman named Delilah from the valley of Sorek. The Philistines offered to pay her if she discovered the source of Samson's unusual strength. She continually hounded him for the secret. Eventually, Samson gave in and revealed that his long hair, a symbol of his connection with the God of Israel, was the key to his power. Delilah told her countrymen what she had learned. Soon after, while Samson slept soundly, someone sneaked in and gently cut off his long hair. Then the Philistines who were waiting outside the door burst in and arrested Samson. Samson tried to fight them off but couldn't. The invaders poked out Samson's eyes, blinding him, and carried him away to prison.

Later, during a large Philistine festival, his captors took Samson to their temple stadium to make fun of the blind Israelite man. Thousands of men, women, and children were there to watch. Samson pretended to be tired and asked if he might lean against the temple pillars. Resting there, he prayed, "Oh, Lord, I have sinned, please forgive me, and strengthen me one last time." The Lord answered his prayer. Samson pushed against the two weight-bearing pillars, they gave way, and the whole temple stadium collapsed, killing himself and all the people.

Samson's story shows that our strength and our effectiveness for God's mission comes exclusively from and depends entirely on our faithfulness to God.

> Would that all who have not chosen Christ might realize that He has something vastly better to offer them that they are seeking for themselves. Man is doing the greatest injury and injustice to his own soul when he thinks and acts contrary to the will of God. No real joy can be found in the path forbidden by Him who knows what is best, and who plans for the good of His creatures. The path of transgression leads to misery and destruction; but wisdom's "ways are ways of pleasantness, and all her paths are peace." Proverbs 3:17.
> —*Patriarchs and Prophets*, 600

The Child Samuel

Back in Israel, a man named Elkanah, who was rich and loved the Lord, had two wives. His first wife, Hannah, had not been able to have children. Eager for heirs, Elkanah took a second wife, who bore sons and daughters. Hannah longed for the same privilege, and her heart was crushed that she could not seem to bear children.

Hannah went alone to pray by the sanctuary curtains. She begged that the Lord would give her a son, and if He would, she promised to dedicate him to God. She started to cry and wept so hard that she began to groan. The high priest wondered if she were drunk. She said, "No, my lord, I have not been drinking. I feel hurt because I can't have children, and I'm asking the Lord to help me." Then the high priest blessed her and said, "Be at peace; may the Lord answer your prayer."

God did answer Hannah's prayer. She had a baby boy and named him Samuel. Hannah loved little Samuel with all her heart. She told him how much God loved him, and he grew up loving God. When Samuel was still a young boy, Elkanah and Hannah went back to the sanctuary to worship. They took Samuel with them and explained to Eli, the high priest, that they had promised to give Samuel back to God. Eli was glad to have a young helper, and Samuel, who was willing and kind, did his best to help the high priest in whatever way he could.

Eli and His Sons

Eli, the high priest, had two sons, Hophni and Phinehas, who were very rebellious. He had not raised them right and had always given in to them, and soon they were controlling him. Though unfit to help in the sanctuary, Eli let them work there. When people brought their offerings, his sons stole some of it for themselves. They even molested the women when they came to worship. Eli kept excusing their terrible behavior.

Then God sent a man to talk to Eli and told him that he was honoring his sons more than he was honoring God, bringing disgrace on God and on His people. Eli scolded his sons, but it didn't do any good. It was too late; Eli should have disciplined them when they were growing up.

The Ark Taken by the Philistines

Through all this, young Samuel remained loyal to God. As time went on and Eli got older, his eyes began to fail and he stayed in bed a lot. One night the Lord called Samuel by name. Samuel thought Eli was calling him, so he went to Eli's room and said, "Did you call me?" Eli said, "No, I didn't call you. Go back to bed." This happened three times. Finally, Eli said to Samuel, "Maybe the Lord is calling you. Say, 'Yes, Lord, I'm listening. What do you want me to do?'" The Lord spoke again and said, "I can't let things go on like this. I'm going to punish Eli's family and all of Israel." This scared young Samuel.

In the meantime, the Philistines were planning to attack Israel again. Israel was in rebellion and didn't consult God about their defense, and they were defeated. Disheartened, they returned to their camp and decided to take the ark with them as a good luck charm, as if the box itself held power. However, God hadn't given them permission to take the holy symbol into battle. The Philistines fought extra hard, because they were especially afraid of the Israelite army when the ark was in their midst, and they won the battle and took the ark. Thirty thousand Israelites died, including Eli's sons. When Eli learned his sons were dead and the ark had been captured, it was too much for him; he collapsed, broke his neck, and died. God allowed the Philistines to punish the Israelites for their sins.

The Philistines took the ark to the city of Ashdod and put it in their temple, which had a statue of their god Dagon in it. When they came in the next morning, the statue had fallen on its face before the ark. They lifted it, and again it fell, this time breaking into pieces. The Philistines decided this was a bad omen and took the ark to a field and left it. Even then, they were plagued and wanted to be rid of its influence.

Finally, they decided to send the ark back with an offering for the God of Israel. Some Philistines opposed it, but finally they placed the ark on a new wagon with an offering and hitched two cows to the wagon to pull it. They let the cows go, and the pair took a direct route to Israel as if someone were leading them. A few Philistines followed just to make sure the wagon and the ark were safely in the hands of the Israelites.

> There are many whom He has called to positions in His work because they have a humble and teachable spirit. In His providence He places them where they may learn of Him. He will reveal to them their defects of character, and to all who seek His aid He will give strength to correct their errors.
> —*Patriarchs and Prophets*, 633

The Schools of the Prophets

God wanted His people to be happy, healthy, and intelligent. He directed the Israelites to set up an educational system to help everyone mentally, physically, and spiritually, but especially the priests. If a young man wanted to become a spiritual leader, he would attend "the schools of the prophets." Samuel had been called by God to be a prophet, and he would often visit students. Training in these schools included spiritual disciplines, physical labor, health education, and music lessons to deepen their devotion and gratitude to God.

The First King of Israel

The Lord knew that Israel would eventually want to have a king like other nations. But a king in Israel needed to understand that he would rule under God as His representative and help people live by the principles God had given them.

Samuel, who was a prophet and functioned as judge and priest, was an excellent leader. The people respected Samuel and listened to him but were not totally committed to God as they should have been. Samuel was getting older, and Israel wanted to be like other nations and have a king.

God warned the people that a king would set up an army; draft men; force women to cook for the royal house, which would get bigger and bigger; and tax the nation. The people didn't realize how blessed they were to have a good government under Samuel without a king. They insisted on having a strong and powerful king, so finally God gave them what they wanted.

Saul was a young man who worked with his father, taking care of their herds and flocks. Some of the animals had strayed, so Saul and one of the servants went looking for them. They looked for three days but couldn't find them. They decided to go to Samuel the prophet for help.

When they got to the city where Samuel lived, the people told them that Samuel was on his way to a special religious service. Saul encountered Samuel along the road and explained what he needed. Samuel said, "Your animals have been found and are being taken home." Then he asked Saul to come with him and the elders to worship God on the high place. They were humbled and agreed. When they got there, Samuel asked Saul to sit in a place of honor. When the meeting was over, Samuel took Saul and his servant to his home to get a good night's rest.

The next morning, Saul thanked Samuel and he and his servant left for home. Samuel walked with them for a short way to say goodbye. As they were walking along, Samuel stopped and asked Saul's servant to go on ahead so he could have a private conversation with Saul. Samuel took a small vial of oil, poured it on Saul's head, kissed him on his cheeks, and said, "The Lord has anointed you to be king of Israel." Then to confirm this, he told Saul that on the way home, he would meet three men going to Bethel to worship God. One man would be carrying three baby goats, the other man three loaves of bread, and the third man a bottle of grape juice for the sacrificial feast. They would stop and salute Saul and give him two loaves of bread. And that's what happened.

As Saul neared home, he met some spiritual leaders coming out of the city, praising God and playing instruments. He joined them in singing, and the Holy Spirit came on him. He realized that God was calling him to lead Israel and would give him the strength he needed to do it.

The people of Israel didn't know that Saul had been anointed king. Samuel called the people together and had them decide who they wanted to be king by casting lots. God was guiding the process, and Saul was chosen. He was a head taller than all the men of Israel, and when the people saw him, they shouted, "God save and bless our king!"

The Presumption of Saul

In the second year of Saul's reign, he decided to reduce his army, which had so far been successful against their enemies, to only two thousand men. He figured that's all he needed to fight Israel's other enemies because God would help him, but that was presumption, not faith. When God asks us to do something, we need to do all we can to prepare for it.

Samuel had told Saul to wait with his men at Gilgal so that Samuel could offer sacrifices to the Lord and pray for their success. Saul waited a couple of days, got impatient, and decided to offer the sacrifices himself. That was a mistake, because Saul was not a priest. When Samuel arrived, Saul proudly told him what he had done. Samuel said, "Do you realize what you have done? You followed your own impulse and disobeyed God." Yet Saul did not humble himself.

A little later, Saul's son Jonathan and his armor-bearer went to find out how strong an army the Philistines had. They made their way down a gorge that separated the two armies. When the Philistines saw them, they shouted, "You two, why don't you come up to fight us and not sneak around down there like you are afraid?" Jonathan and his armor-bearer found a way to sneak up to the Philistine camp without being noticed, surprised the sentinels, and killed them. The other Philistine soldiers thought they were being attacked by the Israelite army and started fighting against one another.

When Saul and his men heard fighting, he ordered them to go after the Philistines and, under penalty of death, not to stop and eat anything until the battle was over. Jonathan and his armor-bearer hadn't heard that, and as they joined the others going after the Philistines, they found a beehive and ate some honey. Other Israelite soldiers were also ravenous during the exhausting fight, and they ate. When the Philistines were defeated, Jonathan got a lot of the credit. Saul was jealous, and when he heard that Jonathan and his armor-bearer had eaten during battle, he determined to kill them for it. However, the people stopped him from doing it. Saul's pride nearly led him to murder his own son.

> Oh, how precious is the sweet influence of the Spirit of God as it comes to depressed or despairing souls, encouraging the fainthearted, strengthening the feeble, and imparting courage and help to the tried servants of the Lord! Oh, what a God is ours, who deals gently with the erring and manifests His patience and tenderness in adversity, and when we are overwhelmed with some great sorrow!
> —*Patriarchs and Prophets*, 657

Saul Rejected

When Saul got back home, Samuel confronted him about his bad decisions at Gilgal. While Saul respected Samuel, he did not like to be corrected, so he began avoiding

Samuel. God told Saul to attack the Amalekites and to destroy them all. It was the most brilliant victory Saul had ever had, and he became very proud of himself. Saul captured Agag, the Amalekite king, but decided not to kill him as he should have. He also saved the enemy's flocks and herds to use them for offerings to the Lord so they wouldn't have to use their own animals.

When Samuel heard about this, he went to see Saul. However, Saul's heart was hardened. He justified himself and blamed everything on the people. Samuel told him that to obey God is better than all the sacrifices we might bring to the Lord and told Saul that God had not rejected him. Saul repented, not because he was sorry for what he did but because he was scared of being punished. When Samuel turned to leave, Saul grabbed the prophet's robe so hard to keep him from leaving that it tore. Then he killed the enemy king and did not use the flocks and herds of the Amalekites as sacrifices to the Lord.

Finally, because Saul repeatedly refused to humble himself and return to God, the Lord decided he was not fit to be king.

The Anointing of David

A few miles south of Jerusalem was Bethlehem, where little David was born and where his family lived. The Lord said to Samuel, "I have rejected Saul as king of Israel. I want you to go to Bethlehem, call the family of Jesse together, and have a special worship service with them."

When everyone was together, including the elders of the town, he asked Jesse if all of his sons were present. Jesse said, "Yes, except David, the youngest one, who is taking care of the sheep." Samuel told Jesse to send for David, because everyone needed to be there before he could have this special worship service. Then the Lord told Samuel to anoint one of Jesse's sons king. Samuel had a hard time deciding which one, because they were all so big and strong. When young David finally came, the Lord told Samuel to anoint him. When Samuel hesitated, the Lord told him not to judge people by their appearance but to consider their hearts, which only the Lord knows. So Samuel anointed David Israel's next king.

David and Goliath

As time went on, Saul realized that God was not with him, and he became depressed. His counselors advised him to get a harpist, because the music would make him feel better. David was chosen, and for a while, he went back and forth between the palace and his flocks in the field. Being in the palace gave David a glimpse of what it was like to be a king.

In the fields, David had learned to use his sling against wild animals to protect his sheep. One time a lion jumped at him and knocked him down, but David was able to kill the lion with the sling. David was very courageous.

Once, David went to Saul's camp to visit his brothers, who were at war fighting the Philistines. The enemy had challenged Israel's fighting men with one of their biggest soldiers. He was huge, about nine feet tall, and all muscle. He shouted at the Israelite camp, "Send a man over here to fight me. If he wins, we will be your servants. If I win, you will be our servants." All the Israelite men knew they couldn't defeat this giant. Even Saul went to look at him from a distance and gave up.

Angered by the giant's mocking of God and His people, David told Saul that he would fight the giant. Saul hesitated but eventually relented. He insisted that David should at least wear some armor. David tried on the armor, but it restricted his movement and he refused to wear it. As he made his way up the hill toward Goliath, David stopped at a little stream to pick up some stones for his sling. When Goliath saw him, he pushed back his helmet and laughed at his comparatively tiny opponent. That's just the opening David needed. He swung his sling with all his might. The stone flew and hit the giant in his forehead. Goliath stood there, surprised, for a moment and then collapsed. David ran up to him, cut off his head with his sword, and took it back to camp.

David a Fugitive
After David killed the giant, Saul put him in charge of part of the army and wouldn't let him return home. This made David depend more on God. While at the palace, David and Saul's son Jonathan became best friends, like brothers. One day when Saul and David returned from battle with the Philistines, the women of Israel came out to meet them with dancing and singing. One group would sing, "Saul killed thousands!" Another group responded, "And David killed tens of thousands." This made Saul jealous and angry. One day when David was playing the harp for him, Saul got up, grabbed his spear, and threw it at David. David ducked to avoid being hit and ran out as fast as he could. However, Saul kept looking for an opportunity to kill David. Pride leads to jealousy, and jealousy often leads to revenge and even murder.

Saul noticed that David liked his youngest daughter, Michal, and her feelings were mutual. Saul said he would allow them to marry if David would kill a certain number of Philistines. He hoped David would be killed in battle, but God protected David and he was successful. He and Michal were married, making him Saul's son-in-law. Even that didn't make Saul give up his quest to kill David. Time after time, the king sent soldiers, spies, and messengers to kill him, and time after time, God thwarted his efforts and protected David.

David asked Jonathan, "What have I done that your father hates me so much?" Jonathan said, "My father won't do anything against you without telling me." David knew he could be killed at any moment.

At that time, a sacred festival was being held in Israel. David decided not to go to the palace but instead went to see his brothers in Bethlehem. When Saul asked Jonathan where David was, Jonathan said, "I gave him permission to go home and visit his family." This made Saul so mad that he hurled his spear at Jonathan but missed. By this, Jonathan knew his father would not relent until David was dead, so he went to a prearranged spot where he would meet David to warn him not to return. When they saw each other, they hugged each other, cried, and said goodbye.

David didn't know where to go, so he went to see the high priest at the tabernacle in Nob. Under extreme stress, his faith faltered and he lied to the high priest, saying that the king had sent him on a secret errand and he needed bread. The only bread the priest had was the holy bread, and he decided to give David five small loaves to help him because he was on the king's business. He also asked for Goliath's sword, which was stored there, so the priest gave him that too. From there David went to the mountains and hid in a cave. Soon family members and others who sympathized with David joined him there, afraid that Saul would kill them too.

Saul planned to capture David at the cave, but David had already escaped. Saul decided there must have been spies in his camp who had tipped off David. For revenge, he decided to kill the high priest who had helped David, along with his whole family—eighty-five people total.

> All earthly powers are under the control of the Infinite One. To the mightiest ruler, to the most cruel oppressor, He says, "Hitherto shalt thou come, but no further." Job 38:11. God's power is constantly exercised to counteract the agencies of evil; He is ever at work among men, not for their destruction, but for their correction and preservation.
> —*Patriarchs and Prophets*, 694

The Magnanimity of David
Abiathar, one of the sons of the high priest, escaped the slaughter, found David, and told him what had happened. David was heartsick and blamed himself for having stopped to see the high priest. David invited Abiathar to stay with him, because he knew Saul would be hunting him too.

David was never sure where to go for safety. Saul always found out where he was. As he hid in Engedi, Saul went after him with three thousand men. David had only six hundred. As Saul was leading his men up a mountain, he went to rest alone in a large cave, which happened to be the same cave where David and his men were hiding. David's men told David that he should sneak up and kill the king. David refused, because God had anointed Saul as king, but he did crawl up and cut off a piece of the bottom of Saul's robe that he had laid aside. Shortly, Saul stood up, put on his robe, and left the cave.

When Saul got back to his men, David came out of the cave and shouted, "My lord, the king!" Saul was shocked to see him. David continued, "Why do you believe that I'm out to kill you? Look what I have!" David showed Saul the piece of the king's robe that he had cut off. Saul responded, "David, you are a better man than I am. If a man has a chance to kill his enemy, will he let him go?" Saul acknowledged that David would surely be king, and David agreed that when he was in power, he would allow Saul and his family to continue in peace.

It was about this time that Samuel the prophet died. From the time he was a little boy until his old age he had always been true to the Lord. What a contrast between the leadership of Saul and Samuel. The people now realized the mistake they had made when they insisted on having a king. With Samuel now gone, they wondered whether God would forsake them.

David and his men decided to stay in an area that belonged to Nabal, who had lots of sheep. They protected his sheep and shepherds from robbers. All they asked from Nabal in return was some food. Nabal was selfish and unhappy, and just for spite, he refused. This made David upset, and impulsively he decided to punish Nabal by attacking him. Nabal's wife, Abigail, was kind and felt differently than her husband. When she heard about the impending attack, she prepared food for David and his men and took it to them. She apologized for the harshness of her husband and asked David to forgive him. Her kindness impressed David; he realized he had overreacted, and he forgave Nabal.

Abigail returned home and told Nabal what she had done. When he realized how his inhospitable action had nearly cost him everything, he was so stricken that within ten days, he died. David had been so impressed with Abigail's kindness and love of the Lord that he decided to take care of her by marrying her, even though he already had a wife. The decision to take multiple wives, based on the custom of the perverse nations around, caused David pain throughout his life.

After a few months of peace, Saul again began trying to kill David. One time David sneaked into Saul's camp with Abishai. Everything was quiet, and Saul and all his men were asleep. Abishai was ready to kill Saul on the spot, but David stopped him. Instead, they took Saul's spear and water bottle and left camp.

When they reached a nearby hilltop, David shouted down to Abner, Saul's personal guard, "Abner, wake up! Why didn't you guard the king? We came over to your camp, crawled up to Saul's tent, found both of you sound asleep, and left. Here is proof that we were there." Then David held up Saul's spear and water bottle for Abner to see. This was the second time David had a chance to kill Saul but didn't do it.

After running for his life for so long, David's faith grew weary and he went to the Philistines for protection, which dishonored God. He was cordial with the king there and implied an allegiance with the Philistines, but he knew he would not ultimately betray God.

The Death of Saul
War broke out again between Israel and the Philistines. Saul asked God what to do, but God didn't answer him because of his stubborn, persistent disobedience. Saul decided to consult a witch, a practice clearly forbidden in Israel. He disguised himself and went with two attendants to see her during the night.

She recognized the king and asked, "Have you come to kill me?"

He said, "No, I need your help. Please bring up the prophet Samuel from the dead so I can ask him for advice."

The witch did her incantations, and an apparition that looked like Samuel came up covered with a mantle. It was actually the devil disguising himself as Samuel. He said, "The Lord will deliver you into the hands of the Philistines." At that, Saul fell to the ground as if he were dead. He had thus completely abandoned God.

The next day Saul and his men fought the Philistines with all the strength they had, but it didn't do any good. The Philistines won the battle, killing many Israelites and three of Saul's sons, including Jonathan. When Saul determined that his escape was impossible, he decided it would be better to die than to be taken captive and be mistreated. Saul's armor-bearer refused to kill him, so he threw himself on his own sword, killing himself.

Ancient and Modern Sorcery
Some people believe that the witch conjured Samuel from the dead, which isn't true. God uses other tools to communicate His messages and does not use Satan's methods to do so. This misunderstanding of the Bible story has led people to believe that if witches or sorcerers could communicate with the dead, then anyone could. It is Satan who makes predictions and then does his best to make them come true.

Through witchcraft and spiritualism, Satan also teaches that men do not really die but have an immortal soul that lives forever. That is not what the Bible teaches (see Ecclesiastes 9). In addition, Leviticus 19 tells us that those who communicate with spirits are an abomination to the Lord.

David at Ziklag
God prevented David and his men from fighting with the Philistines against the Israelites. God convinced the Philistine war leaders than it wasn't safe to have David fight with them, because he might turn on them during battle. They convinced their king to send him home.

A couple of days later, a messenger came to tell David about the death of Saul. He thought that David would be happy that Saul was dead. The messenger lied and said that he found Saul on the battlefield wounded, and that on Saul's request he had killed him. To prove it, the man showed him the golden bracelets he had taken from Saul's arm. David ripped his robe in half, and he and his men cried and mourned for Saul and Jonathan. When the initial shock of their death wore off, David killed the messenger for killing God's anointed king.

> Whoever under the reproof of God will humble the soul with confession and repentance, as did David, may be sure that there is hope for him. Whoever will in faith accept God's promises, will find pardon. The Lord will never cast away one truly repentant soul. He has given this promise: "Let him take hold of My strength, that he may make peace with Me; and he shall make peace with Me." Isaiah 27:5.
> —*Patriarchs and Prophets*, 726

David Called to the Throne

After a time of mourning, God told David to go to the city Hebron in the territory of Judah. When David and his men got to the city, they found the people waiting to make David king of the tribe of Judah. The Philistines did not interfere or go to war over it.

Eventually, the other tribes decided to make David king over all of Israel, not just the territory of Judah. Officials, priests, soldiers, officers, and elders all gathered in Hebron, dressed in their sacred garments for the ceremony. The high priest poured holy oil on David's brow and anointed him as king over all Israel. They placed a crown on his head and the royal scepter in his hand, and all the people promised to support him and be loyal to him.

The Reign of David

As soon as David was crowned king of all Israel, he decided to make Jerusalem (also known as Salem and Jebus) the capital of Israel. Hiram, the king of Tyre, made an alliance with David and sent men and supplies to help build a palace for him. This alliance bothered the Philistines and they decided to attack Jerusalem. David asked the Lord what he should do. The Lord said, "I'll help you defeat them." So David fought against the Philistines and defeated them. He was now firmly on the throne and had no more threats from foreign enemies.

David's next project was to bring the ark, the golden chest holding the Ten Commandments of God, to Jerusalem from where it had been left by the Philistines when they returned it via ox and cart. David took thousands of leading men with him to make it a festive and joyous occasion. The priests placed the ark on a wagon pulled by two oxen. The men, singing thanksgiving and praises to God, followed the wagon with shouts of joy. However, when the cart hit a bump in the road and a man named Uzzah steadied it with his hand, God struck him dead on the spot. David and his group had not followed God's instructions for how to move the ark (only the priests were to see it uncovered or touch it, and the sons of Kohath were to carry it by the staves on their shoulders). The joyful party ended in tragedy because David had not fully understood how sacred and important God's law is. David decided to leave the ark where it was, near Obed-Edom the Gittite's home. His family was blessed.

Three months later, David decided to try to bring the ark to the city again. This time, he was very careful to follow all of God's instructions. David was so happy that he took off his royal robe and jumped for joy in front of the wagon with the ark on it. When the procession got to Jerusalem, the gates were opened, and the ark was taken off the wagon by the priests and set in the place prepared for it.

The ark was placed in the portable sanctuary that Moses had built under the direction of God. David thought to himself, "I have built a palace for myself, but the Lord's presence is still with the ark in the tent. I need to build a suitable temple for the Lord."

That night the Lord spoke to Nathan the prophet and told him to tell David, "The Lord does not want you to build a temple for Him, because you are a warrior and have shed too much blood. Instead, God wants your son to build it." David accepted this message with humility, knowing that if he built the temple, people would give him the credit and he would become proud.

When neighboring nations saw the unity and strength of Israel, they decided it was useless to attack them. The Ammonites were an exception, and, along with their allies, they planned to attack Israel. David didn't wait to be attacked; instead, he instructed his military commander, Joab, to invade the Ammonite capital. The enemy was defeated but tried again the following year. This time, David himself took to the battlefield, and, with God's blessing, the entire enemy was soundly defeated.

David's Sin and Repentance

David had so much success and influence that he began to think he could do whatever he wanted. This pride and self-confidence led him into sin. One day as he was walking on the balcony of his palace, he looked down on Jerusalem and saw a beautiful woman washing herself in her backyard. He was smitten and sent for her. Bathsheba was flattered that the king would want to see her, so she dressed properly and went to the king. David told her how beautiful she looked and asked her about her husband. She told him that Uriah, her husband, was one of the officers under Joab's command fighting the Ammonites.

David and Bathsheba became attracted to each other and ended up committing adultery. A couple of months later, she told him she was pregnant. In order for David to cover his sin, which was punishable by death, he asked Joab to let Uriah come home on furlough, hoping he would sleep with his wife. That way, the pregnancy could be explained. That didn't work, so he sent word to Joab to put Uriah on the front lines of the fight so that he would be killed.

When Bathsheba got the news that her husband had been killed in battle, she was shocked and mourned for him. When her days of mourning were over, David brought her to the palace and married her. God knew what David had done, and soon the people knew about his sins of adultery and murder.

God sent Nathan the prophet to see David. Nathan greeted the king respectfully and then told him the story of two men, one rich and one poor. The rich man had many sheep, but the poor man had only one sheep. One day visitors came to see the rich man. He didn't want to take a sheep from his own flock to feed the visitors, so he killed the poor man's sheep as a meal for the visitors. David was furious at the injustice and said that the rich man deserved to die and that he should give the poor man four of his own sheep. The prophet said, "You are that rich man." Nathan then told David that since he had ordered Bathsheba's husband killed, his wives would be given to other men and four of his own sons would die. David mourned and repented sincerely.

No one, meek or mighty, is above God's law, and no sin, great or small, is too big for the Lord to forgive if we humble ourselves before Him and repent. However, just because the Lord forgives doesn't mean that we won't yet suffer the consequences of our rebellion. Those errors also reduce our influence for good.

The Rebellion of Absalom

Amnon, one David's sons, raped his sister. Absalom, David's other son, was very angry about this, and because for two years David had not done anything to avenge the crime, Absalom killed Amnon. Then he fled the country. Two years later, Joab convinced David to allow Absalom to return home but not to see David; after another two years, he was permitted to see his father.

Absalom was extremely handsome and ambitious, and the people regarded him as a hero. He would stand at the gates of the city, making friends with people. They told him about their problems and the inefficiency of the government to help solve them. Absalom sympathized with them and told them that if he were king, he would do a better job. The people supported him, and it soon looked like there could be an uprising. David couldn't believe it. Absalom even started to get an army together.

To keep Jerusalem from being destroyed by war, David left Jerusalem with his bodyguards. A number of priests brought the ark and joined David, but the king sent them back. God hadn't told him to take the ark, and David knew better than to use it for selfish purposes. Others decided to stay with David, and he thanked them for their friendship and support. What a scene—David, the king, walking along in bare feet, without his royal robe, feeling awful about his sins and mistakes, and asking God to forgive him.

As soon as David left Jerusalem, Absalom and his army marched in without a fight. Then his advisers told him to find and kill David who, together with his troops and followers, had already crossed the Jordan River for safety. Absalom and his men caught up with David and began to fight. God was with David's forces, and Absalom's troops were defeated. Joab, David's unscrupulous commander who had twice tried to reconcile father and son, caught up with Absalom, killed him, and ordered his body to be thrown into a pit and covered with rocks. Then Joab ordered the trumpet to be blown to stop the fighting.

When David heard what had happened to his son Absalom, he was heartbroken. He cried out loud, "My son, my son, Absalom! Oh, I wish I had been killed instead of you." When Joab heard that, he got upset with David, because God had given them the victory and it was time to thank his people for their effort. David knew Joab was right, so he stopped crying and went to watch his troops march by, blessings them for what they had done.

The Last Years of David

David did not immediately go back to Jerusalem, because a large number of Absalom's followers were still there. Finally, when David did go back, he decided to increase the army by instituting the draft, which required military service of every able-bodied man. The people didn't like this, because it gave other nations the impression that Israel's greatness was because of its army and not because of its commitment to God.

David became more interested in having a large army with officers and commanders than having the priests and magistrates needed for a good government. He even ordered a census. Even Joab, David's military commander, asked him why he was doing this. David listened but went ahead with his plans anyway. Soon David was convicted that what he was doing was wrong, and for the sake of the people, God decided to discipline David.

God let David choose his own punishment. He could choose three years of famine, three months of running from his enemies, or three days of a plague. David said, "Lord, it's too hard for me to make that kind of a decision. You know what is best. You decide." So the Lord sent the plague, which killed seventy thousand people.

As David aged, his health began to fail and he couldn't continue to carry the responsibilities of being king. Because of his feebleness, David was not able to work with his counselors and officials to handle the transition of power to Solomon. David's oldest surviving son, Adonijah, wanted to be king, and it looked like there might be a rebellion over it. God gave David a boost of strength and David appealed to the people, telling them that it was God who had chosen Solomon to be the next king and to build a temple for Him. Zadok the priest, Nathan the prophet, and Bathsheba, Solomon's mother, let David know that Adonijah was planning to fight for the throne, so David immediately abdicated his rule and pronounced Solomon king. After David's death, Adonijah was executed for his part in the attempted coup.

When David felt that he would soon die, he said to Solomon, "Son, I feel like death is approaching, and I will pass away and be buried like all other men. So love God, be loyal to Him, and be a man of courage and conviction. Keep God's commandments, and He will bless you." Then David died and was buried after reigning over Israel for forty years.

THE
KINGS

Insights From
Prophets and Kings

Solomon

Before King David passed away, he anointed his son Solomon as king of Israel. As a youthful ruler, Solomon needed not only to be able to lead an army, but also be a political leader and a good man, loving and serving God. He kept the law of God, because he knew that in order to carry his heavy responsibilities he must have strength beyond his own.

One day when he was praying, Solomon said to God, "I feel like a little child. How am I going to govern a whole country? Please give me understanding and wisdom." The Lord answered and said, "I have heard your prayer, and because you did not ask for riches, honor, a long life, nor for the death of your enemies but for wisdom and knowledge to govern My people, I will give you what you asked for." He stood before God as a learner.

Solomon was a witness to the countries around him about the kind of God he served. As the years went by, his knowledge of God and

> Those who today occupy positions of trust should seek to learn the lesson taught by Solomon's prayer. The higher the position a man occupies, the greater the responsibility that he has to bear, the wider will be the influence that he exerts and the greater his need of dependence on God. —*Prophets and Kings*, 30

His love for Him increased. All the nations nearby began to admire the kind of God that Solomon served.

The Temple and Its Dedication

It had been David's plan to build a temple for the Lord, but because he had fought so many wars and shed so much blood, God decided that a man of peace should build the temple. Per his father's instructions, David's son Solomon went ahead with the project, and for seven years Jerusalem was a busy place. The temple would be built on Mount Moriah near the spot where Abraham had nearly sacrificed Isaac many years before. All the preparations were made ahead of time, and all the cutting and hammering were done outdoors so that the interior construction was completed in silence. Even the King of Tyre sent skilled workers to help Solomon. When it was complete, Solomon set a date for its dedication, and leaders from many nations were invited.

During the event, Solomon had the sacred items from the portable sanctuary, including the ark with the Ten Commandments inside, moved into the grand new temple. The procession featured singing and the blowing of trumpets. When all the sacred items had been carefully put into the Most Holy Place, God's glory filled the place, and it was so bright and dazzling that the priests couldn't go back in. Solomon knelt down, raised his hands to the Lord, and dedicated the temple to the God of Israel. Everything about the temple inspired reverence and showed how holy God is.

During the night, the Lord appeared to Solomon in vision and promised that, if the people continued to follow God, the kingdom would be there forever. Then He warned Solomon about the dangers ahead. He told him that wherever there is prosperity, there is the danger that people will forget God.

> Christians are to keep themselves distinct and separate from the world, its spirit, and its influences. God is fully able to keep us in the world, but we are not to be of the world. His love is not uncertain and fluctuating. Ever He watches over His children with a care that is measureless. But He requires undivided allegiance.
> —*Prophets and Kings*, 59

Pride of Prosperity

As long as Solomon remained humble and upheld the law of God, the Lord was with him and continued to give him wisdom to govern Israel. God had told Moses that all of Israel's rulers should daily read His law and statutes to keep their minds focused. But after having built the temple, Solomon began making choices based on ambition for power and riches that undermined his loyalty to God.

To build his alliance with Egypt, Solomon befriended the pharaoh and married his daughter. At first glance, this seemed to be a blessing, because his wife joined him in worshiping God. However, Solomon decided to make other political alliances the same way, and soon he had married a number of princesses of heathen nations. His fame, honor, and wealth changed him, and he began to lose his dependence on God and became a greedy tyrant.

To please his idol-worshiping wives, Solomon built beautiful shrines for their gods on Mount Moriah near the temple. He even worshiped them himself and participated in horrific heathen rituals, including child sacrifice. Israel was horrified at first, but gradually began to follow suit and lose their commitment to God.

To avoid Solomon's fate, we must always submit ourselves to God and obey Him. Daily reading of God's Word and time in prayer will help guard against the devil's snares. If we aren't careful, we will go the direction that Solomon did and let our emotions and impulses overtake reason and truth.

Results of Transgression

Commitment to God and a willingness to give up things for Him is the foundation of our relationship with the Lord. We need to give God the credit for everything good, because it's all about Him and not about us. He is the one who helps us. God doesn't place as much importance on what or how much we do for Him as He does the spirit with which we do it.

When the Queen of Sheba heard about Solomon and all the things that he had accomplished, including building the magnificent temple, she decided to go meet him and see it all for herself. Solomon welcomed her, and they talked for a long time. She told him all about the wonderful and mysterious things that she had seen in nature but didn't understand. Then Solomon taught her about the wonderful God who created everything. He gave God credit for every good thing.

While she was there, she admitted that everything she saw was even greater than what she had heard. She said, "I was told only half of what I see." As she left for home, she praised the God of heaven and earth.

> The true penitent does not put his past sins from his remembrance. He does not, as soon as he has obtained peace, grow unconcerned in regard to the mistakes he has made. He thinks of those who have been led into evil by his course, and tries in every possible way to lead them back into the true path.
>
> —*Prophets and Kings*, 78

Solomon's Repentance

Over time, Solomon had become disobedient to God and his heart hardened against the Ten Commandments. He kept admiring what he had done to build up the kingdom of Israel and became proud. Finally, the Lord sent a prophet to Solomon telling him that since he had been disobedient the kingship would be taken away from his descendants. But the way the prophet said it, there was a glimmer of hope in it for Solomon. He saw the extreme error of his self-serving ways, repented, and asked the Lord to forgive him.

In Ecclesiastes 12:13, Solomon wrote: "Have reverence for God, and obey his commands, because this is all that we were created for." He thought especially about the young people and warned them not to follow his example. Security does not come from the things we have but from the principles we live by. No matter how intelligent a man is, and no matter how faithful he is to God, he should never trust in what he can do. Solomon's repentance was sincere, but the harm he had done, both to himself and to Israel, could not be erased. So, too, our choices can affect others for generations, for good or evil.

The Rending of the Kingdom

Solomon grew old, died, and was buried in Jerusalem where his father, David, was buried. Solomon's son Rehoboam became the next king. Solomon had wanted to prepare and train him for the responsibilities of being a king, but Solomon's selfish pursuits of pleasure and riches had kept him too busy. Rehoboam's mother was originally from Ammon. She didn't have a strong character, so Rehoboam was never fully committed to God.

When Rehoboam became king, the leaders of Israel asked him to lower the heavy taxes Solomon levied on the people. Rehoboam told them to come back in three days for his answer.

He first counseled with the old men who had served under his father. They told him to be kind to the people by lowering their taxes so they would be grateful and gladly serve him. Then Rehoboam counseled with the young men he grew up with. They told him to demonstrate his authority by making the people's burden even heavier. Rehoboam liked that idea because it made him feel powerful. Unfortunately, they failed to look at the bigger picture.

Hearing the king's plan to increase their taxes, Israel rebelled against Rehoboam and the country split. The ten northern tribes became known as Israel and the two southern tribes, with Rehoboam as their leader, as Judah. When Rehoboam's tax man visited the north to make amends, they stoned him to death.

When he heard this, Rehoboam formed an army with more than 180,000 men to go to war against Israel. That's when the Lord sent Shemaiah the prophet to tell

Rehoboam and his men that a war was contrary to God's will, so they disbanded and went home. For the next three years, Rehoboam focused on developing the country, recognizing that God was the Supreme Ruler. For a time, things went well for Judah.

Then the king began to focus on building cities, fortresses, and a defense system. Soon he forgot that God was their protector and returned to idolatry, and so did the people. God allowed the king of Egypt to attack the kingdom of Judah. When Israel cried out to God, humbled themselves, and prayed for help, the Lord did not allow Egypt to destroy Jerusalem. They did, however, take many of Jerusalem's treasures back home with him. The people were grateful that the pharaoh didn't destroy Jerusalem, but soon forgot that it was God who had protected them and returned to their idolatrous ways. Within a few years, Rehoboam died and was buried in Jerusalem. His son Abijah became king of Judah.

Jeroboam

Jeroboam, a former servant of Solomon, became ruler of the northern kingdom of Israel. He could have been a great leader if he had trusted God. Instead, he worried that his people might try to reunite with Judah when they went to visit the temple in Jerusalem. To prevent this, he set up two worship centers, each marked by a golden calf to represent God, in Israel—one in Bethel and the other in Dan. Many of the Levites living there fled to Israel to be with others who still worshiped God.

> The Lord seeks to save, not to destroy. He delights in the rescue of sinners. "As I live, saith the Lord God, I have no pleasure in the death of the wicked." Ezekiel 33:11. By warnings and entreaties He calls the wayward to cease from their evil-doing and to turn to Him and live.
> —*Prophets and Kings*, 105

The king's actions did not go unrebuked. The Lord sent a prophet to the altar where Jeroboam was worshiping to deliver His message of disapproval. The altar broke in two and the ashes of the sacrifices poured onto the ground. Then the hand Jeroboam raised in anger shriveled and atrophied. Seeing this should have led Jeroboam to repent, but he hardened his heart and determined more than ever to do what he wanted to do.

After ruling Israel for twenty-two years, Jeroboam suffered a big defeat by Abijah, king of Judah. During the fighting, Jeroboam was wounded and soon died. Even through their apostasy, God didn't give up on His people. He continued to draw them to Himself, and many of them responded.

National Apostasy

After Jeroboam's death, the people of Israel continued to slide further into idolatry for the next forty years. Eventually, Asa, who was ruling in Judah and obedient to God, took away all the altars of idolatry.

Asa's faith was put to the test when armies from Ethiopia came against Judah. He had prepared a small army for war and kept putting his faith in God. He prayed, "Lord, it doesn't matter to You whether I have a large army or a small one; if You're on our side we will not be defeated." King Asa's prayer was answered; he and his small army defeated the armies of Ethiopia.

Out of gratefulness, Asa continued to destroy everything related to idol worship. He committed himself to the Lord and commanded all in the land do the same. Later, fearing invasion from the northern kingdom of Israel, Asa made an alliance with the king of Syria and began to depend on him for help. The prophet Hanani brought a rebuke from God, which made Asa mad. He put the prophet in prison. After more than forty years as king of Judah, Asa died from a disease in his feet and legs.

Two years before Asa died, Ahab became king in the northern kingdom of Israel. He was an evil, apostate man and worshiped Baal. His wife, Jezebel, made things even worse by building altars to heathen gods all over the land and had her priests teach the people all sorts of blasphemous things. The whole nation declined into moral bankruptcy.

> Our hope is not in man, but in the living God. With full assurance of faith we may expect that He will unite His omnipotence with the efforts of human instrumentalities, for the glory of His name. Clad with the armor of His righteousness, we may gain the victory over every foe.
> —*Prophets and Kings*, 111

Elijah the Tishbite

During Ahab's rule, God called Elijah the Tishbite to speak for Him. Elijah was very sad when he saw that the people were worshiping a god called Baal instead of the real, true God. God told him to deliver a message to King Ahab. He marched into the palace unannounced and told the king that because of the nation's idol worship, there would be no rain for three years. The king was shocked, and before he could come back to his senses, Elijah had left.

On his way home, Elijah saw flowing streams and green foliage; it had been this way for years. No rain for three years would certainly bring about a change. The Lord directed him to go to a flowing mountain brook and hide there for a while. He could drink the water and ravens would deliver food. When the people heard about Elijah's message to the king, most of them laughed and didn't believe it would happen. But time passed, there was no rain, and the streams began to dry up. Because the people believed Baal controlled nature, they worshiped him more fervently, asking for rain.

Queen Jezebel was outraged. She refused to admit that the drought was because of their Baal worship. God used this punishment to let the people know that He controls nature, not Baal. Ahab and Jezebel wanted to kill Elijah, but they could not find him, so instead, they killed many of God's prophets in Israel. Not during the entire three years of drought did the people repent.

The Voice of Stern Rebuke

Elijah continued hiding by the brook until the drought dried the stream. Then the Lord told him to go into the neighboring heathen country of Sidon to the city of Zarephath, where a non-Israelite widow who believed in God would take care of him. When he came to the outskirts of the city, he saw a woman picking up sticks. He asked her for a drink of water, and as she went to fetch it, he asked her to bring him some bread too.

This widow treated all strangers with kindness, but she had hardly any food left in her house. She had only a tiny bit of oil and flour, and she told Elijah that this would just be enough for her and her little son's last meal. Then they both would starve to death. Again Elijah asked her for some water and a piece of bread, and then added, "If you do this, the Lord will bless you for it." Acting in faith, she gave him all she had. God rewarded her kindness and faith; after feeding Elijah, she never ran out of water, oil, or flour again. God blesses His people when they give unselfishly by faith.

Soon after, the widow's young son got very sick and died. She held her dead son close to her, showed him to Elijah, and asked if he had brought destruction on her family because of her sins. Elijah carried the boy upstairs, laid his body on the bed, and stretched himself over the little body three times, crying to the Lord to give the boy's life back. God heard his prayer and restored the little one to life. Then Elijah carried him downstairs to his mother, who saw that Elijah was in fact a man of God.

After the third year of drought, the Lord told Elijah to go see King Ahab. On his way he met Ahab's governor, Obadiah, who had remained faithful to God. At Elijah's request, Obadiah went to tell Ahab that Elijah was coming to see him. Ahab took some bodyguards and went to meet Elijah. The king looked at Elijah and said, "So here you are, the one who is bringing all these troubles on Israel." Elijah responded,

> The widow of Zarephath shared her morsel with Elijah, and in return her life and that of her son were preserved. And to all who, in time of trial and want, give sympathy and assistance to others more needy, God has promised great blessing. He has not changed.
>
> —*Prophets and Kings*, 131, 132

"No, it's not me. It's you and your house who worship Baal." Because Elijah trusted God, he wasn't afraid to deliver a painful, truthful message.

Carmel

Elijah asked Ahab to call the priests and the prophets of Baal to come to Mount Carmel. Early one morning Jezebel's priests and prophets, led by the king of Israel, gathered. Elijah challenged them saying, "Make up your minds. If God is God, follow Him. If Baal is your god, then follow him." No one declared loyalty to God.

Then Elijah told them to prepare a sacrifice, place it on Baal's altar, and pray that he would send fire down to burn up the sacrifice. The followers of Baal sacrificed a bull, placed it on Baal's altar, and danced and shouted to Baal, asking him to send down fire. Nothing happened.

Elijah got the Lord's altar ready, placed the sacrifice on it, and asked the men to dig a trench around it. Next he asked them to pour water all over the sacrifice until it overflowed into the trench. Then Elijah prayed, "Lord, let the people know that You are the God of heaven and earth." For a moment everything was quiet; then suddenly fire came down from heaven, burned up the sacrifice and part of the altar, and consumed the water in the ditch. The people were afraid that the fire would burn them up too, so they fell on their knees and cried out, "The Lord, He is God! The Lord, He is God!"

However, the priests of Baal refused to repent, so Elijah said, "These priests must be killed." The people were furious that they had been misled, so they took the priests and prophets of Baal down from Mount Carmel to the brook Kishon and killed them all.

From Jezreel to Horeb

Elijah stayed on Mount Carmel and prayed in faith for rain. When his servant reported a small cloud on the horizon, Elijah told Ahab to go back to Jerusalem as fast as he could before the storms came. Soon the wind-whipped sky filled with black clouds and it began to pour. The king couldn't see his way, so Elijah, strengthened by the power of God, sprinted in front of Ahab's chariot to guide the king back to Jerusalem.

When Ahab got back and told the queen what had happened on the mountain, Jezebel was furious and said Elijah must be killed because he had humiliated the

> The whole universe is watching with inexpressible interest the closing scenes of the great controversy between good and evil. The people of God are nearing the borders of the eternal world; what can be of more importance to them than that they be loyal to the God of heaven?
> —*Prophets and Kings*, 148

king and killed all the priests of Baal. When a messenger told Elijah about Jezebel's threat, he ran for the mountains to hide. It looked as if he had forgotten how God had protected him from the same threat a few short years before. He ran and ran in the rain until he was so depressed and exhausted that he sat down under a juniper tree and fell asleep.

God showed gentle mercy in response to Elijah's sinful despondency. As he was sleeping, an angel woke him and said, "Get up and eat. You have a long journey ahead and you haven't eaten for a while." Elijah sat up and saw a little fire, some baked bread, and a big bottle of water. Elijah was amazed and gladly ate, then went back to sleep. Twice this happened. After good rest, food, water, and warmth, he was strengthened enough to walk forty days to Horeb, where he found a hiding spot in a cave.

"What Doest Thou Here?"

One day, God spoke to Elijah through a powerful angel by the entrance of the cave. He asked, "What are you doing in here?" Elijah answered, "I've been faithful to God and stood up against the priests and prophets of Baal, but now the king and queen of Israel are trying to kill me. So I had hide." Then the angel asked him to stand just outside the cave's entrance, because the Lord was going to come by.

Immediately, a powerful wind blew and broke off some of the rocks on the mountain; then an earthquake shook the ground; and finally a roaring fire passed over. However, God wasn't in those displays. Finally, Elijah heard a small, quiet voice. Elijah pulled his robe over his face and ran to the cave's entrance. The Lord whispered, "What are you doing here, Elijah?" He again told God that he was hiding from Ahab and Jezebel.

Then the Lord told Elijah to go back where he came from and anoint Hazael king of Syria and anoint Jehu king of Israel. He was also to anoint Elisha as a prophet who would be Elijah's apprentice and successor. So this is what Elijah did. God was with him every step of the way.

God never leaves those who love and work for Him. We must often ask ourselves, "What doest thou here?" Are we following God in faith or succumbing to discouragement?

> If, under trying circumstances, men of spiritual power, pressed beyond measure, become discouraged and desponding, if at times they see nothing desirable in life, that they should choose it, this is nothing strange or new. Let all such remember that one of the mightiest of the prophets fled for his life before the rage of an infuriated woman.
>
> —*Prophets and Kings*, 173

"In the Spirit and Power of Elias"

People today, as in the days of Elijah, are worshiping the world's gods—money, fame, and pleasure. They don't give God credit for all He has done and created. Others get involved in spiritualism and witchcraft. Some make gods of themselves, praising their own accomplishments.

God gave us the Bible and the Ten Commandments, including the Sabbath, to show us the best way to achieve happiness on earth and entrance to heaven. When Christ was here, He kept the Sabbath. In unmistakable language Jesus said, "Don't think that I have come to change the law or what is written. As long as heaven and earth exist, God's law will exist. Those who tell people that God's law has been changed are not sent by God." The Sabbath is a sign of loyalty to God.

Those who gradually conform to worldly practices and customs eventually lose their connection with God. As the earth's history comes to an end, God will send people to call other people back to Him, back to keeping His law. All over the world, people who have remained faithful to God will be like stars brightly shining in a dark night.

Jehoshaphat

Jehoshaphat became king of Judah when he was thirty-five years old, and he followed the example of his father, King Asa, who loved the Lord. Jehoshaphat told the people not to follow the idolatrous practices and Baal worship going on in the northern kingdom of Israel under King Ahab. Over time, he destroyed the idol shrines within his territory. Under his leadership, the Sodomites living in the land began leaving, which freed the people of Judah from their influence. He set up a system to teach the people about God's law, because they had long since forgotten most of it. This resulted in a revival.

For many years, Jehoshaphat lived in peace, protected by God from nearby enemy nations. Unfortunately, Jehoshaphat agreed to let his son, Jehoram, marry Athaliah, the daughter of King Ahab and Jezebel in Israel to the north. This created an alliance between Judah and Israel that God did not ordain. Once, when the two kings met, Jehoshaphat and Ahab agreed to fight the Syrians to take the city of Ramoth. Jehoshaphat asked Ahab to pray about it, so Ahab asked his false prophets. Jehoshaphat didn't trust Ahab's prophets, so he said to ask the prophet Micaiah for advice. Micaiah told them they should not attack the Syrians, but Ahab was determined to do it and Jehoshaphat didn't have the courage to back out. During the battle, Ahab was hit by an arrow and died, so Jehoshaphat and all the soldiers went home.

Jehu the prophet came out to meet Jehoshaphat and said, "Was it right for you to have made an alliance with Ahab, who had no respect for God? But God sees a lot of good in you."

From then on, Jehoshaphat did his best to strengthen the country and to keep its focus on God. He also set up a judicial system, which guarded the rights and liberties of the people. God expected him to do this, because He is a God of justice. Jehoshaphat also fortified the cities and strengthened the army.

Near the end of Jehoshaphat's reign, the Moabites, Ammonites, and others joined forces to attack Judah. Jehoshaphat had prepared Judah for battle, but he knew he couldn't win without God's blessings. He asked the people to fast, pray, and come to the temple for a special meeting. There, Jehoshaphat cried out to God, claimed His promises, confessed their helplessness, and begged for divine protection from their enemies. The people also humbled themselves and asked God for help. Then Jahaziel, a Levite working at the temple, stood up and delivered a message from God: "Don't be afraid of your enemies; the winning battle will be yours, not theirs."

Early the next morning, Jehoshaphat and his men marched toward the battle zone. The choir, singing and praising God, led the procession. When they got to the battlefield, they learned that the enemy armies had turned on one another, and all their fighting men were dead. Shocked and overjoyed, Jehoshaphat and his army returned to Jerusalem, praising God for what He had done for them.

Every battle God's people face belongs to God. No matter what odds are stacked against us, if we trust God to see us through, He will, for His glory and our good.

The Fall of the House of Ahab
Ahab, king of the northern kingdom of Israel, became even more wicked in his later years than he had been in his early years. His wife, Jezebel, encouraged him in this wickedness. He became so hardened that he couldn't stand anyone not doing what he wanted them to do.

Near the palace there was vineyard Ahab wanted to buy for an herb garden. The owner, Naboth, refused to sell it because it had originally belonged to his father and ancestors. Selling that type of property was forbidden by the Levitical code. Ahab was disappointed and went back to the palace and told Jezebel what had happened. Jezebel said, "You're the king; you can do whatever you want. Don't worry, I'll get it for you." She wrote letters in the king's name accusing Naboth of cursing the king and God and suggested that he be stoned to death. Sadly, the elders of the city did as she said, and Ahab took the vineyard. The Lord told Elijah to confront Ahab and tell him that because of the terrible thing he did, his entire family would be killed. Ahab repented,

> A man may be in the active service of God while engaged in the ordinary, everyday duties—while felling trees, clearing the ground, or following the plow. The mother who trains her children for Christ is as truly working for God as is the minister in the pulpit.
>
> —*Prophets and Kings*, 219

and God delayed the punishment until after his death.

Three years later the Syrians attacked Israel, and Ahab was killed. Then Ahab's son Ahaziah took over as king. He did all the same wicked things his father had done. One day he fell and hurt himself and was laid up in bed, wondering about his future. The Lord sent Elijah to see him and deliver a message: "Since you followed Ahab your father and did the wicked things that he did, you will die in your bed." And that's what happened.

Ahaziah's brother Jehoram became king and reigned for twelve years. He didn't follow God either, so God punished him by allowing the neighboring enemies to attack and take everything the king had, including his wives and all of his children except his youngest son, Jehoahaz. Then Jehoram got a terrible bowel disease, which killed him within a couple of years. Jehoahaz took over, but he was just as bad.

God decided it was time to keep His promise to Ahab, so he had Elijah anoint Jehu king of Israel and commanded him to kill the rest of Ahab's surviving family, plus all the remaining prophets of Baal and everyone associated with their dynasty.

After that, Israel crowned young Joash king. He was the only remaining royal descendant of David. Then Israel experienced a reformation.

The Call of Elisha

As Elijah was getting up in years, the Lord told him to go and see a young man named Elisha, who was working on his father's farm. Their family loved the Lord and had raised Elisha to respect God. Elijah went to the farm to see Elisha, walked up to him in a field, and threw his robe over Elisha's shoulders, a sign to follow him. Elisha was free to follow Elijah or not. Because the family was familiar with Elijah's work, Elisha decided that he would accept the invitation. He said goodbye to his father and went with Elijah. When God calls us, we are to do as Elisha did and willingly leave behind whatever keeps us from His work.

Elisha's duties were not always glamorous. He provided Elijah, a great prophet, with humble service. Elisha never wavered. He always relied on God and did whatever Elisha asked him to do. He didn't fully realize it then, but the Lord was preparing him to take Elijah's place. The full work of ministry should always involve training younger

> The religion of Christ reveals itself as a vitalizing, pervading principle, a living, working, spiritual energy. When the heart is opened to the heavenly influence of truth and love, these principles will flow forth again like streams in the desert, causing fruitfulness to appear where now are barrenness and dearth.
> —*Prophets and Kings*, 234

workers to step in and complete the circle of service.

Samuel's schools of the prophets were in disrepair and enrollment had declined, so Elijah decided to make the schools grow again. Young people could go to the schools for an education and spiritual training. Elisha was excited to see what these schools were doing to help the young people, and he spent time teaching there.

God had told Elijah that he would be translated and taken to heaven without dying. God had also revealed this to Elisha and the leaders at the schools. One day when Elijah and Elisha were walking along, Elijah asked him what he could do for him before he left. Elisha said, "I would like to have twice as much of the Holy Spirit as God has given to you." Elijah said, "You are asking a lot. But that's God's decision. If you see me taken, then it's yours." When they got to the Jordan River, Elijah took his cape, rolled it up, and hit the water. The river parted and the two of them walked across on dry ground. As they walked, a chariot of fire pulled by horses of fire appeared in the sky, speeding toward the earth, and Elijah was picked up and taken to heaven. The Lord did not want him to die and be buried in some lonely grave in the desert.

When Elisha realized Elijah was gone, he cried out, "My father! My spiritual father!" Out of grief, he took his robe and tore it in half. Then he saw Elijah's cape left on the ground, so he picked it up, approached the Jordan River, rolled up the cape, and hit the water with it like Elijah had done. The river parted, and he walked across on dry ground. The students and followers watching knew that God had transferred the calling to Elisha, so they bowed before him.

The Healing of the Waters

The Jordan Valley was a beautiful place to live, but the spring that provided water had become polluted. Drinking from it was making people and cattle sick. The men of the city told Elisha about the problem and asked for his help. Elisha said, "Bring me a large container of salt." They did, and Elisha sprinkled the salt into the river. The water became pure again and stayed that way forever. That event illustrates how our lives need to be purified by the salt of God's Word and how we are to be the salt that brings life and purity to our environment.

A Prophet of Peace

The work of Elijah and Elisha was different. God called Elijah to condemn sin and idol worship and get the king and the people to repent. Elisha was to gently teach the people and students how to walk with God and live for Him.

One day as Elisha was on his way to the school in Bethel, some young men from the city who had heard about Elijah being taken to heaven laughed and made fun at such a thing. They said to Elisha, "You should go up, too, you bald head!" They became ruder and more disrespectful, and on and on they went. If Elisha had said nothing and just taken it all, then the mocking mob may have continually interfered with his ministry. So Elisha turned and God, through Elisha, cursed the group. Suddenly, two female bears came out of the woods and mauled all forty-two of them. That taught the boys and everyone else who heard the story to respect and show courtesy to Elisha, as well as to their ministers, teachers, and parents.

As Elisha was making his way through the area, he stopped at the village of Shunem to get some rest. One of the women recognized him and invited him in to eat. She did this every time he passed through town. One day she said to her husband, "Let's make a little room for him with a bed, a chair, a table, and a light." This was a nice, quiet retreat for Elisha, and he really appreciated their hospitality. The Lord also blessed their kindness by giving the barren woman a son.

Some years later, the little boy was out in the harvest field and suffered a heatstroke. They carried him to his mother, and he died in her arms. She placed him gently on Elisha's bed and went out looking for Elisha. She told him what had happened and insisted that Elisha come home with her. Elisha did as she asked. When they arrived, the prophet went into the bedroom, closed the door, and prayed to God. Then he lay on top of the boy and breathed into his mouth, and the boy's body got warm. Elisha left the room and walked around, praying, then came back and did the same thing again. The boy sneezed seven times and then opened his eyes. Elisha called for the mother. She could hardly believe her eyes; she rushed in, picked up her son, and left the room holding him, crying for joy.

> We know not in what line our children may be called to serve. They may spend their lives within the circle of the home; they may engage in life's common vocations, or go as teachers of the gospel to heathen lands; but all are alike called to be missionaries for God, ministers of mercy to the world.
> —*Prophets and Kings*, 245

Naaman

During one of the Syrian raids on Israel, some Israelites were taken captive. One young girl became a slave in the house of Naaman, captain of the Syrian army. The girl had been raised in a family that loved the Lord, and they taught her respect and reverence. Unfortunately, Naaman had leprosy. The little girl felt sorry for him, and she told her master's wife that there was a prophet in Israel who could heal him. Naaman heard this, so he decided to go to Israel to see the prophet.

When Naaman and his servant got there, Elisha didn't come out to see him in person. Instead, he sent his servant to tell Naaman to go dip himself in the Jordan

River seven times, and he would be healed. The captain was insulted and angry. He thought Elisha would come out and call down God's magic to heal him on the spot. So he turned away in a huff and left. The captain's servant said, "Master, why not try it? It can't hurt. He told you to do a simple thing, and a simple thing is simple to do." Naaman's faith won out, and on the way home they stopped by the Jordan River. The captain waded into the water and dipped himself seven times. The leprosy disappeared!

Naaman immediately went back to see Elisha and offered to pay him for the trouble, but Elisha refused. He said, "It was your faith in the God of Israel that brought you here and your obedience of dipping in the Jordan River that healed you." Naaman thanked Elisha, praised the God of Israel, left to go home, and worshiped the Lord ever afterward.

Gehazi, Elisha's servant, secretly raced after Naaman and told him that the prophet had changed his mind and would take some pay after all. Naaman gladly gave him some silver and fine clothes. However, Gehazi had lied and planned to keep the money for himself. When he came back, Elisha knew where he had been and what he had done. He said to Gehazi, "The leprosy of the captain will be on you and your children for the rest of your life." And it was. God hates lies and deceit, because He is a God of truth and faithfulness.

Elisha's Closing Ministry

The Syrian king decided to kill Elisha because he kept telling the king of Israel about the Syrians' battle plans. The king of Syria told his servants to find Elisha and bring him back to Syria. Elisha's servant heard about this and began to panic. Elisha prayed that the Lord would open his servant's eyes so he could see how the Lord was protecting them. The Lord answered Elisha's prayer, and the servant saw the surrounding hills filled with horses and chariots of fire. God had sent these angels to protect His people.

The Syrians kept coming for Elisha, but the prophet prayed that the Lord would make the Syrian troops blind, and He did. Then Elisha led them to see the king of Israel in Samaria. When the king saw them, he asked Elisha whether he should kill them. Elisha said, "No, don't kill those you captured. Give them something to eat and drink, and send them back to their king." Then Elisha prayed for the Lord to open the eyes of the men so they could see, which He did. The king fed them and sent them back home. For some time, Syria left Israel alone.

Eventually, though, the Syrian king decided to attack again. His troops surrounded Samaria and attacked. Famine had ravaged Samaria and the attack was fierce. Just as the king of Israel was about to give up and surrender, Elisha told him they would be delivered the next day. Sure enough, the next morning, God made a great noise, causing the Syrian soldiers to hear what they thought was the thunderous noise of many chariots and horses, as if a large army were about to attack them. They got scared and ran for their lives, leaving their tents and horses and food. Elisha thanked the Lord and praised Him for saving Israel.

After this Elisha continued to encourage the people and visit the schools and the students. One time some of the students decided to go to the Jordan River and cut down some trees to build a place where they could stay while they visited Elisha. As they were cutting down the trees, one student's ax head flew off the handle into the river and sank. He called to Elisha and said, "Sir, that ax is not mine; I borrowed it." Elisha asked where it fell, cut a little stick, threw it in the same spot, and the iron ax head floated up to the surface.

When Elisha got old and wasn't feeling well, young King Joash came to visit him and to ask for advice about the constant threat of Syrian invasion. Elisha said, "Pick up your bow and shoot an arrow out the window toward the east." Joash did as he was instructed. This represented Israel's total victory over the Syrians in Aphek. Then Elisha said, "Pick up the other arrows and hit the floor with them." The king hit the floor with the arrows three times. Elisha said, "You should have done it five or six times to show your complete determination. So now you will defeat the Syrians only three times."

Soon after, Elisha died and was buried.

"Nineveh, That Great City"

Nineveh was a great city, but it was full of crime and wickedness. However, some of its people wanted to know more about God. God asked Jonah the prophet to go tell the people to repent and turn back to Him. Jonah was overwhelmed as he thought of the nearly impossible task, so he decided to get on a boat going in the opposite direction. He forgot that God can overcome any obstacle.

Then the Lord sent a huge storm to the sea, and the frightened sailors prayed to their gods to save them. Jonah was down in the ship sleeping. The sailors were desperate, so they woke him up and asked him to pray to his God to save them. That didn't work, so they asked him who he was, where he was from, and where he was going. He told them that he was an Israelite and worshiped the God of heaven and earth. He also confessed that he was running from God's mission and that they should toss him overboard if they wanted to survive the storm. As soon as they did that, the storm stopped.

As Jonah sank into the ocean, God sent a big fish to swallow him up and take him on a three-day, three-night ride to the shore near Nineveh. There, the fish vomited him out onto dry land. This time Jonah obeyed God's command, went into the city, and walked from street to street, warning the people that God would destroy the city because of their wickedness. When the people heard that, they repented. The king announced a day of fasting and prayer. God forgave them and didn't destroy the city. When Jonah saw this, he should have celebrated, but he didn't want to be known as a false prophet since his prediction of doom didn't come true. Jonah went and sat outside the city to pout and see if anything would happen to Nineveh. God made a little plant grow up over Jonah for shade, and he loved the plant.

Then God taught him a lesson by sending an underground worm to chew on the roots of the plant so that it withered up as the sun rose, leaving him without shade. Jonah was despondent and angry about losing the plant. Then God said, "Why are you so upset about a tree you didn't even work to grow? You loved that little tree, didn't you? So why shouldn't I love the people of Nineveh when they turn to Me and repent?" The Lord wants his messengers of hope to be faithful and not to become discouraged and give up.

> In the last days of this earth's history, God's covenant with His commandment-keeping people is to be renewed.... "I will break the bow and the sword and the battle out of the earth, and will make them to lie down safely."
> —*Prophets and Kings*, 299

The Assyrian Captivity
The last few years of the kingdom of Israel were full of violence and bloodshed. Kings were assassinated to make room for more ambitious ones, and all principles of right and justice were set aside. Through the prophets Hosea and Amos, God gave the people message after message inviting them to repent and change, but it didn't do any good. They still loved and worshiped Baal and their other idol gods.

As a result, the Lord let the Assyrian army kill thousands; thousands more died from hunger and disease. Others were captured and taken to locations throughout Assyria. Some of those were still faithful to God, but the invasion put an end to the literal kingdom of Israel.

"Destroyed for Lack of Knowledge"
God loved Israel and its people, but when they rebelled against Him, He could no longer protect them. He had given them the Ten Commandments to guide them, but gradually the people became worse and worse. Satan was behind all this disobedience. Throughout the generations, the Lord had sent messages warning them that if they rebelled against God, He could no longer protect them from their enemies.

Hosea the prophet specifically said, "Because you have rejected the Lord and have forgotten His law, you opened the floodgates of wickedness to lying, killing, cursing, stealing, and committing adultery, and God has no choice but step in and do something about it." Had the people listened to the many messages God sent, they would have been spared the invasion of Assyria and the humiliation that followed. However, they persisted in doing what they wanted, and the Lord had no choice but to discipline them for their disobedience.

Even so, God's covenant with His people remains to this day. And we, too, must love Him and keep His Commandments.

The Call of Isaiah

When he was only sixteen years old, Uzziah became king of Judah and ruled for fifty-two years. He did what was right in the eyes of the Lord and ruled with wisdom. The country prospered as it had not since Solomon had died nearly two centuries before. However the people did not have a corresponding spiritual growth. Their worship of God was just a formality mixed with pride and rituals.

However, Uzziah got into spiritual trouble during the last years of his life. Though he was not a priest, he went into the sanctuary to burn incense on the altar. The high priest and his assistants stopped him, which hurt his ego. He got very angry with the priests, so God gave him leprosy right then and there.

During the final years of Uzziah, his son Jotham carried some heavy responsibilities for him. When his father died, Jotham became king.

It was during this time that the Lord called the young man Isaiah to be a prophet. He witnessed the fall of the kingdom of Israel to the north as it was attacked and overpowered by the Assyrians. The kingdom of Judah might be next. Isaiah saw that the prosperity of Judah had corrupted the people, and only a few remained loyal to God.

One day as Isaiah stood in front of the temple, the Lord gave him a vision. He was allowed to see into the Most Holy Place and saw God surrounded by thousands of angels singing, "Holy, holy, holy is the Lord, the whole earth is filled with His glory." When Isaiah saw that, he was overwhelmed to think that he was part of the chosen people of God and felt totally unfit to be their prophet. So an angel was sent to relieve him of his concern and the voice of God was heard saying, "Who will I send to the people to be a prophet and speak for Me?" Isaiah

> The heart of Infinite Love yearns after those who feel powerless to free themselves from the snares of Satan; and He graciously offers to strengthen them to live for Him. "Fear thou not," He bids them; "for I am with thee: be not dismayed; for I am thy God: I will strengthen thee; yea, I will help thee; yea, I will uphold thee with the right hand of My righteousness."
> —*Prophets and Kings*, 316

responded, "Lord, I'm willing, send me." Isaiah served God's people for more than sixty years, delivering messages of hope and triumph.

"Behold Your God!"

In the days of Isaiah, the people thought of God as harsh, waiting for any chance to punish His people. They had forgotten how patient God had been with them through the years. Isaiah remembered, however, so he continually reminded the people that God was their Creator, that He had brought them out of slavery in Egypt, and that He had given them Moses as their leader. He also told them that God is loving and merciful, forgives sins, and blesses those who are humble and depend on Him.

Then Isaiah called the people to repentance and said, "Seek the Lord, forsake your wicked ways. Turn to the Lord, and He will have mercy on you and forgive your sins." Isaiah's appeals were not useless. The people started to see their Maker as a loving God, and many turned away from their idols.

Ahaz

When idolatry began to surface again, it became worse than it had ever been, and some who had been against it gave in and participated in these evil practices. Even so, the people still considered themselves God's people. The prophet Isaiah also told the people that they were becoming like Sodom and Gomorrah and that if they didn't ask God to help them overcome their sins, things would go badly.

God's prophets had appealed to Israel and Judah to be humble, to depend on God, and to live a life of practical godliness, loving their neighbors and helping those in need. When there was no response, the only recourse the Lord had was to discipline His people. The Lord asked Isaiah to go see King Ahaz, who was worried about an attack from Syria, and tell the king, "Don't worry, God will be with you and protect you."

It would have been good for Judah if Ahaz had listened, but instead he asked the king of Assyria to come help defend Judah against its enemies. The Assyrians helped, but then the people of Judah constantly worried about the Assyrians taking over their country. Still, Ahaz did not repent and turn to God for help as he should have. In fact,

> Far more than we do, we need to speak of the precious chapters in our experience, of the mercy and loving-kindness of God, of the matchless depths of the Saviour's love. When mind and heart are filled with the love of God, it will not be difficult to impart that which enters into the spiritual life.
> —*Prophets and Kings*, 347, 348

he even closed the temple, stopped the services, and set up heathen altars on street corners throughout Jerusalem. Nevertheless, there were some in Judah who were loyal to God, and Isaiah and Micah did all they could to encourage them.

Hezekiah

When Ahaz died, his son Hezekiah became king. Hezekiah did all he could to keep the country from idolatry. The northern kingdom of Israel had already fallen into the hands of the Assyrians, and it looked like Judah would be next unless God worked a miracle. It was time for action, so Hezekiah asked the priests and Levites to help him repair the temple and restore the services there. The elders joined the king in asking God for forgiveness, the priests placed offerings on the altar, and the king and all those with him bowed and worshiped the Lord. The courts of the temple rang with shouts of praise.

Next, an invitation to celebrate the Passover feast went to everyone in both the northern and southern kingdoms of Israel. This festival brought such a huge revival that, although it usually lasted for one week, the people decided the week went by too fast, so they celebrated the Passover for a second week. The people were so convicted of their own sins that they all went out and broke down the idolatrous shrines and altars Ahaz had constructed around the kingdom.

During the reign of Hezekiah, it was obvious that God was with the kingdom of Judah. The Assyrians had taken the northern kingdom of Israel, but the kingdom of Judah was protected and prospered.

> The Holy Spirit is implanting the grace of Christ in the heart of many a noble seeker after truth, quickening his sympathies contrary to his nature, contrary to his former education.
> —*Prophets and Kings*, 376, 377

The Ambassadors From Babylon

Near the end of his reign, Hezekiah became deathly ill. The Lord sent him a message through the prophet Isaiah telling him to prepare for death. Hezekiah turned his face to the wall, cried, and prayed to live. The Lord heard his prayer and told Isaiah to go back and let the king know that not only would he be healed and live fifteen more years but that God would also deliver Judah from the Assyrians.

At this message Hezekiah rejoiced, but he had trouble believing it was true. So the prophet asked Hezekiah, "Is it easier for the sun's shadow to go forward or backward?" The king said, "It's easier for the shadow to get longer than shorter." So the prophet prayed, and the Lord shortened the shadow (essentially reversing time enough that it showed on the sundial clock). Hezekiah witnessed the miracle and believed.

Now there were astrologers in Assyria who had noticed this phenomenon and were shocked. They knew that the God of heaven must have done this, and they came to congratulate Hezekiah on being healed and to learn more about God. Instead of telling them all about God's power and mercy, Hezekiah tried to impress them by showing them the wealth and treasures of his kingdom. Because he had sinned by taking credit for all the good things, and because he had blown a huge opportunity to tell others about God, Isaiah prophesied, "The Babylonians will come soon and everything you have shown these visitors will be taken by the king of Babylon." Hezekiah felt terrible about what he had done, humbled himself, and asked for forgiveness. The Lord forgave him.

Every day, life is full of opportunities and responsibilities to move God's mission forward. The consequences of failing to make the most of them can be dire, both for us individually and for God's church corporately.

Deliverance From Assyria

When the Assyrians invaded the kingdom of Judah, they turned it into a wasteland. Hezekiah encouraged his troops by telling them that God would be with them. Finally, the Assyrian officers came to the gates of Jerusalem to demand a complete surrender. They shouted over the wall of the city to Hezekiah's officers, demanding they surrender and yelling all sorts of blasphemous things. Hezekiah's men asked him what to do, because the numbers were not in their favor. The Lord sent Isaiah to tell Hezekiah that he should not surrender, because the Lord was going to give them victory. Hezekiah continued to pray fervently for his people and the kingdom.

That very night, God sent an angel to kill the whole Assyrian army—185,000 of them. When the news reached the Assyrian king, he was shocked. He returned home in shame and was soon assassinated.

Hope for the Heathen

Throughout his ministry, Isaiah had made it plain to the people that God loved everyone, no matter their nationality, and that many others would respond, give their hearts to the Lord, and become a part of His people. The Jewish people thought back to their deliverance from Egypt and became proud of who they were. They didn't like to think of anyone else being part of God's special people. They forgot, or refused to grasp, that God makes no distinction between nationalities and races but that all who love Him, obey Him, and keep His commandments are His people.

Isaiah was shown the future and could see that many false teachers would deceive people's thinking with philosophy and spiritualism. Others would have empty religious rituals and practices and yet not know God. He also saw the plan of salvation and the people of God sharing the good news. Isaiah was known for his bold, direct, and plain telling of the full plan of salvation.

Manasseh and Josiah

Judah prospered during Hezekiah's reign, and when he died, his son Manasseh became king. Manasseh was only twelve years old when he became king. He was the most evil king ever. He reinstituted the worship of Baal and Asherah, justice was perverted, and wickedness and violence were everywhere. Manasseh even sacrificed babies, including his own son, to these idols. He didn't hesitate to kill those he didn't like or who dared oppose him, including the prophet Isaiah. The king and the people were warned again and again that they must turn from evil, but it didn't do any good.

Finally, a band of Assyrian soldiers invaded Jerusalem, captured Manasseh, and put him in prison in Babylon. This brought Manasseh to his senses, so he humbled himself and prayed earnestly to the Lord. He was released and returned to Jerusalem. There, he tried to undo all the idolatry, false worship, and injustice that he had brought in before, but it was too late. He reigned fifty-five years, and when he died, his twenty-two-year-old son, Amon, took the throne. He did all the wicked things that his father had done. He had been king only two years when his servants assassinated him, and his eight-year-old son, Josiah, became king of Judah. He did what was right and ruled for thirty-one years.

During the reign of the evil kings, those who remained true to God had prayed and prayed for better days. The prophet Habakkuk bowed in submission to the Lord and prayed, "Lord, how long do I have to pray and cry? When will You help us and save us?" The prophet Zephaniah had the same concerns and reminded the people of the results of their continued disobedience.

The Book of the Law

A decided spiritual change took place during Josiah's reign as the people began studying the holy Scriptures. One day, Hilkiah the high priest found a long-lost copy of God's book of the law in the temple. He told Shaphan, a learned scribe, to take it to Josiah and read it to the young king. Josiah's heart was touched as he heard the Scriptures read. He didn't know that the Scriptures were so plain and full of blessings and warnings.

Josiah had come to the throne when he was only eight years old. At that time, he didn't know much of the history of his country. He fully consecrated himself to the Lord when he was sixteen, and when he was twenty, he decided to remove the temptations for idolatry in his country by destroying the altars and images of Baal and Asherah, which had been set up all over the land. He had the pagan priests arrested and executed and had their bones burned on their pagan altars. He was so passionate about it that he went throughout the territory that had been the northern kingdom and tore down all the idols there too.

The more Josiah read of the book of the law, the more he was convicted of Israel's impending doom because of its sins. The king asked the prophetess Huldah to ask God if there was anything he could do to save Judah. Through her, God sent a message saying that, because Judah had forsaken Him, He would destroy them, but because Josiah had humbled himself and prayed, God would delay the punishment until after his death. When Josiah heard that, he did all in his power to bring the country back to God. He called a meeting of the elders and magistrates, and together with the Levites and priests, they met in the courtyard of the temple. The king read from the book of the law, and then he proposed that they join him in consecrating themselves to God and working together to bring about a change in the country. He also told them to reinstate the yearly celebration of the Passover as a reminder of Israel's deliverance from slavery in Egypt. All of these efforts brought about a great reformation in Judah.

When he was thirty-nine, Josiah was killed in battle with the Egyptians. He was buried with his fathers, and the whole country mourned for him, especially the young prophet Jeremiah.

Jeremiah

Jeremiah, a Levite, received a call to the prophetic ministry when he was young. He was part of the family of priests and was training for the priesthood. When God called him, he felt too young and unprepared, but God saw in Jeremiah a courageous servant. So the Lord said to him, "Don't say, 'I'm too young.' I'll go with you." The reformation under Josiah had cleared the land of idols, but the hearts of many people had not changed. Jeremiah kept encouraging the leaders of Judah to lay a foundation for continued spiritual growth. He also emphasized the importance to the Sabbath, which the people had forgotten. Yet most people did not respond.

> When man has sinned against a holy and merciful God, he can pursue no course so noble as to repent sincerely and confess his errors in tears and bitterness of soul. This God requires of him; He accepts nothing less than a broken heart and a contrite spirit.
> —*Prophets and Kings*, 435, 436

The Lord told Jeremiah to go stand in the temple courtyard and speak plainly to the people without mincing words. Jeremiah obeyed and said to them, "Listen to the Lord, change your ways. Don't fight with your neighbor, mistreat visitors, take advantage of orphans and widows, or kill people. If you don't repent and change, the Lord will have to discipline you."

Because they didn't like what he said, the leaders and people of Judah turned against Jeremiah. If Jeremiah had cowered or changed his message to please them, it would have meant nothing and they would have killed him anyway. However, men of influence pleaded with the people for Jeremiah and reminded them of the story of Micah; as a result, his life was spared. All through his ministry, Jeremiah stood for what was right. He had a naturally timid personality and longed for peace and quiet, so the constant criticism and mocking seemed like knives piercing his heart. He learned to pray, "Lord, help me and correct me, but don't turn away from me. I need You to help me carry out Your mission." His words in Lamentations proclaim, "Great is thy faithfulness."

Approaching Doom

Without much warning, the Babylonian Empire replaced the Assyrian Empire as the major political and military power in the region. God would ultimately use the Babylonians to discipline and destroy the kingdom of Judah. King Nebuchadnezzar sent troops to Jerusalem again and again, each time taking more and more people captive.

Jeremiah continued to call the people to repentance. The Lord said to Jeremiah, "Go and remind the people that I was the one who brought their ancestors out of Egypt and that I have given you the land that you now have. I guided and directed you through prophets and teachers, but you wouldn't listen." Jeremiah reminded the people that God's name means "the Lord is our righteousness," and he repeated the promises of deliverance. Eventually, the king of Judah got so mad at Jeremiah for constantly predicting the fall of the kingdom that he put him in prison.

While Jeremiah was in prison, the Lord told him to write down all the messages God had given him. King Jehoiakim demanded to hear the writings read aloud, got angry, slashed the scroll into pieces, and threw it in the fire. God had Jeremiah rewrite the whole thing. Through Jeremiah, the Lord told King Jehoiakim to honor his allegiance to the Babylonian king and surrender to Nebuchadnezzar so that Jerusalem would not be destroyed. Jehoiakim refused and was despised by everyone. When Nebuchadnezzar came against Jerusalem and took the city, he freed Jeremiah, because he had heard that Jeremiah had counseled Jehoiakim to surrender to the Babylonians. Little was left of Judah, but the Babylonian Empire allowed it to continue operating as a state. Nebuchadnezzar changed the name of Josiah's youngest son, Mattaniah, to Zedekiah and made him king.

The Last King of Judah

Nebuchadnezzar trusted King Zedekiah because the prophet Jeremiah was his adviser. Jeremiah had long counseled the king to cooperate with the Babylonians. Eventually, he delivered a message from God commanding Judah and those in nearby nations to submit to the king of Babylon indefinitely. However, false prophets, both in Judah and in Babylon, kept encouraging insurrection. Hananiah was one such false prophet. He kept telling the people and the king that they would defeat the Babylonians within two years and that the kingdom of Israel would regain its power and position. Jeremiah told the people that failing to submit to the Babylonians would have consequences and that time would show whether Hananiah's words were true.

Then, because he wasn't getting anywhere with the king and the people, Jeremiah decided to leave Jerusalem and go home. Before he got far, the Lord told him to go back and tell Hananiah that because he had claimed to speak for God and had sold the people a lie, he would die. Less than two months later, he died.

King Zedekiah again promised allegiance to Nebuchadnezzar, who had gotten to know more about God through Hebrew captives, such as Daniel. It was during this time that God called Ezekiel, one of the captives, to prophesy against the idol worship going on back in Jerusalem and even inside the temple. The people mocked Ezekiel's words, and it was clear that God could no longer delay Israel's final destruction.

King Zedekiah was leading Israel's charge into ruin. He disregarded the oath he had taken to cooperate with Nebuchadnezzar and turned to Egypt for help. But the Babylonians caught him, poked his eyes out, and put him in a Babylonian prison until he died.

Carried Captive Into Babylon

When Zedekiah was still king of Judah, he asked the Egyptians to help stop the Babylonians from attacking Jerusalem. The Babylonians, also known as Chaldeans, briefly pulled back, giving Zedekiah hope that they would be spared. He sent a message to Jeremiah, asking him to pray that God would help protect their country. Unfortunately, Judah's rebellion against God had been so severe and so prolonged that God did not hold back the attackers any longer. Jeremiah told Zedekiah that the Babylonians would invade and destroy Jerusalem.

There were a few righteous people left in Jerusalem, and they wanted to protect the ark before the Babylonians took the city. They hid the ark, the golden chest with the Ten Commandments in it, in a cave without telling anyone where it was. It has never been found, and will remain hidden until Jesus comes back and takes it to heaven.

As the enemy advanced and it became clear that Judah would fall, the false prophets began telling everyone that Jeremiah was planning to join the Babylonians. The

> Humbled in the sight of the nations, those who once had been recognized as favored of Heaven above all other peoples of the earth were to learn in exile the lesson of obedience so necessary for their future happiness. Until they had learned this lesson, God could not do for them all that He desired to do.
> —*Prophets and Kings*, 475

leaders of Judah arrested Jeremiah and threw him in a dungeon. King Zedekiah eventually sent for him and asked him what God's purpose was for Jerusalem. Again Jeremiah advised him to peacefully surrender to Nebuchadnezzar, because if he didn't, the Babylonians would come and destroy the city. He also asked the king not to send him back to the dungeon, so the king ordered that he be kept in the prison courtyard with the guard.

Zedekiah had gone against the counsel of Jeremiah so often that he thought it would be too embarrassing for him to listen to Jeremiah now. With tears, Jeremiah urged Zedekiah to do what God commanded, which would save his life and the lives of many of his people. Not surprisingly, the cowardly and morally weak Zedekiah instead decided to fight against the Babylonians as the false prophets had urged. When Nebuchadnezzar came against Jerusalem again, Zedekiah ran. Nebuchadnezzar caught him, killed his sons in front of him, put out his eyes, took him to Babylon, and put him in prison, where he stayed until he died.

Nebuchadnezzar set a governor over one of the areas of Judah, but some of the remaining Jews refused to live under that arrangement because it was still controlled by Nebuchadnezzar. Against Jeremiah's counsel, they decided to flee to Egypt. Jeremiah pleaded with them not to go because things would not go well for them there. But they wouldn't listen, left for Egypt, and forced Jeremiah to go with them. He not only told them about the bad things that would happen to them there but also about the wonderful promises of God on condition of repentance and obedience.

While they were in Egypt, Jeremiah continued to urge them to love God and obey Him. Finally, they got so upset with Jeremiah that they decided to stone him to death, which they did.

> A noble character is not the result of accident; it is not due to special favors or endowments of Providence. It is the result of self-discipline, of subjection of the lower to the higher nature, of the surrender of self to the service of God and man. —*Prophets and Kings*, 488

Light Through Darkness

The Lord would have saved the kingdom of Judah if the people had listened and done what He had asked them to do. He gave them plenty of warnings through Daniel's prophecies, Ezekiel's warnings, and Jeremiah's pleadings in Jerusalem. Sadly, during the closing years of Judah, the people paid little attention to what the prophets said, and they kept Jeremiah under close surveillance. Reverence for and obedience to God's law would have changed the course of human history entirely.

To show his faith that God would someday restore the Jews to their land now controlled by the Babylonians, Jeremiah bought a small piece of property in the area that the Babylonians occupied. He gave the deed to his servant, Baruch, and told him to make sure it was preserved. He hoped this would inspire others to look to the future and remain true to God.

In the Court of Babylon

When Nebuchadnezzar invaded Judah at the beginning of the seventy years of captivity, he intentionally took some exceptionally bright young men with him as captives to Babylon. Among those chosen were Daniel, Hananiah, Mishael, and Azariah. Nebuchadnezzar also took with him the sacred things of the temple and placed them in the temple of the Babylonian gods as evidence that they were more powerful than the God of the Jews.

The prince in charge decided to rename the boys after Chaldean gods, so they became known as Belteshazzar, Shadrach, Meshach, and Abednego. The king wanted to educate them and gradually change their faith. To show the boys that he was giving them special treatment, the king offered them access to his finest foods and wine. However, the food had been offered to idols, so they didn't want to partake of it and possibly give the impression that they were denying their faith. They also had been taught that God doesn't approve of alcohol, because it dulls both physical and mental powers. Daniel and his three friends could have excused themselves and eaten the Babylonian diet because they were captives, but they decided to obey God.

The prince in charge, Ashpenaz, cared for Daniel and took their request for exemption kindly. However, the prince worried that if they lost weight or got sick and the king heard about it, he would be in trouble. Daniel and his friends then appealed to Melzar, the king's officer, for a ten-day trial during which the Hebrews would eat simply and not have wine. The other young men from different nations ate their fill of whatever they were served from the king's bounty. After ten days, it was obvious to everyone that the Hebrews' simple diet was superior. In every test, they were stronger, faster, smarter, more attractive, and wiser than their peers, so they were selected for special service to the king.

God gave guidelines for living our best, healthiest lives, and following those statutes brings many blessings. When God's people seek Him, work hard, and use their talents to honor Him, God brings true success. It can happen today just as powerfully as it did for Daniel.

Nebuchadnezzar's Dream

After Daniel and his friends qualified for special service to King Nebuchadnezzar, they had an opportunity to show the idolatrous nation the power of God. Nebuchadnezzar had a dream that really bothered him, but when he woke up, he couldn't remember the details. He asked his advisers—magicians, astrologers, and sorcerers—to tell him what he had dreamed and what it meant. They wanted him to tell them the dream first, but he couldn't recall all of it, only bits and pieces that didn't make sense. After a lot of back-and-forth between the king and advisers, the king said, "You're just stalling for time so you can come up with who knows what. For me to know that you're on the right track, first tell me the dream I had." They couldn't, which made the king so angry that he decided to kill all of them.

Daniel heard about this and decided to risk his own life by going to see the king. Daniel told the king that if he had a few days, he would come back with the dream and its interpretation. The king agreed. Daniel and his friends got together and prayed that God would reveal what he needed to know. In a night vision, God showed Daniel the dream and its meaning.

Appearing before King Nebuchadnezzar, Daniel started by giving God credit for the revelation. Then Daniel explained that he had seen a huge image of a man with a head of gold, arms and chest of silver, hips and thighs of brass, legs of iron, and feet mixture of iron and clay, and these represented different kingdoms, one following another. When Daniel finished telling the king his dream and its meaning, he added, "The dream is certain, and God will eventually set up a kingdom that will never be destroyed." The king, awed by this interpretation, fell down and worshiped God. He stayed the execution of the advisers and made Daniel his chief assistant.

> The history of nations speaks to us today. To every nation and to every individual God has assigned a place in His great plan. Today men and nations are being tested by the plummet in the hand of Him who makes no mistake. All are by their own choice deciding their destiny, and God is overruling all for the accomplishment of His purposes.
> —*Prophets and Kings*, 536

The Fiery Furnace

In time, Nebuchadnezzar's pride and ambition got the better of him, and he returned to idol worship. He decided that Babylon would be the kingdom that would last forever. So he made a huge image of a man, about ninety feet high and nine feet wide, all of gold, to represent Babylon. Then he called together the nobles, leaders, and people for a day of festivities and worship. He commanded everyone to bow down to the massive golden image representing Babylon as a sign of respect and loyalty to him and the nation. Those who refused were to be thrown into the nearby fiery furnace.

Daniel was away that day on some urgent business for the king. Shadrach, Meshach, and Abednego did not bow down to the image. The king's jealous wise men reported their rebellion to the king. The young men told Nebuchadnezzar they would not worship the golden image, regardless of the consequences. God could deliver them, they told the king, but if He did not, they would still not worship the image. The king became furious and ordered the nearby furnace to be heated seven times hotter than normal and the three young men to be thrown in. The guards tied them up and took them to the door of the furnace. As they pushed the trio in, the flames jumped out and the soldiers burned to death.

The king watched the furnace, expecting to see the three young men burn up. Instead, he saw them walking around in the flames as if it were nothing. Nebuchadnezzar also saw a fourth Man in the furnace who looked like the Son of God he had been told about. Nebuchadnezzar ran to the furnace and called to the young men to come out. When they did, they had no burn marks on them, and their clothes didn't even smell of smoke. The fire had only consumed the ropes binding their hands. The fourth Man had disappeared.

King Nebuchadnezzar was humbled and said, "Blessed be the God of the Hebrews. There is no one like Him!" The Babylonians abandoned the golden idol and praised God because of the faith of the young Hebrew men who were faithful to the Lord. In the closing days of the earth's history, God will walk through trials with His faithful servants, just like He did in the fiery furnace.

True Greatness
Nebuchadnezzar decided to beautify the great city of Babylon, and when he looked at the beauty he had created, he became proud. He also conquered several smaller nations and added them to his empire. His ego was growing dangerously big, so one night, God gave him a vision of a huge tree whose top seemed to reach to heaven and whose branches spread to the ends of the earth. Flocks and herds enjoyed gathering under its branches and birds built their nests there. Then Nebuchadnezzar heard a loud voice from heaven call out, "Cut down that tree, cut off its branches, and scatter its fruit, but protect its stump."

Nebuchadnezzar was really troubled about this dream, so he sent for Daniel, told him the dream, and asked him for its meaning. The Lord gave Daniel its meaning, and he was shocked. It was not good news for the king. He told Nebuchadnezzar that the tree represented him and that God had decided to humble him by taking away

> Babylon, with all its power and magnificence, the like of which our world has never since beheld,—power and magnificence which to the people of that day seemed so stable and enduring,—how completely has it passed away!
> —*Prophets and Kings*, 548

his reasoning. He would crawl on his hands and knees and eat grass like an animal for seven years, but his throne would be protected. Then Daniel urged the king to repent, give his heart to God, do righteously, and stop being so prideful. This made a real impression on Nebuchadnezzar, and he changed his ways for a few months. Soon enough, he began to question the interpretation of the dream, decided he was being paranoid, and returned to his oppressive ways.

A year after the dream, as he was walking in his palace thinking about the great nation of Babylon that he had built, his reasoning ability was suddenly taken away and he could only think like an animal. His advisers were shocked and decided to take the king away from the palace, out of the city, to a field. Nebuchadnezzar stayed there seven years, eating grass and living in the elements like the animals but protected by God.

After seven years, God restored his sanity and the king returned to the throne. He publicly acknowledged the sins that led to his just punishment by God. He later wrote, "After my thinking came back, my throne was given back to me, and I had learned that God is the King of all kings, the Lord of all lords. He is able to take away man's pride, but all His goodness is true goodness." The once heathen, idol-worshiping king had become a humble and godly servant-leader.

The Unseen Watcher
Near the end of Daniel's life, great changes had taken place. Nebuchadnezzar had died and his grandson Belshazzar was in charge. One day he decided to hold a royal banquet for thousands of the land's most important men and beautiful women. As they were feasting and drinking wine from the golden vessels taken from the temple in Jerusalem, suddenly a bloodless hand appeared and began writing on the wall words of fire that no one could read. The revelers froze with terror and everyone watched as the hand of fire finished writing and scenes of their sins passed before them.

King Belshazzar panicked and called his advisers to interpret the mysterious writing. They couldn't, so the queen mother suggested that Belshazzar call the old man Daniel, who had interpreted things for Nebuchadnezzar, to come interpret the words on the wall. Daniel reminded the king that he had not humbled himself before God, even though he knew his grandfather's history. Then he looked at the words, "MENE, MENE, TEKEL, UPHARSIN," and said, "MENE means that God has numbered the days of your kingdom; TEKEL, your behavior has been judged; and the last word means that the Medes and Persians will come take the kingdom." The king and the party guests stood there shocked, and while they were still in the banquet hall, the armies of the Medes and Persians captured the city. During the fighting, Belshazzar was killed.

Today as then, we must pay attention to God's warnings and turn to Him. The days of human history are numbered and we, too, will be judged.

In the Lions' Den
After Belshazzar died, Darius took over the Babylonian territory and decided to reorganize the government. He gave 120 princes responsibilities over various sections of the kingdom, and he put three presidents over the princes—Daniel was lead president. The other two presidents were jealous of Daniel and began plotting to get rid of the Hebrew. They went to Darius and suggested that everyone in the kingdom should show their loyalty by praying to no one but Darius for thirty days. If they did pray to anyone or anything else, they were to be thrown into the lions' den. Darius was flattered by the idea and signed it into law.

These men knew that Daniel prayed to God three times a day with his window wide open looking toward Jerusalem. They watched him all day until they had plenty of evidence then went and told the king that Daniel disregarded the decree and must be punished. At that, Darius realized what they had done. He was heartsick about it because he loved Daniel and respected him. However, in Persia, once the king signed a law, it couldn't be changed. So the king reluctantly gave his permission for Daniel to be arrested and thrown into the lions' den.

> In his own strength, man cannot meet the charges of the enemy. In sin-stained garments, confessing his guilt, he stands before God. But Jesus, our Advocate, presents an effectual plea in behalf of all who by repentance and faith have committed the keeping of their souls to Him.
> —*Prophets and Kings*, 586

The king tossed and turned all night; he couldn't sleep thinking about Daniel. First thing in the morning, he went to the lions' den and called out, "Daniel, has God delivered you from the lions?" Daniel called back, "O king, live forever. God sent an angel to shut the hungry lions' mouths. I'm OK!" The king was thrilled to hear Daniel's voice and to know that he was alive. He immediately ordered that Daniel be released from the lions' den and his accusers thrown in, along with their wives and children. All of them were quickly devoured. Once again, the king of a heathen, idolatrous nation publicly declared the supremacy of the God of heaven.

Daniel continued to live for many more years, during which God gave him visions, dreams, and prophecies. Many of those are included in the book of Daniel in the Bible. Daniel didn't understand them all, but God assured him that their meanings would become clear closer to the end of time.

The Return of the Exiles

After King Darius died, his general, Cyrus, took over the throne. The prophet Isaiah, speaking for the Lord, had long before prophesied, "Cyrus is My shepherd, doing what I ask him to do, even letting the temple in Jerusalem be rebuilt." So Daniel went before the king and asked that he might release the Jewish people so they could go home and rebuild the temple. Cyrus respected Daniel and was touched that he was favored by God, so he agreed to let them go. He made a proclamation that it was his desire for the Hebrews to go back home and rebuild the temple and sent it throughout the kingdom. At this, the Hebrews rejoiced and praised the Lord.

Fifty thousand Jews prepared to leave Babylon. Their friends in Babylon gave them silver, gold, flocks, and herds as gifts to take with them. Cyrus even sent some money to help rebuild the temple. Cyrus appointed Zerubbabel, one of King David's descendants, as their governor, and Joshua went back with him to serve as high priest.

As soon as they got home, the people immediately built an altar on the site of the old temple altar and celebrated the Feast of Tabernacles. They also began gathering the building materials for the temple itself. Joy and gratitude filled their hearts, and mixed with the older generation's sadness at the thought of Solomon's glorious temple, which would not have been destroyed if God's people had been obedient. Even so, they sang and shouted for joy as they watched the workers getting ready to rebuild the temple.

"The Prophets of God Helping Them"

The Samaritans were a group of people that had sprung up from a small number of Jews who had married heathen colonists from Assyria. They claimed to worship the God of heaven, but they were prone to idolatry. They came to Zerubbabel, governor of the returned Jews, and offered to help rebuild the temple. The Jews needed help, but God had told them not to make friends with their neighbors, and they remembered that the Lord had allowed them to be taken captive because of their disobedience and because they allowed themselves to be influenced by idol worship.

When the Jews refused their help, the Samaritans did all they could to keep the Jews from rebuilding Jerusalem and the temple. Satan caused discouragement and strife among the workers, and many of them turned their attention to building their own houses and lives. This made the Lord very unhappy. But there was a glimmer of hope. The prophets Haggai and Zechariah told the people that, out of respect for God, they should make building His temple a priority. This time the people didn't dare disregard the Lord's message. Then the building of the temple resumed and God gave them the courage they needed. The people knew that His promises never fail.

As the building project moved forward, the Samaritans and others gave them no end of trouble. Finally, King Darius decreed that the entire project and all its related needs should be funded by the king's treasury and that anyone who interfered would be punished.

Joshua and the Angel
Satan put forth a great effort to keep Jerusalem and the temple from being rebuilt. God gave Zechariah the prophet a vision to give His people courage. In the vision, he saw Joshua the high priest standing before the Lord; Satan was there, accusing Joshua of his sins and the sins of his people. Joshua was dressed in a filthy garment, and Satan kept pointing it out. Joshua had no excuse and couldn't defend himself. He stood there, ashamed of himself. Then Zechariah saw the Son of God rebuke Satan, remove Joshua's filthy garment, and place a clean, white garment on his body and a crown on his head as symbols of forgiveness and acceptance.

What Zechariah saw in vision applies also to us. We have made mistakes and sinned, but forgiveness awaits us through Jesus Christ, the Son of God. If we repent, confess our sins, and ask Him to help us be good and do good, He will.

"Not by Might, nor by Power"
Immediately after Zechariah's vision of Joshua the high priest, God gave him a vision of two small olive trees standing on either side of the seven-branched candlestick in the temple. These small olive trees were feeding oil into the candlestick to keep it burning. This meant that the Holy Spirit provides the power in everything that is done in the temple and in the lives of God's people, who are to keep burning brightly for God.

God promised Zerubbabel, the governor who began building the temple, that it would be finished during his reign, and it was. This temple did not equal the splendor of Solomon's, yet the prophet Haggai said this temple would be greater than Solomon's, because the Son of God would one day walk in it.

In the Days of Queen Esther
When the Jews went back home to rebuild the temple, about fifty thousand of them went, but that was just a small fraction of those still living in Media-Persia. Some years later, the king issued another decree giving the Jews permission to go back home. The prophet Zechariah pleaded with the Jews to take advantage of it and go. Some did, but many decided they were happy where they were and didn't want to leave.

Soon the political situation changed, and Xerxes took the place of Darius as king of Persia. Xerxes's advisers led the king to believe that the Jews were against him, so Xerxes issued a decree that all the Jews were to be killed and their property confiscated. By God's providence, Xerxes's wife Esther was a faithful Jewish woman. Mordecai, her relative, asked her to appeal to Xerxes on behalf of the Jews. Because she had not made an appointment to see the king, appearing before him unannounced could mean she would be arrested and killed, but in faith she said, "I'm going in to see him, and if I die, I die."

When she appeared, the king held out his scepter, giving her permission to come into the throne room and talk to him. She told him that she was a Jew and pleaded for her people. As a result, Xerxes modified his decree and allowed the Jews to defend themselves. When the Jews heard this they thanked the Lord, and their enemies weren't able to kill them because angels protected them and caused the killers to freeze in fright. Many non-Jews saw this as a miracle from the God of heaven and decided to become Jews.

Ezra, the Priest and Scribe
Some decades passed and Artaxerxes became king of Persia. He issued a third decree that Jerusalem be rebuilt, walls and all. He ruled for some time and did what he could to help God's people. Ezra and Nehemiah were good friends with the king, who showed favor to God's people. Ezra loved God and was a spiritual adviser to Artaxerxes. Ezra studied the history of God's people and learned why they had been taken as captives to Babylon. As he continued to study, he experienced a deeper conversion, and God asked him to teach His people about their history. Teaching became his primary life work, and he also had all the copies of God's law copied and distributed as widely as possible.

> God's children are not only to pray in faith, but to work with diligent and provident care. They encounter many difficulties and often hinder the working of Providence in their behalf, because they regard prudence and painstaking effort as having little to do with religion.
> —*Prophets and Kings*, 633, 634

The king did all he could to help God's people, even paying for their priests from the treasury of Persia. He told Ezra and his helpers that when they got back to Jerusalem they were to appoint civil officers, magistrates, and judges to help govern the people according to God's laws.

The king again told the Jews in Persia that if any of them wanted to go back home, they could. A small number responded; the rest decided to stay in Persia for they had gotten comfortable there. It would take several months for those going back home to get to Jerusalem. Before they left, they fasted and prayed, asking God to give them a safe journey. God protected them, and their enemies didn't bother them, so their four-month trip was a good one.

A Spiritual Revival
When Ezra and the people got back to Jerusalem, they saw that the temple had been finished and the walls of the city partially rebuilt. Over the years, some of the Jews

back home in Jerusalem had remained faithful to God, but others had not, and no one had encouraged them to obey God.

Four days after Ezra and the others arrived in Jerusalem, they took all the gifts that King Artaxerxes had given them to the temple, added their own thank offerings, and sacrificed burnt offerings as an expression of gratitude to God for a safe trip home.

Soon after, the leaders shared a problem with Ezra. Some of the Jewish men had married women from the nearby heathen communities. Ezra knew this issue had been one of the biggest problems in Israel's past, and when he heard it was happening again, he tore his robe in grief, pulled hair from his head and beard, and fell on his knees before God, confessing the sins of his people. The people also recognized their error and confessed.

This was the beginning of a wonderful revival and reformation as Ezra and his fellow teachers worked kindly and gently to bring the people back to God and to obey Him in every aspect of their lives. God's word through the holy Scriptures is very powerful, but if God's people lay it aside and neglect it, its power on our behalf is lost. We must study the Bible earnestly and apply it diligently to our lives.

A Man of Opportunity

Nehemiah, one of the exiled Jews, had a very responsible position in the Persian court. He was the cupbearer for King Artaxerxes. This meant he had to make sure that the king's food and drink were not poisoned. The king fully trusted him.

Nehemiah learned that the temple had been rebuilt but the protective walls around Jerusalem were not finished and that non-Jews were harassing the Israelites. Overwhelmed by what he heard, Nehemiah prayed for his people, and the more he prayed the more he was convicted that something had to be done. He prayed and waited for the right time to talk to King Artaxerxes about it then asked permission to go home and help his people.

The king could feel Nehemiah's pain, so he granted him time off to go to Jerusalem and help his people finish building the walls. When the king granted Nehemiah's first request, Nehemiah got the courage to make a second request: that might go with a military escort and documents verifying that Artaxerxes approved of his mission.

The Builders on the Wall

Nehemiah's long trip to Jerusalem was a safe one. The king's letters to the local governors along the way helped prevent any trouble. However, the fanfare surrounding his arrival wasn't unnoticed. Nearby heathen tribes were jealous and Nehemiah knew they would try to cause trouble. When Nehemiah got to Jerusalem, he confided in a few trusted leaders the reason why he had come. Three days later, he got up at midnight and with a few companions to survey the city's broken-down walls. He spent in prayer the rest of the night in prayer because in the morning he planned to talk to the people about rebuilding Jerusalem's protective walls.

Nehemiah's determination and courage inspired others as he said to them, "The God of heaven will help us, and we will build the unfinished walls." The priests and the majority of the princes and leaders responded enthusiastically, and the work began. Their enemies watched from a distance and began planning how to stop the construction. This only inspired Nehemiah, and he was more determined than ever to do what needed to be done. The workers were just as determined, so they strapped swords to their sides, ready to defend themselves if they needed to while they continued building the wall. Through all of this, Nehemiah put his trust in God, no matter what opposition he faced.

> In the work of reform to be carried forward today, there is need of men who, like Ezra and Nehemiah, will not palliate or excuse sin, nor shrink from vindicating the honor of God. Those upon whom rests the burden of this work will not hold their peace when wrong is done, neither will they cover evil with a cloak of false charity.
> —*Prophets and Kings*, 675

A Rebuke Against Extortion

The wall around Jerusalem wasn't finished yet, but Nehemiah's attention was turned to the poor in the country. To buy food for their families, they had to borrow money and pay it back with high interest. This was in addition to the taxes they had to pay to the kings of Persia. When the poor who had little or no money decided to take out a mortgage on their property, they got deeper and deeper in debt.

Nehemiah told the Jews not to take advantage of the poor by loaning them money to be paid back with interest. He was especially upset about rich, greedy Jews taking advantage of other Jews. He confronted them for not having pity on their fellow citizens. Nehemiah and others also paid the ransom to free those who had sold themselves or family members as slaves to heathen neighbors.

Every wrong that God's people do is recorded in the books of heaven. And everything done to help others in need, such as widows and orphans, is also recorded.

Heathen Plots

The enemies of the Jews didn't dare attack them openly because the king of Persia favored the Jews. So they came up with another plan to try to draw Nehemiah away from finishing the wall. Pretending to want friendly dialogue about compromise, they invited him to come meet with them in a little village outside the city. An angel alerted Nehemiah to their true purpose, so he responded, "I am doing God's work, so I can't come down from the wall and talk to you right now." They persisted, but so did he.

Satan can come up with all kinds of schemes to lure us away from doing what God wants us to do. He can even work through friends, who may not even realize what they're doing.

Nehemiah did all he could to inspire the people to finish rebuilding the wall of the city, and he worked tirelessly to relieve the burdens of the poor and needy. He never did anything for his own advantage; everything was about God and what He wanted, not about Nehemiah.

Instructed in the Law of God
The time came for the Festival of the Trumpets, a special Sabbath. Some parts of city itself were still in ruins and needed attention, but the protective walls of the city had been finished, and the people celebrated. Ezra, now an old man, decided to talk to the people one last time, so he called them together with the priests and Levites supporting him. He stood on a platform to speak to the people, who had come from many parts of the country to celebrate the special Sabbath.

Ezra looked at the people, bowed his head in prayer, and thanked the Lord for bringing them back home to Jerusalem and for what He had helped them accomplish. The people responded with "Amen! Amen!" They bowed their heads in gratitude and worshiped the Lord. Then Ezra explained the law of God to the people to make sure they understood things correctly. Some of them spoke other languages because they had been living among non-Jewish people for so long, but God made sure everyone understood what Ezra said. The people listened and determined to do things right. They also observed the Day of Atonement and celebrated the Feast of Tabernacles. Every day, Ezra read and explained God's law.

The people were so convicted of their sins that they even put out all the heathens they had brought in for any reason, and promised not to intermarry with the heathen in the future. They also pledged to honor the Sabbath by keeping it holy, to pay a faithful tithe, and to fund the work of the temple. The day ended with rejoicing as the people recounted the blessings of the Lord.

> Let us by faith behold the blessed hereafter as pictured by the hand of God. He who died for the sins of the world is opening wide the gates of Paradise to all who believe on Him. Soon the battle will have been fought, the victory won.
> —*Prophets and Kings*, 731, 732

Reformation

The people had pledged to obey and honor God, but when Ezra and Nehemiah weren't there, they began slipping away from God again. To make things worse, Eliashib, the high priest who had a room for himself at the temple, had made arrangements for his friend Tobiah the Ammonite, an enemy of the Jews, to have a room there too.

Nehemiah had returned to Persia to serve the king, but when he came back for a visit to see how things were going and heard about this, he was rightfully upset. The storage room reserved for the offerings to support the temple had been turned into a bedroom for Tobiah. Eliashib and Tobiah also misused the offerings, so people stopped bringing them. Temple workers could no longer be paid, so they left to look for work elsewhere. Nehemiah reprimanded the high priest and told Tobiah to take his things and leave. When the people saw this, they once again brought their offerings to support the temple.

Another problem Nehemiah faced had to do with the Sabbath. Jews and others regularly stood outside the gates of the city, buying and selling their wares and crops. However, Nehemiah saw that they were doing this on the Sabbath as if it were any other day. The leaders had the authority to stop it, but they were profiting from the sales. Nehemiah rebuked them and announced that the city gates would be closed before Sabbath on Friday and stay closed until Sabbath ended.

Nehemiah's other primary mission was to awaken Israel to the danger of intermarrying with unbelievers. He reminded them of all the times throughout their history that this had caused catastrophic damage to Israel. Nehemiah and the spiritual leaders decided that all remaining idolaters must be exiled, including spouses of Jews. Some sent their unbelieving spouses away; others joined them in exile.

The success that attended Nehemiah's leadership shows what prayer, faith, and wise action can do. Nehemiah was not a priest or a prophet, and he claimed no title. He was just a man whom God had called to set things right.

The Coming of a Deliverer

From the time of Adam and Eve to the time when Jesus would come, the hope of Israel centered on the promised Deliverer. The Son of God had told Adam and Eve that He would come to earth and crush the serpent's head. The patriarchs and prophets kept the hope of a Deliverer alive for God's people. God's promise to send His Son came from His heart of love, even as Satan tried to frame God as hateful and mean by twisting the Scriptures.

Prophecy foretold how the Son of God would come and how He would be treated. He loved people and was willing to die for them. He asked only that humanity accept Him as the promised Messiah and Savior and by their obedience show that they loved Him and appreciated what He had done for them.

The exact time when Jesus would come, be baptized, and die on Calvary was prophesied ahead of time and recorded in Scripture. Also recorded in Scripture was the fact that Satan would severely tempt Christ to sin but that he would not be successful because Jesus always depended on God to help Him.

"The House of Israel"

In every age, God promised to love and bless His people, and they were to show that they loved Him by obeying Him and by telling others about His goodness, faithfulness, and mercy. He wants us to ask Him to help us spread His love around the world.

What God wanted the Jewish people to do for the world is what He wants His followers today to do for the world. The good news of salvation is to go to every nation, kindred, tongue, and people. We are to be like a shining light in a dark place, no matter how bad things get.

When the apostle John was old, he was arrested and put on the prison island of Patmos. It was there that God gave him a vision of the future. John saw a great multitude of people from every nation dressed in white robes standing before God and saying, "Amen! Blessings, glory, honor, and power belong to our God and to the Lamb forever and ever!"

Visions of Future Glory

As we near the end of the world, we must keep in mind the descriptions of future glory as recorded in Scripture. Jesus will come back as He promised, clear the world of wickedness, and end the lives of wicked men and women. As the prophet Isaiah said, "This is our God, we have waited for Him, and He will save us, and we will be glad and rejoice!"

We will hear the voice of Jesus resurrecting those who loved Him and had given their hearts to Him. They will come out of the grave healthy and young forever. No one will ever again have to say, "I'm sick." God will say to them, "Be glad and rejoice forever, and I will rejoice with you!" The music and songs will be like no one has ever heard before, and the redeemed will join in the singing, praising God and His Son for Their love and for what They have done for them. There will be no more sin, sickness, or death, but instead, happiness and joy forever.

THE
SAVIOR

Insights From
The Desire of Ages

"God With Us"
Jesus has always been one with the Father. Through Creation, Christ carried out the Father's will and revealed God's glory. Jesus was the reflection of the Father's glory. He came to this earth as one of us to show how much the Father loves us. It is the glory of God to love and to give. This is the law of heaven and earth. Force of any kind is contrary to God's government.

Conversely, sin exalts self and misrepresents God. It began in heaven when Lucifer said, "I will be like God and place my throne above the stars of God." Some of the angels admired Lucifer and decided to join him. Their rebellion had to be stopped, so they were expelled from heaven.

Lucifer decided to tempt Adam and Eve to sin, and he succeeded. To save humankind, Jesus chose to give His kingly scepter to the Father, get off His throne, come to earth in a human body, and give His life for us. This plan wasn't crafted after Adam and Eve sinned; it had been "kept in silence through times eternal" (Romans 16:25, ASV). Forevermore, Christ will be the Son of God in a human body like one of us. He is forever our Brother.

While on earth, Jesus gave us an example of obedience. Satan believed that God's law was unreasonable and impossible to keep, but Jesus kept the law of God without using any power that is not also offered to us. He gives us the power to obey if we ask Him, and through Christ we become more united to the Father.

By dying willingly on the cross, Christ proved Satan wrong and showed heavenly and earthly creation that God and His government are fair and based on love. One day Satan will be destroyed completely and sin will never again enter the universe. Our union with God will never again be broken.

The Chosen People

God planned for His people to show others the love of God. However, the Israelites thought only about themselves, disobeyed God, and fixed their hopes on becoming a great nation. So like a loving human father would, God had to discipline His selfish and disobedient children. Yet there were some who loved and obeyed Him no matter what.

As time went on, the Israelites began to forget that their various spiritual rituals pointed forward to the coming of their Redeemer. The priests tried to strengthen the people's commitment to God by adding burdensome requirements of their own to the religious ceremonies. The people soon began losing their love for God.

In the time of Christ, the Romans occupied Israel, and the Jews wanted to be free from that tyranny. However, as they looked forward to the coming of the Messiah, they thought of Him as a King who would come to defeat the Romans and make Israel a great political power again. They lost sight of the scriptures that said He would come to earth and die to set them free from sin, not the Romans.

"The Fullness of the Time"

Christ came at a time when people had heightened interest in the future and life beyond the grave. Even outside the Jewish nation, people talked about the coming of a Messiah. Philosophers had studied the mystery of the Hebrew beliefs, which kindled hope in their own hearts and in the hearts of thousands of others. The Scriptures had been translated into Greek and spread throughout the Roman Empire. Some Greeks understood better than the Jews the purpose of the Messiah.

Satan had been doing all he could to deceive people since Creation. The Son of God looked down from heaven and saw that humans had become the victims of Satan's cruelty. He manipulated their senses, nerves, passions, and bodily organs to indulge the vilest lust. Sin had become like a science and was even integrated into false religion. Angels and the unfallen worlds expected God to step in and wipe out the mess

> In the light from Calvary it will be seen that the law of self-renouncing love is the law of life for earth and heaven; that the love which "seeketh not her own" has its source in the heart of God; and that in the meek and lowly One is manifested the character of Him who dwelleth in the light which no man can approach unto.
> —*The Desire of Ages*, 20

that was the human race. Instead, the Son of God came with love and grace to restore in man the image of God.

Unto You a Saviour
The Son of God decided to come and take on human nature. The angels watched with anticipation as the plan unfolded. The angel Gabriel appeared to a young virgin named Mary and told her, "You will become pregnant through the power of the Holy Spirit, and your baby will be the Son of God." When Mary told Joseph, her fiancé, that she was pregnant, he was shocked and refused to marry her. Then Gabriel told him that she was pregnant through the power of the Holy Spirit and that he should go ahead and marry her, so he did.

About this time, Caesar Augustus announced that everyone must go and register their name at the city of their ancestors. This meant that Joseph and a very pregnant Mary had to travel from Galilee to Bethlehem. Thousands were arriving in town, so when they arrived in Bethlehem, their friends' and families' homes were full of other visitors and the local motels were booked solid. Every place was full. Fortunately, an innkeeper pitied the pregnant woman and allowed Mary and Joseph to set up their beds in the barn where the guests kept their animals. So that's where Jesus was born.

All heaven rejoiced and angels hovered above the hills, waiting for the signal to share the good news with the shepherds. During the night in the fields of Bethlehem, shepherds were talking to one another about the promised Messiah when suddenly the sky lit up and an angel appeared and said to them, "Don't be afraid. I have good news for you. Go into Bethlehem and you'll find a new baby bundled up and sleeping in an animal feeding box in a stable." Then a host of angels appeared and began praising God and singing a song of peace for all people.

It would have been very humbling for Jesus to take on human nature when Adam was alive, but instead He took on human nature after it had been weakened by four thousand years of physical degeneration. Christ grew up facing the same possibility of sinning that everyone must face, but He did not sin. He died for us that we may have eternal life. This is amazing love, beyond the comprehension of those in heaven and on earth.

> Heaven and earth are no wider apart today than when shepherds listened to the angels' song. Humanity is still as much the object of heaven's solicitude as when common men of common occupations met angels at noonday, and talked with the heavenly messengers in the vineyards and the fields.
> —*The Desire of Ages*, 48

The Dedication

About six weeks after Jesus was born, Joseph and Mary took Him to the temple in Jerusalem to be dedicated. They needed to bring a lamb for an offering, but since they couldn't afford a lamb, they were allowed to bring a couple of healthy pigeons. The priest, who didn't see anything unusual about Him, took the Baby in his arms, held Him up before the altar, handed Him back to Mary, and wrote the name "Jesus" on the logbook of firstborn children.

As Joseph and Mary were presenting Jesus to the priest, an old prophet named Simeon came into the temple and saw Jesus being dedicated. As he looked at the Baby, he was impressed by the Holy Spirit that this was the promised Messiah. He took the Baby from Mary and lifted Him up to heaven, saying, "Lord, now that I have seen Him as you said I would, I can die in peace." He handed the Baby back to Mary and Joseph and blessed them. Then Anna, a prophetess, came in. Her face lit up as she looked at the Baby and poured out her thanks to God that she was allowed to see the promised Messiah.

Mary held Jesus in her arms and tried to understand everything she saw and heard. At the time, she had no idea of His mission. Some years would pass before she would understand Jesus' mission and the suffering He would have to go through, especially dying on Calvary.

"We Have Seen His Star"

When Jesus was born in Bethlehem, three noble philosophers from the East came to Jerusalem to meet the King of Israel. They had copies of the Hebrew prophecies that predicted the coming of a Divine Teacher, and from these they understood that His coming was near. They had also studied astronomy, and one night they noticed an unusually bright star in the sky close to earth. As they watched the star, it kept moving, and they wondered what this meant. The bright star was a company of angels guiding them, but they didn't know that. Through their dreams, the Holy Spirit told them to follow the light to find the promised Prince. They loaded gifts for the Savior into their packs and set out on the long journey. When they got to Jerusalem, the star stopped over the temple, then faded away.

King Herod heard about the arrival of the three men from the East and visited with them to find out if they were plotting an overthrow of his regime. When they told him

> Men acknowledge Christ in history, while they turn away from the living Christ. Christ in His word calling to self-sacrifice, in the poor and suffering who plead for relief, in the righteous cause that involves poverty and toil and reproach, is no more readily received today than He was eighteen hundred years ago.
> —*The Desire of Ages*, 56

why they had come, he told them to go to Bethlehem to find the Baby and then come tell him so he could honor and worship Him too. Of course, what he really planned was to kill any potential rival.

The bright star reappeared and led the men to Bethlehem. When they found the house where Joseph, Mary, and little Jesus were staying, they expected to see some royal guards protecting the King, but there were none. But when they looked at Jesus, they felt a Divine Presence and fell on their knees and worshiped Him. Then they gave gifts of gold, frankincense, and myrrh to Mary and Joseph for the Baby King. What an amazing faith these three men showed!

When they were ready to leave, an angel told them in a dream not to go back to Herod to tell him that they had found the Baby, so they went home via a different route. When Herod learned this, he was furious. God told Joseph to quickly take Mary and the Baby to Egypt and to stay there until they were told to come back, so he did, just in time. The enraged King Herod ordered his soldiers to go through Bethlehem and kill all babies under the age of two. This terrible atrocity left mothers and fathers weeping all over the city. However, if God's people had been faithful to Him and recognized Jesus as the promised Savior, God would have protected them from the king.

> If we have given our hearts to Jesus, we also shall bring our gifts to Him. Our gold and silver, our most precious earthly possessions, our highest mental and spiritual endowments, will be freely devoted to Him who loved us, and gave Himself for us.
> —*The Desire of Ages*, 65

A few years later, Herod died, and God told Joseph in a dream that it was now safe to go back home. So Joseph took Mary and little Jesus back to Israel. The family settled in Nazareth in Galilee, where Joseph opened a carpenter shop.

As a Child

Jesus grew up learning how to work and help his father in the carpenter shop. He was always ready and willing to do whatever needed to be done. He was honest, truthful, courteous, and kind and always lived by principle. With deep interest, Mary watched Jesus grow up learning and trying to understand things. His body and mind grew and developed like other children's, but Mary received guidance from the Holy Spirit on how to work with Him to develop His character and to teach Him the holy Scriptures.

No one has ever lived under such constant temptations as Jesus did, because Satan's primary mission was to defile Him. Jesus' parents were poor and had to work hard to keep food on the table. Because of their poverty, Jesus had no free time to get into trouble. All through His life, He worked hard, always making sure to do everything to the best of His ability. Jesus' example shows us that hard work for the benefit of others builds strength in our minds and our characters.

Jesus never made a distinction between classes of people. He did all He could to help those in need and to encourage anyone He could, and He identified personally with the poor. In everything, Jesus kept a cheerful spirit. He did not complain about anything; only songs and words of praise for God spilled from His lips. This brought light and cheer to those around, drawing them closer to God, and serves as an example for us all.

> It would be well for us to spend a thoughtful hour each day in contemplation of the life of Christ. We should take it point by point, and let the imagination grasp each scene, especially the closing ones. As we thus dwell upon His great sacrifice for us, our confidence in Him will be more constant, our love will be quickened, and we shall be more deeply imbued with His spirit.
> —*The Desire of Ages*, 83

The Passover Visit

In Jewish culture, the age of twelve was considered the border between childhood and adulthood. All adults were expected to come to Jerusalem for three yearly festivals: Passover, Pentecost, and the special Sabbath called the Feast of Tabernacles. Of these three, the Passover was considered the most important; it celebrated Israel's deliverance from slavery in Egypt more than a thousand years before. People came from everywhere, even from other countries. People traveled with friends and relatives, and when they saw Jerusalem in the distance, they would break out in song.

Jesus was twelve years old when he first attended the festival with Mary and Joseph. It was the first time He had seen the temple. With all the other worshipers, Jesus went in and bowed in prayer. While inside, He watched all the rituals and rites with great interest. He saw a lamb being sacrificed, and the mystery of His mission began to open up to Him. Jesus wanted to be alone, so He stayed in the temple after His parents and the other worshipers left.

In a classroom attached to the temple, the learned rabbis met with their students, and Jesus went there to listen to the discussions. When the time came for questions, Jesus asked about the prophecies concerning the coming Messiah. Noting the depth of His thought, the rabbis began to ask Him questions. He always answered with verses from Scripture that led the teachers to consider ideas they hadn't before. If Jesus had come with an attitude that indicated He knew more than the rabbis, they never would have listened to Him. But He approached them as a humble learner, so they didn't put up their defenses, and their hearts were stirred.

Meanwhile Jesus' parents left with their friends and relatives to go home, assuming Jesus was with the group. When they tried to find Him that evening and couldn't, they asked their friends and relatives if anyone had seen Him that day, but no one had. Joseph and Mary were really worried, and they rushed back to Jerusalem. The next day they found Jesus talking with the theological leaders in the temple school. Mary and Joseph called Jesus aside and said anxiously, "Where have You been? We've been looking all over for You; we were worried sick!" Jesus answered, "You should know that I would be about My Father's business." For three agonizing days, Joseph and Mary had been separated from Jesus, just like when he would later die on the cross and be in the tomb for three days.

As with Mary and Joseph, when we take our eyes off the Savior, we risk forgetting Him and allowing the idle chatter of life to replace holy pursuits. People attend church and feel encouraged by the preaching, but without private meditation and prayer they lose the blessings they gained. Spending time each day thinking about God's goodness and praying to Jesus would benefit us much more than simply attending religious services. Making space for Him in our hearts and minds leaves us more and more filled with His love and more like Him.

> He taught all to look upon themselves as endowed with precious talents, which if rightly employed would secure for them eternal riches. He weeded all vanity from life, and by His own example taught that every moment of time is fraught with eternal results; that it is to be cherished as a treasure, and to be employed for holy purposes.
> —*The Desire of Ages*, 91

Days of Conflict

As Jesus was matured, He noticed that the social practice of religion and the requirements of God were in constant conflict. Men exalted their own ideas above the law of God. He wanted no part of it. When anyone challenged Jesus about His simple faith, He showed them from Scripture the reasons why He lived that way.

Conversely, Jesus' brothers always did what the priests and the rabbis said to do. Like the priests and rabbis, They accused Jesus of being independent, stubborn, and proud. The rabbis didn't like it when Jesus refused to participate in the man-made religious requirements. Even though it was obvious that He knew the Scriptures better than they, their pride made them cold to the truths He shared. Very young, Jesus had to learn how to patiently endure the abuse brought on Him by others.

Jesus never contended for His right to do what He wanted. He went about His work and took insults without complaining. He lived above all this by getting up early in the morning, finding a secluded place to read the Scriptures, and praying to His heavenly Father.

Christ loved and respected His parents, especially His mother, who watched Him grow up amid the hardships and difficulties He faced. Sometimes she would urge Him to conform to what the priests and rabbis said in order to make things easier for Himself. But when He showed her that His behavior was based on Scripture, she was satisfied.

In every case of suffering that young Jesus saw, He did what He could to help. He would often give the hungry His own lunch. And when He saw people, including His own brothers, speak harshly to the poor and homeless, He would go out of His way to help them. All this upset His brothers, and they accused Him of thinking He was better than they because He refused to take part in their mischievous acts. They often threatened and intimidated Him, but He returned only kindness.

Jesus taught people to see the valuable gifts of God within themselves. In every interaction, He taught lessons from Scripture and encouraged people to keep their eyes on God. Though He loved everyone, He was really alone, both because He was so different and because He was bearing the heavy burden of His divine mission.

The Voice in the Wilderness

The mothers of John the Baptist and Jesus were relatives. John was born about six months before Jesus. His parents were Zacharias and Elizabeth. Zacharias was a priest and was scheduled to go to Jerusalem to serve in the temple for a time. One day while he stood by the altar in the Holy Place, an angel appeared to him and said, "Zacharias, your prayer has been heard; your wife will have a baby and you should call him John. He will remind people about their duty to God and get them ready for the coming Redeemer." Surprised, Zacharias responded, "How is this possible? She is passed childbearing age."

The angel said, "I am Gabriel, and I stand in the presence of God. With God all things are possible. He sent me here to give you this good news." Zacharias still doubted, so Gabriel said, "Because you doubted my words, you will not be able to talk until the baby is born." When Zacharias came out of the temple to bless the people, he couldn't talk, so he just raised his arms as a sign of blessing. When the baby was born, Zacharias's speech returned, and he named his son John.

For John to grow up and carry out his mission, he had to be healthy and strong. During his childhood and youth, John had to learn self-control and how not be influenced by the sin around him. This would help him become the kind of man he needed to be. Self-discipline is essential for mental, spiritual, and physical strength. God asked him to live in an isolated place in the desert for a while to prepare for his ministry through meditation and prayer. He dressed like the ancient prophets and ate whatever he found in the hills.

From time to time he would go into the city to mingle with people and learn about how they were handling life's problems so he could know how to help them. He spent the rest of his time studying the Scriptures and prophecies and learning about God in nature. Through the Holy Spirit, he also learned about the methods that Satan uses to get people to sin and how to combat those methods. At the time, John did not fully understand the ministry of Christ. He thought the Messiah would get rid of the Romans and set up Israel as a holy nation once again.

When John's ministry began, the nation of Israel was on the verge of revolution, but amid all this unrest, John did not tell the people to go ahead and free themselves from Roman occupation. Instead, he focused on talking to them about God. He said, "Repent and be baptized because the kingdom of God is almost here." Many people turned from their wicked ways and asked to be baptized; even some scribes and Pharisees joined. The Holy Spirit told John that many of the Jewish leaders were not sincere in their repentance and were only trying to strengthen their influence with the people. John called them out and told them to stop being so proud and selfish; instead, they should go and help people, especially the poor.

The Baptism

The news of John's ministry spread everywhere. When it got to Nazareth, Jesus decided to go to the river Jordan to be baptized as others were doing. Though they had never met, John had heard about Jesus and believed that He was the Messiah, but he had no proof. God told John that Jesus would come to be baptized and that at His baptism evidence would show him that Jesus was the Messiah. But John thought, *If Jesus was the Messiah, how could he, a sinner, baptize the sinless Messiah?*

Jesus didn't *need* to be baptized as people do, but He did it as an example for others. When he arrived at the river's edge and asked for baptism, John hesitated. "You should baptize me!" he told the Savior. Jesus responded, "This is the way it's supposed to be." So John led Jesus into the water and buried Him under the surface. At that moment, the heavens opened and the Holy Spirit came down as a dove hovering over Jesus' head, and God said aloud, "This is My beloved Son, in whom I am well pleased." Only those in the crowd whose hearts were open to God noticed these signs.

> By sin, earth was cut off from heaven, and alienated from its communion; but Jesus has connected it again with the sphere of glory. His love has encircled man, and reached the highest heaven. The light which fell from the open portals upon the head of our Saviour will fall upon us as we pray for help to resist temptation.
>
> —*The Desire of Ages*, 113

Jesus got out of the river, knelt on the shore, and poured out His soul in prayer. He asked the Father to help Him break Satan's power over people. Never before had the angels heard such a prayer. Suddenly, the light of heaven surrounded Him as a promise from the Father that He would help His Son. At this, John announced that all the people should look at Jesus, because He was the Lamb of God who had come to save humanity.

Like Jesus, we must pray earnestly, asking the Father to help us overcome temptation and reach people for Him. Jesus has opened the way for us to know that we, though sinners, are still God's sons and daughters, and we can reach out directly to Him.

The Temptation

After Jesus was baptized, the Holy Spirit led Him into the wilderness to fast and pray and get ready for His ministry. After He had been there fasting and praying forty days, Satan, disguised as an angel, came to see Jesus. Satan pointed to some stones and, appealing to the Lord's appetite, said, "If You are the Son of God, why don't You use Your power and turn one of these stones into bread for Yourself?" He continued his attacks, but every time Satan tempted Jesus, the Savior answered him with Scripture, "It is written . . ."

There is power in the Bible, and if we study it diligently and know its verses well, we will always have a ready answer to the deceiver's temptations.

> The tempter can never compel us to do evil. He cannot control minds unless they are yielded to his control. The will must consent, faith must let go its hold upon Christ, before Satan can exercise his power upon us.
> —*The Desire of Ages*, 125

The Victory

Then Satan changed his tactics, took Jesus to the roof of the temple, and said, "If You are the Son of God, jump off and God will send His angels to catch You before You hit the ground." Jesus refused to do such a dumb thing just to prove that He was the Son of God. True faith and love for God leads us to do sensible things to show that we love Him. Plus, there is a distinct difference between faith and presumption.

When this second temptation failed, Satan tried a third one. He took Jesus to the top of a nearby mountain, gave Him a view of all the beautiful things on earth, including its prosperity and riches, and said to Jesus, "This earth and all that I've shown You is mine. I'll give it to You if You just bow down and acknowledge my authority."

Christ rebuked him again, "Go away and stop tempting me, Satan. The scriptures say that we must worship and serve the Lord God and none other." Jesus' divinity flashed through His humanity and Satan could not stand to be in the presence of holiness any longer. This last temptation is the same one that Satan uses on people today. He promises to give us all the good things this world has to offer if we only acknowledge his supremacy and do what he says. Yet with all his promises, Satan cannot force us to do anything evil. To sin, we have to let go of our faith and choose the course of wrong.

After Satan left, Jesus slumped to the ground, exhausted and dying. Angels had been watching all this, and as soon as Satan was gone, they rushed to the Savior with food and water to strengthen Him and with words from His Father to comfort Him. As His strength returned, Jesus thought about all the people needing help, so He got up to do the work that He came to do.

"We Have Found the Messias"
John the Baptist was still calling the people to repentance and baptizing them. But he also focused his preaching on the prophecies that pointed to the time when the Messiah would come.

One day as crowds of people were listening to John, Sanhedrin leaders came to the river dressed in their rich robes. They asked John, "Who are you?"

John knew what was on their minds and said, "I am not the Messiah, and I don't pretend to be."

Then they asked, "So then, who are you? Are you Elijah raised from the dead?"

John said, "No!"

Then they asked, "So who are you?"

He said, "I'm just an ordinary man. What you need to do is to smooth out the spiritual road ahead of the Savior's journey."

The rabbis and priests continued to question him, "Why are you baptizing people if you are not the Messiah or even Elijah?" They believed that before the Messiah would come, Elijah would be raised from the dead to announce His coming. If the rabbis and priests had seen that John's work was like Elijah's work, they would have expected the coming of the Messiah.

When John spotted Jesus among the people, he said, "The Savior is among us!" The priests turned to look, but they didn't see anyone who appeared kingly. Jesus was just an ordinary-looking Man, and even more so now that he was emaciated and weary. John hoped Jesus would say something, but He didn't. The next day when John again saw Jesus among the people, he pointed to Him and said, "Behold the Lamb of God!" It seemed impossible to the people that such an ordinary Man could be the Messiah. They expected a kingly warrior, an impressive physical specimen.

The next day John again spotted Jesus in the crowd and said, "Look, there He is, the Lamb of God!" Two of John's disciples looked, saw Jesus walking away, and decided to catch up to Him. Andrew and John, the brother of James, approached the Savior.

Jesus turned and asked, "What can I do for you?"

They said, "Where are you staying? We would like to talk with you."

Jesus said, "Come and see." So they followed Him and stayed with Him the rest of the day.

The next day Andrew went to find his brother Simon Peter. When he found him, he said, "We have found the promised Messiah!" Peter had heard John the Baptist talk about the Messiah, so he hurried to see Him. When Jesus saw him, He instantly read his character, his history and future. He knew that one day Peter would die for Him.

Jesus decided to go to Galilee, and there He saw Philip, to whom He said, "Come and follow Me." Then Philip called Nathanael to Jesus. Though a bit put off by the Savior's unimpressive appearance, Nathanael came, because John the Baptist's words had convicted him. Jesus looked at Nathanael and said, "This morning when you sat praying under the fig tree, I saw you." When Nathanael heard that, he said, "You *are* the Son of God!"

> The gifts of Jesus are ever fresh and new. The feast that He provides for the soul never fails to give satisfaction and joy. Each new gift increases the capacity of the receiver to appreciate and enjoy the blessings of the Lord. He gives grace for grace. There can be no failure of supply.
> —*The Desire of Ages*, 148

At the Marriage Feast

Jesus' ministry began quietly. His first stop was a wedding in the little town in Galilee, not far from Nazareth. The bride and groom were relatives of Joseph and Mary. Joseph had died and Jesus had been away from His mother for at least two months. When she saw Jesus, He didn't look the same; He had lost so much weight and seemed more burdened, more powerful. She was glad to see Him and wished He would work a miracle to prove who He really was. The disciples told her all about the things she had missed.

At that time, wedding celebrations usually lasted a few days. Near the end of the wedding, the hosts ran out of wine. Mary was in charge, and running out of wine would seem very inhospitable, so she asked Jesus what to do. He respectfully said to her, "Mother, I must follow the directions of My Father in heaven and do what He tells me to do." He said this because otherwise Mary might think she could tell Him what to do as she did when He was growing up.

To honor Mary's belief and to strengthen the disciples' faith, Jesus decided to work His first miracle. Mary sensed this and said to the servants, "Whatever He tells you to do, do it."

Now there were six large water pots nearby. Jesus pointed to them and said, "Fill those with water." They did, and He turned the water into wine, which was then served to the master of ceremonies.

When he tasted the pure, unfermented grape juice, he said, "Why did we save the best for last? We usually serve people the best drinks first, and after they've had so much to eat and drink that it doesn't really matter anymore, then we serve them the lesser wine."

In His Temple

After the wedding, Jesus and the disciples went to Capernaum, where Peter lived, and stayed there for a while. When the Passover came, they joined a large caravan headed to Jerusalem. People came from all parts of Palestine and even from neighboring countries. Because of the distance, people could not easily bring animals with them to offer as a sacrifice, so they had to buy them when they got there. Upon entering the temple courtyard, they had to exchange their foreign money for local money, which gave the money changers a chance to make a dishonest profit. From there, the people would buy the overpriced animals from greedy vendors also set up inside the courtyard. The temple was a jam-packed madhouse rather than a sacred space.

When Jesus arrived and saw what was going on, the disrespect for God's house was too much to tolerate. As Jesus stood looking over the masses, silence slowly filled the courtyard. The priests and rabbis and businesspeople felt as if Jesus were looking into their souls and revealing the darkness of their hearts. They couldn't look away from him. The Savior, for whom the temple had been built, spoke in a ringing, commanding voice and told the merchants to take their things and get out. Then, with a bundle of cord in His hand that seemed to them as deadly as a flaming sword, He turned their tables over, money and all. No one could oppose His authority. Without a single question about His authority, they all fled, and silence prevailed.

This display marked a public announcement of Jesus' ministry and mission. The corrupt had been cast out; the faithful, poor, and needy remained. They pressed around Jesus, saying, "Master, please help us," and told Him about their needs. Right there,

> **When the Spirit of God takes possession of the heart, it transforms the life. Sinful thoughts are put away, evil deeds are renounced; love, humility, and peace take the place of anger, envy, and strife. Joy takes the place of sadness, and the countenance reflects the light of heaven. No one sees the hand that lifts the burden, or beholds the light descend from the courts above.**
>
> —*The Desire of Ages*, 173

He healed everyone who was sick, lame, deaf, blind, sad, or in any way burdened. As the temple officials and priests moved slowly back into the space and saw what Jesus was doing, they were amazed, afraid, and filled with hate.

Nicodemus

Nicodemus was a member of the Jewish National Council. He was highly educated, respected, and honored, yet unlike so many other Jewish leaders, he was sad about the spiritual condition of Israel and was impressed by Jesus' teachings. When the priests and rulers of the Sanhedrin plotted to get rid of Jesus after He cleansed the temple courts of money changers, Nicodemus advised caution, because it would be dangerous to cause harm to someone vested with authority from God.

Late one night after everyone in town was asleep, Nicodemus went to see Jesus to ask Him some questions. Jesus looked into his soul and said, "You need to know that unless a man is born again, he can't be taken into heaven." Nicodemus was shocked and said, "How can a grown man be born again?" Jesus said, "I'm not talking about physical birth but spiritual birth by the power of God." As He never had before and never did again in personal conversation, Jesus explained to Nicodemus His mission and the plan of salvation. Nicodemus embraced everything Christ had said and he quietly accepted Him as the Messiah.

Though Nicodemus didn't make a big public statement about his faith, whenever the National Council met and the priests and rulers talked about harming Jesus, Nicodemus did all he could to stop them. After Jesus was finally crucified, Nicodemus used his wealth and position to help the disciples spread the gospel as far and wide as they could.

"He Must Increase"

John the Baptist continued his ministry, which had more influence with the people than the teachings of the priests and rulers. He kept preaching about Jesus being the Messiah and took no credit to himself. John was so effective that, gradually, people began to turn to Jesus and away from John.

John's disciples became jealous of Jesus and His disciples. They talked about the importance of John's preaching and baptism and how Jesus hadn't offered to baptize anyone. They questioned whether Jesus and His disciples even had a right to baptize. Because John still had a lot of influence, had he gone along with their murmurings, he could have damaged Jesus' ministry. Fortunately, John had dedicated himself so fully to Jesus that he resisted their attempts to stir jealousy and kept directing the people to Jesus as the Messiah. He said, "He must increase, and I must decrease." Any true messenger of God will say the same thing.

Jesus knew that the Jewish leaders would intentionally create a rift between His disciples and John's just to cripple the work. To avoid conflict, He and His disciples moved on to Galilee.

At Jacob's Well
On the way to Galilee, Jesus had to go through Samaria, whose citizens were enemies of the Jews. It was lunchtime when they arrived, tired, thirsty, and hungry, so Jesus stopped by a well near the edge of the valley to rest while the disciples went into town to buy food.

For generations, the Jews and Samaritans had hated each other. When the Jews had returned from Babylonian captivity and wanted to rebuild the temple, the Samaritans tried and failed to stop them. The Jews also rejected the Samaritans' religion. Samaritans were considered unclean, so the Jews were not to talk to them, ask favors of them, or anything beyond necessary business transactions.

As Jesus rested, a Samaritan woman came to the well with her bucket to get water. Watching her made Him even thirstier, so He asked her for a drink. In those days no one would refuse a thirsty traveler a drink of water. However, when she realized that Jesus was a Jew, she said, "How come a Jew would ask a Samaritan for a drink of water?"

Jesus said, "If you knew who I was, you would ask Me for a drink."

She said, "You don't have a bucket, so how could You offer me a drink?" She didn't realize that Jesus was talking about spiritual water. Something about Jesus and what He said made a deep impression on her, and spontaneously she said, "Lord, give me the water You're talking about, then I won't have to keep coming to this well."

Jesus changed the subject and said, "Go get your husband."

She said, "I don't have a husband."

Jesus said, "I know, you've had five husbands and the one you're with now is not your husband."

The woman was shocked and began to shake. How did this Jewish stranger know her history? She finally got control of herself and said, "Are You a prophet?" Then she changed the conversation. "You Jews say that we should worship at the temple in Jerusalem, but our ancestors had their own temple."

Then Jesus decided to break down her prejudice and said, "True worship is not so much where we worship but the spirit in which we worship."

Never before had she felt such a deep spiritual need. She said to Him, "One thing we know is that when the Messiah comes, He will tell us the truth."

Jesus looked at her and said, "I am the Messiah." The woman stood there speechless and accepted what He said as truth.

While the two talked, the disciples came back with food and were surprised when they saw Jesus speaking to a Samaritan woman. When she left, Jesus didn't seem to be interested in eating. His face was shining, and He was deep in thought and prayer. They didn't want to disturb Him, but finally they suggested that He eat something. Gently, Jesus responded, "I have had a special kind of food that you don't know about."

The woman was so excited by what Jesus had said that she forgot her water bucket and ran back to her village, announcing to the people, "Come, see a Man who told me everything that I ever did. This must be the Messiah!" There was such an expression of joy on her face that the people felt compelled to stop what they were doing and go see this Messiah. Jesus stayed in Samaria for two whole days teaching them, and many accepted Him as the Redeemer.

Like the Samaritan woman, when we spend time with the Savior in prayer and through reading His Word, His beauty shines through our faces and draws others closer to Him too. That is our first Christian duty.

> There are many who realize their helplessness, and who long for that spiritual life which will bring them into harmony with God; they are vainly striving to obtain it. In despair they cry, "O wretched man that I am! who shall deliver me from this body of death?" Romans 7:24, margin. Let these desponding, struggling ones look up. The Saviour is bending over the purchase of His blood, saying with inexpressible tenderness and pity, "Wilt thou be made whole?" He bids you arise in health and peace.
> —*The Desire of Ages*, 203

"Except Ye See Signs and Wonders"

When the Galileans who had been at the Passover in Jerusalem came back home, they told the people about the miracles that Jesus had done there. So when Jesus returned to Galilee and stopped at Cana, the news spread everywhere that He was back. This caught the attention of a Jewish nobleman who worked for King Herod. The man's son was gravely ill, so he went to Cana to ask Jesus heal him. He had some degree of belief that Jesus was the Messiah, though he wasn't sure, especially after seeing the ordinary man, dusty and worn with travel. Nevertheless, he pressed his way through the crowd to get close to Him.

Even before the officer had left home, the Savior already knew the problem and what he would ask Him to do. Jesus also knew the questions in his mind. So while the officer was waiting, Jesus looked in his direction and said, "Unless you see Me do miracles, you won't believe I'm the Messiah." At this, the man saw his own lack of faith and selfish motives. In desperation, he said, "Sir, *please* come to my house and heal my little son before he dies!"

Jesus said, "Go on home, your son has been healed." The man was immediately flooded with joy and relief; he believed that Jesus had healed his son and that He was the Redeemer. Back at home, the caretakers noticed a sudden change in the little boy: His face began looking healthy. The fever was gone, his eyes opened, and strength had returned to his little body.

The officer arrived home the next day. When he got close, his servants came running out to tell him the good news that his little son was better. He wasn't surprised and asked them what time he began to get better. They said, "Yesterday, in the heat of the afternoon!" The officer knew that it was the exact time he had asked Jesus to heal his little son.

The joyful father rushed inside, put his arms around his boy, and held him close. Then he decided to learn more about Jesus, and when he did, he and his whole family became followers of Jesus. News of the miracle spread all over town and prepared the people's hearts for Jesus' visit.

Bethesda and the Sanhedrin

Near the sheep market in Jerusalem there was a pool of water surrounded by five areas where people could rest. Sick people would come there to wait for the water in the quiet pool to stir. They believed that this was a sign of supernatural power and that the first one to get into the water after it stirred would be healed.

One Sabbath, Jesus walked by the pool on His way to worship at the temple. He saw all the broken people waiting there, hoping for a chance to be healed in the water. His heart went out to them, and He really wanted to heal them all. This would've enraged the Jewish leaders and made it impossible for Him to continue His work, so He couldn't. However, one crippled man on a mat drew His heart. Jesus could tell that the man must have been crippled for some time, but the man was all alone.

Jesus stopped, looked the man in the eyes, and said, "Do you want to be healed?" A spark of hope flashed and he wondered if Jesus would help him into the pool when the water moved again. But then he turned away and said, "Yes, I want to be healed, but there is no one here to help me into the water when it moves." Jesus said, "Get up, pick up your mat, and go home." Suddenly, new life came into his crippled frame. His muscles moved, and he stood up, picked up his mat and blanket, and walked. The overjoyed man turned to thank Jesus, but the Savior had disappeared in the crowd.

On his way home, the man saw several Pharisees and told the spiritual leaders what had happened. Instead of rejoicing with the healed one, they reminded him that he wasn't allowed to carry things on the Sabbath. He said, "The Man who healed me told me to pick up my things and go home." Soon after, the man decided to go to the temple with a thank offering for God.

The man was overjoyed when he saw Jesus in the temple. He ran up and thanked

Jesus for healing him. Then Jesus said, "Be careful and don't do things to bring some other problems on yourself." On his way out of the temple, the man saw some Pharisees, so he pointed to Jesus and told them that He was the one who had healed him.

The leaders charged Jesus with breaking the Sabbath and made Him appear before the Sanhedrin court. Jesus told them that it was lawful to help sick people get well on the Sabbath, and that His Father had told Him to do so. Jesus also said that while they believed that knowing the Scriptures gave them eternal life, they didn't really have the Word of God in their hearts. The council members were stunned by His boldness, but because they didn't have good answers for His claims and because He was so popular with the people, they decided not to punish or kill Him right then. Instead, they plotted to arrest and kill Him the first chance they had without stirring up the people.

> From what dangers, seen and unseen, we have been preserved through the interposition of the angels, we shall never know, until in the light of eternity we see the providences of God. Then we shall know that the whole family of heaven was interested in the family here below, and that messengers from the throne of God attended our steps from day to day.
> —*The Desire of Ages*, 240

Imprisonment and Death of John

John the Baptist was the first one to preach about Jesus being the Messiah. Even King Herod listened to his messages and became convicted that he had done wrong by taking his brother's wife, Herodias, and marrying her. Herodias hated John the Baptist for making her husband consider divorcing her. She eventually persuaded Herod to arrest John and put him in prison.

Being in prison was hard on John, because he had always lived out in nature and had been very active. To sit alone in a cell was depressing. His disciples were angry because Jesus kept busy with His ministry and didn't act like He cared about John's imprisonment or didn't try to help get him out. Satan tried to convince John that maybe Jesus wasn't the Messiah after all, but his whisperings failed. Jesus told John's disciples to first go and tell him about all the miraculous things they had seen Him do. This information comforted John, because that's exactly what he expected the Messiah to do.

Herod was thinking about releasing John, but his clever, wicked wife came up with a plan to stop it. Herodias asked her daughter Salome to go dance at Herod's birthday party. Herod was so impressed with the young lady's performance that, to wow the crowd, he promised to give the girl anything she asked for. Herodias said, "Ask the king for the head of

John the Baptist on a platter." The young woman hesitated, but because her mother insisted, she went back to Herod with her request. The king was horrified and confused, but because he had taken an oath to grant her request, he couldn't back down.

Herod called the jailer and asked him to cut off John's head and bring it to him on a platter. The jailer went back to the prison, cut off John's head, and brought it in on a platter to Herodias.

Jesus did not interfere with the arrest and execution of John, though He wanted to, because it would have hindered or prematurely ended His ministry. Herod heard about the works of Christ and wondered if God had raised John from the dead to ruin him for what he had done. Herodias's plan backfired, because her husband felt tormented by his sin and pushed her further away.

"The Kingdom of God Is at Hand"

Jesus gave the Jewish leaders the first opportunity to believe in Him and lead the way as they carried the gospel message to the world. Instead, they rejected and despised Him, and they did everything they could to turn the people against Him. Since Jerusalem was hostile to Him, Jesus spent more time in Galilee, where people were more open to His message.

Jesus continued preaching and teaching and healing. People flooded to Him from everywhere, to the point He often had to hide from them to prevent a mob that would bring Roman attention. Christ took His messages straight from prophecy. The people should have known from studying the Scriptures how to identify Jesus as the Messiah, but they failed to grasp the messages.

> There is no limit to the usefulness of one who, by putting self aside, makes room for the working of the Holy Spirit upon his heart, and lives a life wholly consecrated to God. If men will endure the necessary discipline, without complaining or fainting by the way, God will teach them hour by hour, and day by day. He longs to reveal His grace.
> —*The Desire of Ages*, 250, 251

As when Jesus came, humanity has reached a point in its history prophesied about in Scripture. The end of our world is coming close, and we must study and know what the Bible says so we can be prepared to know truth from error. One thing we know for sure—when Jesus comes again, no one will be confused about who He is!

"Is Not This the Carpenter's Son?"

People in Galilee responded wonderfully to Jesus' teaching and preaching. But those in His hometown of Nazareth did not accept Him as the Messiah. They would say,

"He's only the carpenter's son." Although they had not seen Him for some time, they had heard about all the good things that He had done. So when He came back home to Nazareth, Jesus went with His mother, brothers, and sisters to the synagogue to worship on the Sabbath.

The rabbi in charge asked Jesus to come up front to have the Scripture reading. He read from the book of Isaiah, "The Sovereign Lord has filled me with his Spirit. He has chosen me and sent me." Then He closed the book and gave it back to the rabbi. The people were enraptured and responded with praises and thanksgiving. Then Jesus explained the Scripture and told the people that it was fulfilled before their eyes in Him. This stoked their fear and prideful self-righteousness, and they closed their hearts again.

Suddenly, in a clamor, the service broke apart and the worshipers turned into an angry mob controlled by Satan. They grabbed Jesus and dragged Him out of the city to the edge of a nearby cliff, intending to throw Him over. Suddenly He disappeared; the angels carried Him to a place of safety.

After that, Jesus' fame grew even more. He tried one final time to reach the people in His home city. They knew He traveled around healing whole villages and bringing hope to the poor. And when they listened to Him speak, their hearts were stirred with the Holy Spirit. Even so, they would not accept Him as the promised Messiah, and because they didn't believe, He wasn't able to work many miracles in that community. Their spiritual pride was just too great, and this is still a problem today.

> Every man is free to choose what power he will have to rule over him. None have fallen so low, none are so vile, but that they can find deliverance in Christ. The demoniac, in place of prayer, could utter only the words of Satan; yet the heart's unspoken appeal was heard. No cry from a soul in need, though it fail of utterance in words, will be unheeded.
>
> —*The Desire of Ages*, 258

The Call by the Sea

So far, Jesus' disciples had kept their regular jobs. Peter and his brother, Andrew, were fishermen; they had been fishing on the Sea of Galilee all night but had caught nothing. They pulled their empty boat ashore and began washing their nets. Jesus had come to the shore hoping to get a little rest from the crowds that thronged Him day after day. But soon people young and old, sick and seeking, found Him and pressed in on Him from all sides, looking for a blessing. Backed to the water's edge, Jesus stepped into Peter's boat and asked him to pull a little bit from the shore so He could sit and teach the people from the boat. What a scene, the little boat rocking back and forth with the Savior in it teaching the people about the good news of salvation.

When Jesus finished talking to the crowd, He told Peter to row farther out into the sea to catch some fish. Peter said, "Lord, we fished all night and caught nothing, but because You say so, we'll try again." They caught so many fish that the nets were almost breaking, so they called for their partners, James and John, to come in their boat to help them. This miracle showed that Jesus was so powerful that He could even control nature. When they finally returned to shore, Peter fell on his knees before Jesus and said, "Lord, I'm too sinful and not worthy of Your blessings!" At that, Jesus told Peter and the other men to follow Him, and they would fish for people instead of fish. And that's what they did.

For the next three years, they followed Jesus and did all they could to tell the people about the good news of salvation, which is not just knowing truth but also having a relationship with Jesus as the Redeemer of the world. Education, social position, and natural ability are not the best predictors of success winning people to Jesus. Rather, those who truly love the Savior the most will do the most good for Him.

At Capernaum

Jesus had made Capernaum on the shore of the Sea of Galilee His hometown. There were beautiful trees, orchards and vineyards, and little villages and towns. Travelers from other countries liked to stop and rest in Capernaum. There they would meet Jesus, listen to His teachings, and carry the good news back home, even to other countries.

Jesus taught them with love in His heart. He made the truth simple, beautiful, and clear. The rabbis would speak about the Scriptures as if they could be interpreted different ways depending on the situation. Jesus taught that the Scriptures had unquestionable authority. His messages fit the different situations and minds of those who were listening, but He never flattered anyone or any group. His love and kindness attracted people.

One Sabbath as Jesus was speaking in the synagogue, a demon-possessed man rushed forward and shrieked, "Leave us alone! You have no business here, Jesus! You are the Holy One of God! Have you come to destroy us?" This brought utter confusion into the synagogue. The man wanted to be free from the power he had given Satan in his life, but the devil controlled him and had put these words in his mouth. Then Jesus commanded the demons to depart, and the man was set free. He fell on his knees and with grateful tears praised God for deliverance.

The congregation sat there spellbound. Jesus quietly left and went to the home of Peter to rest. When He got there, He found Peter's mother-in-law sick with a very high fever. Jesus rebuked the sickness, and immediately she became well, got up, and prepared some food for Jesus and His disciples.

Jesus worked long days, and at night He tried to get some rest. Often He would go to the mountains to be alone with God. He would spend the whole night in prayer and then get back to work in the morning.

"Thou Canst Make Me Clean"

Of all the diseases people had, the most dreaded was leprosy. The Jews believed that leprosy was a judgment of God resulting from a sinful life. The leper had to stay away from family and friends, and wherever he went, he had to call out, "I am unclean! Unclean!" There were many lepers where Christ was working. When they heard about Jesus' miracles, hope sprang up in their hearts. But how could a leper get close to Jesus, who was always surrounded by crowds?

One leper heard that Jesus was teaching by the lake and went to see Him. From a distance, he could see Jesus placing His hands on the sick, the lame, and the blind, healing them. Faith sprouted in his heart, "Would Jesus heal me, a leper?" As he approached the crowd, people drew back in horror at his gruesome, mangled body. The man was so focused on Jesus that he didn't even notice. He got close enough and called out, "Jesus, will You heal me too?" Jesus answered, "I will! You are healed!" Immediately, the man's body became whole and perfect again.

Then Jesus said, "Go to the priest right now, without delay. Don't tell him how you were healed; let him examine you and pronounce you well." The leading Jews were always discrediting Christ's work, so if they found out Jesus was responsible, they would have lied and said the man still had leprosy. Afterward, the man just couldn't keep quiet. Once news of the healing of a leper spread, so many people came to Jesus to be healed that Jesus had to leave the area and take a break from His public ministry for a while.

In another case, a completely paralyzed man heard about Jesus. His friends were determined to carry him on a stretcher to Jesus to be healed. The man had faith that Jesus could heal him, but what he most wanted was forgiveness for his sins. When they got to the house where Jesus was teaching, the crowd was so large they couldn't possibly squeeze into the house, especially with a stretcher. Their desperation gave way to a creative solution. The men forced their way through the crowd outside the house, climbed up on the flat roof, and hoisted up the stretcher with their friend on it. They

> **Thousands are making the same mistake as did the Pharisees whom Christ reproved at Matthew's feast. Rather than give up some cherished idea, or discard some idol of opinion, many refuse the truth which comes down from the Father of light. They trust in self, and depend upon their own wisdom, and do not realize their spiritual poverty.**
> —*The Desire of Ages*, 280

pulled opened part of the roof and lowered their friend on his stretcher down, right in front of Jesus. Christ looked at him and said, "Be happy; your sins are forgiven!" The peace of forgiveness flooded the man's body, and his physical pain was also gone, his body healed. He lay on his stretcher in perfect peace, too happy for words.

The Pharisees who were there looked at one another and determined that something had to be done to stop Jesus. No one can forgive sins except God, and since they didn't believe Jesus was God, they considered his proclamation of forgiveness blasphemous. Jesus looked at them and said, "Why do you think I've done something evil? Is it easier to say, 'You are forgiven,' or 'Be healed and get up'?" Then Jesus turned to the man and told him to get up and go home. The man stood up, picked up his stretcher, and left. The Pharisees stood there—speechless. Christ had shown that He possessed the power they believed belonged to God alone. When the man got home, his family was so thankful that they were ready to give their lives for Jesus.

Levi-Matthew

No one was more hated by the people than those who collected taxes for the Romans. Matthew was one of them. But Jesus saw in him someone whose heart was open to truth. One day when Matthew was sitting at his tax booth, Jesus came by, looked at him, and said, "Follow Me." Matthew got up, turned the tax booth over to his assistants, and followed Jesus. This fifth official disciple left a good income for a life of self-denial and work. This was the same for the other disciples. The sincerity and dedication of very follower of Christ will be tested. The Jewish leaders did not like that one of Jesus' followers was a tax collector.

> However imperfect and sinful we may be, the Lord holds out to us the offer of partnership with Himself, of apprenticeship to Christ. He invites us to come under the divine instruction, that, uniting with Christ, we may work the works of God.
> —*The Desire of Ages*, 297

Matthew wanted his relatives and fellow tax collectors to meet Jesus, so he decided to invite them to his house for a special meal with Jesus as the honored guest. Jesus treated all of them with kindness and respect. During the conversation they were impressed with what Jesus said and never forgot it. Many of them were converted and helped spread the gospel. The Jewish leaders often asked Jesus' disciples, "Why does your Master socialize and eat with tax collectors and sinners?" Before they could reply, Jesus said, "A physician's mission is to heal sick people, not healthy people."

The Sabbath

The Son of God created the earth, then on the seventh day, He rested and blessed the Sabbath as a memorial of what He had done. The Sabbath is both a memorial of Creation and a testimony of the love and power of Christ.

The Sabbath was established at Creation, but its importance was solidified when God wrote out the Ten Commandments on stone tablets for Moses on Mt. Sinai. The Sabbath helped distinguish God's people from the idolatrous nations around them. Satan wants to do away with the Sabbath, because Jesus said, "If you love Me like you say you do, obey My laws," which includes the Sabbath.

The priests who worked at the temple on the Sabbath worked harder on that day than on any other day. To do the same amount of work on the Sabbath for business would be wrong. But the work of the priests had to do with redemption and bringing people to Christ. In the same way, doing necessary medical work and other labor specific to the spiritual and physical restoration of humanity on the Sabbath is allowed. Jesus explained it this way to the Jewish leaders, "If one of your sheep falls into a ditch on the Sabbath, don't you go and pull it out?"

Jesus also pointed out that He was the Lord of the Sabbath, which makes the Sabbath the Lord's Day. That's why Jesus said, "All of you who work hard, come to Me, because you need a day of rest."

> Hearts that respond to the influence of the Holy Spirit are the channels through which God's blessing flows. Were those who serve God removed from the earth, and His Spirit withdrawn from among men, this world would be left to desolation and destruction, the fruit of Satan's dominion.
> —*The Desire of Ages*, 306

"He Ordained Twelve"
One day Jesus asked His disciples to come with Him into the nearby mountains. Jesus loved being in nature, and He wanted to get them away from the distractions of the city. Some of the disciples had spent more time with Jesus than the others. Peter, James, and John had been with Him almost constantly and had the closest relationship with Jesus. Of the Twelve, John was the youngest and the most receptive to the loving and kind spirit of Jesus. The Savior had a special affection for his childlike faith, and John was one of the most effective disciples.

Judas, who had not been invited to join them but had inserted himself into the group, said, "Master, I'll be glad to follow You wherever You go." Knowing that Judas's motives were not based on love for Him, Jesus replied, "Foxes have holes and birds have nests, but I have no place of My own. Are you sure you want to follow Me?" The disciples liked Judas because he was smart, handsome, and well connected. Jesus didn't really want him to be one of His disciples and knew that one day Judas would betray Him, but He let him come along because the other disciples wanted him.

The disciples differed widely in personality. All were flawed. Some were impulsive like Peter, others timid like Thomas and Philip, and some were hot-tempered and ambitious like James and John. They all had to learn to get along with one another, and their uniqueness ultimately expanded the reach of the gospel message.

On the mountainside, Jesus trained His disciples for their coming ministry. When He finished, He gathered them close and asked them to kneel with Him. Then He laid His hands on the head of each of them, prayed, and ordained each individual for ministry. Their responsibility was to preach the gospel, and angels would help them as they went. The same mission applies to each of us today and the same assistance, from the Holy Spirit and the heavenly angels joins our efforts.

> When the soul surrenders itself to Christ, a new power takes possession of the new heart. A change is wrought which man can never accomplish for himself. It is a supernatural work, bringing a supernatural element into human nature. The soul that is yielded to Christ becomes His own fortress, which He holds in a revolted world.
> —*The Desire of Ages*, 324

The Sermon on the Mount
Jesus didn't reserve His teaching and healing for religious people. He welcomed everyone, and spoke truth in ways anyone who earnestly sought truth could understand. Because the crowds that followed Him were so big, Jesus often chose the mountainside to teach, because there was room for everyone. The disciples were always beside Him. After He ordained the disciples, Jesus had a special message for them, but He spoke the Sermon on the Mount so that the huge crowd could also hear. Jesus did not begin by talking against the false traditions of the Jewish leaders but about things that the people had never thought of before and needed to know.

He said:
"Happy are those who recognize their spiritual need.
"Happy are the humble who come to Me for help.
"Happy are those who hunger and thirst for what is good."

Jesus also told the people, "You are the salt of the earth and the light of world." He meant that God would use them to bring the flavor and sunshine of salvation to people all around the world, not just to the Jewish people.

Jesus knew that religious leaders in the crowd were hoping He would say something that broke their laws so they would have an excuse to arrest Him, so He added, "I have not come to do away with obeying the law of God but to confirm it and to fulfill its purpose." The law expresses the thoughts of God. Jesus kept the law and wants us to keep it too.

Jesus wants us to be happy, and He knows that obeying God's law will help keep us from things that make us unhappy. The law points out our sins and shows us that we need a Savior, and that's good. Jesus set an example of keeping the law, and He made it possible for us to resist the devil's temptations too. However, knowing the law and talking about it is not the same as keeping it, and keeping the law without knowing the Savior personally is pointless when it comes to salvation.

Jesus told His disciples not to do things to draw attention to themselves but to always glorify God. He said, "You can't serve two masters—God and yourself. People are like shifting sand. Only what's built on the solid Rock will last." It's important to build our spiritual lives on solid ground, Jesus, for He is our Rock.

The Centurion

Jesus was sad that most of His own people did not believe He was the Messiah. Instead, they were always looking for a miracle on which to build their faith. Others, such as the Roman centurion who came on faith alone to ask Jesus to heal his sick servant, gave the Savior great joy. This man believed the only thing Jesus needed to do was to say so and it would happen.

Because the centurion knew Jesus was busy, and because he didn't considering himself worthy to be in Jesus' presence, he asked the Jewish elders to appeal to Jesus on his behalf. They approached Jesus and told him the man had been good to Israel and had therefore earned His favor. Of course, Jesus didn't care about the deeds he had done but only about the faith in the man's heart. Jesus decided to go to the centurion's house to heal his servant, but because of the crowds, it was slow going. When the man heard that Jesus was coming, he sent Him a message: "Lord, I'm not worthy for You to come to my house. Please, just say the word and my servant will be healed." When Jesus heard this, He marveled at the captain's faith and said to the people around Him, "I have not found anyone in Israel with faith as strong as this Roman's." Then He continued on the way to the centurion's house. The man decided to go meet Him along the way, and Jesus said, "As you have believed, so be it!" His servant was immediately healed.

Who Are My Brethren?

Sometimes Jesus would spend all night in prayer. He would get so busy with the masses of people who came to Him that He often failed to eat. His brothers thought He was nuts, and they were angry that people who didn't like Jesus looked down on them because they were related to Him. They tried to stop Him from doing things the religious leaders didn't like. They even tried to get Mary to help them, thinking that at least He would listen to her.

Jesus also had to deal with the Pharisees telling people that He was casting out demons by the power of Satan. Jesus told them that giving Satan credit for the Holy Spirit's work would align them with the devil, but they didn't listen. Once they gave their opinion about something, their pride was too great to change. So Jesus went on with His work and the Pharisees couldn't stop Him.

When people give their hearts to Jesus, they can resist the devil and don't have to do what Satan tells them to do. It is an insult to Jesus for us to do what Satan suggests.

The brothers of Jesus would often use the Pharisees' arguments against Him. This really hurt Jesus, because He loved His earthly family. Fortunately, Jesus found friendship elsewhere. He loved to visit Lazarus and his sisters, Mary and Martha, and assured them that His Father was their Father too.

The Invitation
Jesus would say to people, "If you're tired and brokenhearted, come to Me, and I will give you spiritual security and rest." The traditions and rituals of the Pharisees did not give the people the spiritual nourishment they were looking for. Hollow religiosity fails us, but Jesus never does. When your soul is exhausted and you just can't bear life's trials anymore, lay them, and yourself, at Jesus' feet, and He will rescue you.

> The only faith that will benefit us is that which embraces Him as a personal Saviour; which appropriates His merits to ourselves. Many hold faith as an opinion. Saving faith is a transaction by which those who receive Christ join themselves in covenant relation with God. Genuine faith is life. A living faith means an increase of vigor, a confiding trust, by which the soul becomes a conquering power.
> —*The Desire of Ages*, 347

If we do only what we want in this life, we will fall into Satan's trap. Instead, we must be willing to do whatever Jesus wants us to do. Jesus often prayed, "Father, I'll be glad to do whatever you tell Me to do. Your law is in My heart." That's what we should say to God when we pray. Our heavenly Father loves us and has a thousand ways to help us that we don't even know about. He will never force us to come to Him. But He will do what He can to help us choose to follow Him.

Many hesitate to give their hearts to Jesus because they're afraid of what it may involve or how it may change our lives. However, if we think only about ourselves and what we want, we'll never have the inner peace that we need and that Jesus wants us to have. Each day, we should pray that He would strengthen our desire for Him, and He will.

"Peace, Be Still"
Exhausted after many full days of teaching, preaching, and healing, Jesus wanted to get away from the crowds and rest. He went down to the Sea of Galilee, got in the disciples' fishing boat, and asked them to take Him to a secluded spot on the east side of the lake, some six or eight miles across the water. The crowds piled into other nearby boats and followed. Exhausted and hungry, He lay down and fell asleep. Soon the sun set and an evening storm came up. The waves beat against the disciples' boat and threatened to sink it. A flash of lightning showed that Jesus was still sleeping. Panicked, the disciples woke Him up and said, "Master, don't you care that we're about to die? Save us!"

Jesus stood up, raised His hand, and said to the waves, "Peace, be still." Immediately the waves went flat, the clouds rolled away, and the stars twinkled peacefully in the night sky. The disciples as well as those in the other boats witnessed what happened and were awestruck. They said, "What kind of a Man is this, that even the weather and the oceans obey Him?"

Jesus was disappointed that the disciples didn't trust Him. No matter what giant storms swirl around us, if we surrender our lives to Him, we can have peace in knowing God is with us.

When they got to the other shore and got out of the boat, two demon-possessed men came rushing down the hill to attack them. The men were wretched and horrifying, an example of how debased humanity would become under Satan's rule. Everyone ran back to the boat, except Jesus, who raised His hand, told the men to stop, and then commanded the demons to come out of them. The men, released from their bondage, fell at Jesus' feet, thanked Him, and worshiped Him. Jesus sent the evil spirits into a herd of pigs, which then ran down the hill into the lake and drowned.

The pig ranchers were angry about losing their herd, and all the superstitious people in that region were so afraid that they told Jesus to leave. As He boarded the boat, the two former demoniacs begged to stay with the One who had set them free. However, Jesus told them to go home and tell everyone what He had done for them. Then Jesus and His disciples left to go back across the lake.

The Touch of Faith
When they got back across the lake, a massive crowd of people had already gathered, eager to see Jesus. He stayed to teach and heal awhile, and then went to Matthew's house to meet with some tax collectors. While He was there, Jairus, the man in charge

of the local synagogue, came and fell on his knees in front of Jesus, begging Him to come to his house and heal his little daughter, who was near death. Jesus left Matthew's house and went with Jairus.

The disciples were surprised that Jesus would respond to a ruling rabbi, because the religious leaders were generally hostile to the Savior. The house wasn't that far away, but it was slow going because people kept crowding around Jesus. Suddenly, a messenger pressed through the crowd and told Jairus that his daughter had died, so he didn't need to bother Jesus after all. Jesus turned to the grief-stricken father and said, "Don't worry; just believe and she will live." When they arrived at Jairus's house, the hired mourners were already there, weeping and carrying on. Jesus said to them, "Stop all this. The little girl isn't dead; she's just sleeping." They scoffed at Him, because they had seen her dead body. Jesus sent them all away and then went into the little girl's room with her parents and three of His disciples. Softly, He said, "Little girl, it's time to wake up." Suddenly she opened her eyes, smiled, and got up. Her parents threw their arms around her and cried for joy.

That same day, a woman who had been sick for twelve years and had spent all her money on doctors who couldn't help her decided to seek healing from the Master. She was feeble and the crowds were massive, so she failed to get close to Him at the shore and at Matthew's house. As He traveled to Jairus's house, Jesus passed close enough to the woman that, although she couldn't get His attention, she thought, "If I can only reach out and touch His robe, I know I'll be healed." She squeezed an arm through the packed masses around Jesus, and as soon as she brushed the edge of His cloak, she was healed. Jesus stopped, turned, and said, "Who touched Me?" Peter laughed and said, "Why would You ask something like that when people are pushing and touching every side of You?" Jesus said, "I felt holy energy go out of Me!" He knew the difference between an ordinary touch and a touch of faith. The woman threw herself at Jesus' feet in gratitude, and He affirmed her faith and blessed her again.

Faith is a powerful thing. Acknowledging truth is the first step, but it is not enough. Talking and thinking about spiritual things or religion doesn't do any good. We must believe with every bit of our souls that Jesus is our Savior and make that faith the foundation of every breath we take. When we remember often, and testify to, all God's gifts to us, large and small, our own faith grows stronger and others see a clearer picture of Him.

The First Evangelists

The twelve disciples were like Jesus' own family, sharing His joys, sorrows, and hard work. They listened to His teachings, learned from His illustrations, and grew with His interpretations of Scripture. Jesus always placed Scripture above tradition, which did not make the Jewish religious leaders very happy.

The time came for Jesus' disciples to go out on their own and share with the people what they had learned from Jesus. He sent them to minister in pairs so they would complement and encourage each other, and He gave them power to heal the sick, cast out demons, and work other miracles. He warned them not to get into arguments with people about whether He was the Messiah. They were to share the gospel with gentleness and tact and inspire people with hope, whether they were Jews or not.

Jesus also told them that if they were taken before the Jewish leaders and questioned, they should never compromise the truth. The disciples could easily talk about what Jesus said and did, but if they were argumentative they would not be representing Him. Jesus promised them, and us, that the Holy Spirit would help them know what to say, and how to say it, at the right time.

Come Rest Awhile

While the disciples were on their mission trips, Jesus continued His work where He was, but the priests, rabbis, and Pharisees watched His every move, hoping to find some reason to arrest Him. During this time, He learned about John the Baptist's death from John's disciples, which served to bring the shadow of His own fate nearer to His mind. His heart was heavy, and Jesus needed to get some rest from the constant crowds and criticism of the people in Galilee.

Returning from their missionary work, the disciples told Jesus about their successes as well as their failures. Jesus knew they needed some rest too; they'd been so busy that they'd barely eaten. They also needed some extra instruction from Him. So He told his and John's disciples, "Let's get away from everything for a while to rest and pray." Everyone who works hard for God must also make time to restore the soul and to remember their dependence on God, just like Moses in the wilderness, David in the hills of Judea, and Elijah along the brook Cherith.

> When trouble comes upon us, how often we are like Peter! We look upon the waves, instead of keeping our eyes fixed upon the Saviour. Our footsteps slide, and the proud waters go over our souls. Jesus did not bid Peter come to Him that he should perish; He does not call us to follow Him, and then forsake us.
> —*The Desire of Ages*, 382

"Give Ye Them to Eat"

The time Jesus and the disciples had to rest and refocus didn't last long. Shortly after Jesus and the disciples left, the crowd noticed He was missing. People ran on foot and jumped into boats to catch up with Him. From the secluded hillside, Jesus and the disciples could see the crowds of people coming to see them. Five thousand men, plus women and children, pressed in. Though He hadn't had time to rest, Jesus' heart longed to minister to the broken people, so He found a place where He could comfortably sit and talk to them, and they eagerly listened to what Jesus had to say. At the end of the day, everyone was hungry, but they hadn't brought any food with them. To test the disciples' faith, Jesus asked them to feed the massive crowd. As usual, they took Him literally, though He was also speaking metaphorically. They said, "It'll take a lot of money to buy enough food to feed all these people, and all we have is a few pennies among us."

Jesus asked how much food could be gathered from the multitude. Andrew said, "The only food nearby is some bread and two small fish in a little boy's basket." Jesus told the disciples to have the people sit in groups of fifty or a hundred. Then He asked to see the little boy, took the basket in His hands, and blessed the bread and fish. Then He handed bread and fish, over and over, to each disciple to distribute. The supply in the basket never ran out. The same happened as the disciples distributed the food to the groups of people. No matter how many times they reached into the baskets, there was always more food in it.

After everyone had eaten their fill, the disciples picked up twelve large baskets of leftovers. Jesus wanted them to share the blessings they received—spiritually and physically—with others back in their villages. What happened that day is an illustration of what happens when we share spiritual food with people. The more we give away, the more we have to give.

A Night on the Lake

As the crowd of likely more than ten thousand people sat in the meadow eating, they were awed by the whole scene. They knew God had provided manna to their ancestors in the desert, and they saw this as a similar miracle. They were sure Jesus was the promised Deliverer, and they wanted Him to be their King and save them from the Romans. They figured that the only reason He had resisted was from humility, so some of the people, including the disciples, decided to crown Him by force. This would really upset the Romans and be disastrous for His ministry, so Jesus told them, sternly, to get into their boats and head for home. Then He dismissed the people with such authority that they stopped in their tracks and left quietly. After all that, Jesus went to the mountain to pray earnestly for His work, for the people's hearts to be receptive, and for the disciples as they labored.

The disciples had waited in their boat just offshore, hoping Jesus would come down the hill and go back to Capernaum with them. They were upset with Him for not allowing them to make Him king when the people were demanding it. They were embarrassed and prideful and were tired of waiting for the Master to establish His kingdom. They even entertained the idea that He was an impostor. When they saw the sky darkening, the disciples decided to get home as quickly as they could. When they were part way home, the massive storm hit. The waves got so high that they began splashing into the fishing boat and it looked like they might sink. They struggled and rowed and bailed and worked to save themselves for hours. Finally, exhausted, they gave up and prayed, begging God for help.

From the mountainside, Jesus could look out over the Sea of Galilee, and He kept His eyes on them. When their pride was broken and they cried for help, He walked down the hill and out on the water toward their boat. The disciples saw a figure coming toward them that looked like a ghost. They were scared out of their wits and thought it was a sign of their impending death. Jesus called out, "Don't be scared; it's Me!"

Peter was beside himself with joy and cried out, "Master, if that is You, ask me to come to You!" Jesus called back, "Come!" So Peter jumped out of the boat and walked on the white-capped waves toward the Master, all the time keeping his eyes on Jesus. This was so amazing, he could hardly believe it. For a moment, Peter took his eyes off Jesus, perhaps to smile proudly back at the others in the boat, and just then a big wave hid Jesus and Peter got scared. Immediately, he started to sink. "Lord, save me!" he cried. Jesus reached out, took hold of his outstretched arm, and pulled him up. Together, they walked to the boat and got in.

Jesus used this event to teach Peter about his own weakness so that he might address it before it became his downfall. He does the same for us by allowing life's circumstances to teach us about Him and about ourselves so that we are prepared when larger tests of faith come. When God calls us, we must not allow any distractions to draw our eyes away from Jesus. Pride, fear, and uncertainty can lead to failure and destruction.

> Christ and His mission have been misrepresented, and multitudes feel that they are virtually shut away from the ministry of the gospel. But let them not feel that they are shut away from Christ. There are no barriers which man or Satan can erect but that faith can penetrate.
> —*The Desire of Ages*, 403

The Crisis in Galilee

Foiling the plans of the great crowd that wanted to crown Him king was a turning point in Christ's ministry. News of Jesus feeding the multitude and the story of Christ and Peter walking on the water spread everywhere. People came from all directions to see Him. Jesus said, "You're only interested in Me because you ate the miracle bread, so you think there might be other material things to gain by following Me. Don't spend your time seeking worldly things. Instead, seek spiritual wisdom and truth and believe in Me."

Then the Jews started to grumble and asked, "Isn't Jesus the son of Mary and Joseph, the carpenter in town? They're a very poor family. What's all this mystery about His birth? Sounds like He was an illegitimate child that was adopted." Never before had Jesus heard such a discussion about Himself, but He said nothing. It would have done no good, because their hearts were hard.

At the synagogue, Jesus spoke many plain truths about Himself from Scripture, but the people took everything He said literally and refused to see the symbolism from the holy writings. The people had been excited when they saw that He could work miracles and heal people, but when He made it clear that He did not intend to use that power to establish a political kingdom and free them from the Romans, they got angry and lost interest in Him. Many of those who had said they were His disciples turned away and left. Jesus turned to the twelve chosen disciples and asked, "Are you going to leave too?" Peter said, "Lord, to whom can we go? You are the Christ, the Son of the Living God!"

After this event, those who believed that Jesus had admitted that He wasn't the Messiah spread that misinformation all over town, so most of the people in His hometown of Nazareth turned against Him.

> The change in human hearts, the transformation of human characters, is a miracle that reveals an ever-living Saviour, working to rescue souls. A consistent life in Christ is a great miracle. In the preaching of the word of God, the sign that should be manifest now and always is the presence of the Holy Spirit, to make the word a regenerating power to those that hear.
>
> —*The Desire of Ages*, 407

Tradition

The scribes and Pharisees had anticipated that Jesus would come to the Passover, so they planned to get Him to say something against traditions so they could arrest Him. He knew what they had in mind, so He didn't attend the event they had staked out. The spies finally found Him among the crowd and accused His disciples of not washing their hands correctly before eating at the Passover.

Jesus made no attempt to defend how the disciples washed their hands, but pointed to the spirit of faultfinding in the hearts of the Pharisees. He told them that they were putting more emphasis on their traditions than on keeping the Ten Commandments.

Then He specifically spoke of their sins in breaking the fifth commandment about honoring and taking care of their parents. Instead, the Pharisees said all the money they had was promised to the Lord, so they couldn't give any to their parents. This was just an excuse.

Jesus never spoke against giving tithes and offering to God. He only highlighted the hypocrisy of the religious leaders, who had created an oppressive focus on some commandments and ignored others for their convenience and personal material benefit. Then He said to them, "You are hypocrites. With your words, you pretend to honor God, but you've never given Him your heart." This made the religious leaders extremely angry, because He made them look petty and foolish.

The disciples said to Jesus, "Master, do You know how angry You made these men?" Jesus answered, "All human traditions that have been substituted for the commandments of God are like worthless weeds that need to be pulled up." Jesus made it very clear that His followers must never confuse human religious ceremonies and doctrines with God's truth.

Barriers Broken Down

After talking to the scribes and Pharisees in the temple courtyard, Jesus decided to leave and go into the hill country near Phoenicia. Looking west, He could see the cities of Tyre and Sidon with their rich palaces and heathen temples and, beyond that, the blue Mediterranean with its many seaports. Just then, a woman who had heard that Jesus and His disciples were nearby came across the border looking for Jesus. When she saw Him she cried out, "Son of David, have mercy on me! My daughter is demon possessed!" This woman had heard what Jesus could do and was determined to ask Him to heal her daughter. Jesus already knew about her daughter's problem; that's why He had come to the area in the first place.

Jesus did not immediately respond to the woman. She was a Canaanite and a heathen. To test her faith and to teach the disciples a lesson, Jesus ignored her the way the Jews would a foreigner. The woman did not give up. As Jesus turned away, she followed Him. The disciples asked Jesus to send her away, so He said to them, "I have not come to save the Jews only. I will save anyone who believes in Me."

Even after the disciples had treated her like a bothersome dog, the woman said that even dogs are fed by their masters. In Jesus' mind she was as much a child of God as the disciples were. So He turned to her and said, "You have great faith. Your wish is granted. Your daughter is healed." Never again was her daughter troubled by a demon.

God hates it when we think we're better than other people. In His sight all people are equally valuable. We all have the same blood no matter where we live or whether we're rich or poor. We were all created by God and belong to Him.

The True Sign

From the border of Phoenicia, Jesus headed back to the Sea of Galilee to Decapolis, where He had healed the demon-possessed men. They had heard about the miracle with the pigs and wanted to see more of this Man. An eager crowd of Gentiles and heathen awaited. When a deaf and stuttering man was brought to Him, Jesus did not heal him with words alone like usual. He took the man aside, put His fingers in his ears, touched his tongue, and then looked up to heaven and prayed that God would heal him. The man was healed.

People from everywhere came to see Jesus, and for three days they listened to Him teach and watched Him heal people. At night they slept in the open air, and in the morning they pressed close to Jesus, listening to what He had to say. After three days, their food was gone. They knew that He had previously fed thousands with five loaves and two fish, so they believed He would feed them too. They brought Him what they had—seven little loaves of bread and two small fish. Then, once again, Jesus multiplied what they had given Him, and four thousand men, plus women and children, were fed.

After this, He went back to Galilee. He was met by a hostile group of Pharisees and Sadducees. These two groups had always been enemies, but now they had joined forces against Christ. They demanded that Jesus give them a sign that He was Lord. Jesus said to them, "You look at the sky and can tell what the weather is going to be, but what about the signs that God gave you at My birth? Shepherds came to see Me, angels appeared, and wise men from the East visited. And at My baptism the heavens opened and a voice from heaven said, 'This is My beloved Son.' Do you want another sign? Let Me give you another one. As Jonah was in the belly of the huge whale for three days and nights before he was vomited out on the shore, I will be buried for three days and nights and then rise again."

The Pharisees were not interested in whether Jesus was really the Messiah. They only saw Him as a threat to their status quo and rejected Him—truth and all. The same thing happens today. Worrying that following Jesus may make their lives more difficult or create a risk to their status, many walk away from His message of truth and forgiveness. Believing Jesus and giving our hearts to Him is what matters most.

> "If Thou canst do anything, have compassion on us, and help us." How many a sin-burdened soul has echoed that prayer. And to all, the pitying Saviour's answer is, "If thou canst believe, all things are possible to him that believeth."
> —*The Desire of Ages*, 429

The Foreshadowing of the Cross

Before Jesus came to earth, He saw everything He would have to go through, from the manger to Calvary. He also saw what He would accomplish, and joy filled His heart as He thought about those who would be saved and live with Him forever. So He chose to endure the shame of crucifixion by being stripped naked and publicly executed by the Romans. As He thought about this, His heart went out to the disciples, who would see Him being crucified. They didn't yet understand Christ's mission, much less what was soon to happen, and He wanted to prepare them for it.

The Jews as a whole did not accept Him as the Messiah. Many were ready to accept Him as a prophet, but not as the Messiah. Jesus asked His disciples, "Who do you say that I am?" Peter spoke for the rest of the disciples and said, "You are the Christ, the Son of the Living God." Jesus responded, "Bless you, Peter. No one told you to say this, but it came to you directly from My Father in heaven. So build your house of faith on Me. I am the Rock!"

Then Jesus began to explain clearly what He would go through at the hands of the religious leaders and the Romans. He told them He would be killed but then be raised in three days. The disciples were shocked and horrified. Peter clung to Jesus and told Him they wouldn't let such things happen. Jesus said, "Get away from Me, Satan! You're thinking about these things like a man rather than like a loving God, and that isn't helping anyone." Though His rebuke was in response to Peter, Jesus was really talking to Satan, who had given Peter the impulse to say what he said. The disciples were profoundly sad and confused, and for nearly a week, as they traveled along the shore toward Jerusalem, they tried to process the meaning of all they'd been told.

He Was Transfigured

As Jesus and His disciples were making their way back to Jerusalem, He asked Peter, James, and John to come with Him up a mountainside to pray. The other disciples didn't ask where they were going, because Jesus had spent nights there praying before, so they stayed behind and weren't worried. After a hard day of traveling, it was a tiresome climb for the four of them.

When they got to the top, Jesus stepped away from them and began praying out loud with pain in His heart and sobbing tears. He knew what was coming; He knew about the sufferings He would have to go through and was praying to the Father for the strength He needed to do it. He also prayed for the disciples. He prayed that their faith in Him would not be crushed. For a while, the three disciples prayed with Jesus, but they eventually got tired and fell asleep like the other disciples down below.

Jesus prayed to the Father to give the three disciples with Him a glimpse of the divinity He had before He came to this world. He thought this would help strengthen their faith in Him when they saw Him crucified. Suddenly, the heavens opened and glory and power came down and surrounded the Son of God. Jesus stood before them, glowing with majesty in garments as white as snow. The brightness of the scene woke the sleeping men; they were stunned and looked at Jesus in awe. Standing beside Jesus were Moses, who had died and had been resurrected, and Elijah, who had been taken straight to heaven without dying. When the disciples saw Moses and Elijah, they thought they had come to make Jesus king.

Suddenly, an extremely bright cloud appeared over the scene and a voice from within it shook the mountain like an earthquake and said, "This is My beloved Son, in whom I am well pleased." The disciples fell with their faces to the ground. Then the quaking stopped and Jesus touched them and said, "Get up, don't be afraid." When they looked up, they were once again alone with Jesus.

Ministry

The three disciples had spent the entire night on the mountain with Jesus, and when the sun rose, they went back down. The three of them would gladly have stayed up there, but there was work to do. So they went down the mountain and found the other disciples with a large group of people waiting for Jesus. He told the three disciples with Him not to say anything about what happened on the mountain until after He had been resurrected.

When the people saw Jesus, they ran to meet Him. They were troubled because a father had brought his demon-possessed son to be healed. The disciples had tried to cast the demon out of the boy, but the demon threw the boy to the ground and made fun of the disciples, who couldn't do anything. Those who were watching laughed and made fun of the disciples too. Just then, Jesus and the three disciples arrived, their faces still shining from the mountaintop experience.

Jesus looked at the situation and immediately knew the problem. He turned to the father and asked, "How long has this been going on?" The father told Him about the years of suffering that he and his son had gone through, and that he couldn't take it anymore. He pleaded with Jesus to heal his boy. Jesus said, "If you believe, all things are possible." The father said, "Lord, I believe; help me not to doubt." Jesus turned to the boy and said to the evil spirit, "Come out of the boy, and don't bother him anymore." As he left, the demon threw the boy to the ground, and it looked like he was dead. Jesus took the boy's hand, helped him up, and gave him

> The human mind is endowed with power to discriminate between right and wrong. God designs that men shall not decide from impulse, but from weight of evidence, carefully comparing scripture with scripture.
> —*The Desire of Ages*, 458

back to his father, perfectly healthy and well. The father and the son embraced each other and praised the Lord together.

Who Is the Greatest?

Jesus returned to his temporary home in Capernaum to get away from the crowds and have some quiet time teaching the disciples and preparing them for His death. Soon after they got there, a temple tax collector came to Peter and asked, "Did your Master pay His temple tax this year?" Peter jumped at the chance to affirm Jesus' compliance with the religious laws and told the man that Jesus would, of course, pay the tax. However, the question was a trick. Refusing to pay it would look as if Jesus were not loyal to the temple. Paying it without hesitation would suggest that He was neither a prophet nor a priest, classes which were exempt from the tax.

Peter went inside the house where they were staying to tell Jesus about it. Jesus said, "Peter, let Me ask you a question. When kings tax people, do they tax their own family, too, or just the citizens?" Peter said, "Just the citizens." Jesus was explaining that the temple was His Father's house, so He would be exempt from paying to support it. Even so, to avoid raising a lot of questions, Jesus told Peter to go to the sea, catch a fish, pry open its mouth, and take the coin from inside the fish to the temple to pay the temple tax for both of them.

Meanwhile, the disciples whispered among themselves about which of them would have the most important position in Jesus' kingdom. They still didn't fully grasp that Jesus was not going to set up a political kingdom, even though He had now plainly told them that He would be killed.

After Peter returned from his errand, Jesus asked the disciples, "What have you all been arguing about? Was it about which one of you was the most important one? And which one of you would be the greatest in the kingdom? Remember that the man who wants to be the top one, in the eyes of heaven, he's the least important one. Look at Me: I have come to serve and to help others, even to die for them and you. So be careful, because if you want to have God's power but not His character, you're turning things upside down."

Jesus also told the disciples that one of them would betray Him. This caused them to review their own behavior and ask Jesus if they had made correct choices. John told Jesus about a time he and James had forbidden a man from casting out demons in Jesus' name. Jesus told them that they were not to judge people who work for Him just because the disciples didn't agree with how they do it. The same applies today.

At the Feast of Tabernacles

Three times each year the people were asked to come to Jerusalem for special meetings to remember God's goodness and to thank Him for the harvest of fruits and grains.

Jesus had not attended these meetings for a while, because He didn't want to antagonize the religious leaders in Jerusalem. This bothered his brothers and others, who urged Him to go. By now, they had been deeply impressed with His ministry and were proud to be His brothers. However, they thought that if He were truly the Messiah, He should announce Himself as king.

The news of Christ's miracles had spread everywhere and people from near and far were on their way to Jerusalem, hoping to see Jesus. Everyone in the city asked, "Where is He?" Meanwhile, Jesus had come to Jerusalem a less crowded way to avoid causing a scene. Early in the week-long festival, He went into the temple courtyard, and everyone was so surprised to see Him there that the whole place fell silent. They were amazed at His courage to come there when the priests and rulers were so against Him. Jesus began teaching and preaching with such authority and wisdom about the Scriptures and about heavenly and earthly things that even the religious leaders felt powerless to take action against Him. Day after day, the pomp and ceremony of the feast dazzled the peoples' senses, and day after day, they gathered to hear the Savior share words of life that dazzled their thirsty souls. Here He spoke the words, "If your soul is thirsty, I can give you what you need to be filled," because He is the Water of Life.

> As an earthly shepherd knows his sheep, so does the divine Shepherd know His flock that are scattered throughout the world. "Ye My flock, the flock of My pasture, are men, and I am your God, saith the Lord God."
>
> —*The Desire of Ages*, 479

Among Snares
During the festival, the priests and Pharisees sent men to spy on Jesus, hoping He would say something they could use to arrest Him. First, they asked by what authority Jesus was teaching, because they believed only those who attended the rabbinical schools should teach. Jesus read their hearts and explained that His teachings did not come from Him but from the Father who sent Him. Then Jesus asked the men why they were plotting to kill him. This question revealed to the rabbis that they were working against Divinity, but because of their pride, they doubled down and suggested that Jesus was crazy, and maybe demon possessed, for thinking anyone was trying to kill Him.

This contentious exchange convinced many around that Jesus was indeed the Messiah, but most of those were led astray by the religious leaders, who declared, based on a false understanding of prophecy, that the Messiah was to set up His kingdom on earth. Jesus didn't do what they expected the Messiah to do—drive out the Romans and set Himself up as king. They said, "We know who You are and that You came from

Nazareth, but when the Messiah comes, no one will know where He came from." Jesus said, "Yes, you know where I came from and where I grew up, but you don't know who I am nor why I'm here."

When the spies heard the crowd expressing belief and sympathy for Christ, they rushed to the chief priests and suggested that they arrest Jesus and take Him to the court to be judged. On the last day of the festival, the chief priests sent officers to arrest Jesus, but they came back without Him. "How can we arrest Him?" they asked. "No one ever taught like this before." The rulers said, "Are you under His spell too?"

Then the priests and rulers discussed how to arrest Jesus without causing a disturbance. As they were discussing this, Nicodemus, who was a member of the leadership group, spoke up and said, "Our law doesn't allow us to condemn someone before we listen to the accused person's side of the story and decide for ourselves what going on." They knew what Nicodemus said was true, so after mocking him for speaking on Jesus' behalf, they dispersed. In the meantime, Jesus left the temple and went to the Mount of Olives to be alone and pray.

The next morning, Jesus returned to the temple area to teach. Suddenly, a group of scribes and Pharisees burst into the gathering, dragging along a frightened woman. They pushed her down in front of Him, accused her of being a prostitute, and demanded that she be stoned to death as the law required. Jesus knew the rabbis were trying to entrap Him. Jesus paused, then gently began to write the rabbis' secret sins in the dust at His feet. He looked at the men and, because the witness to any crime was to cast the first stone, said, "He among you who is sinless, let him throw the first stone." At that, they all dropped the stones they were holding and left in shame. Then Jesus asked the woman, "Is there no one here to condemn you?" She looked around and said, "No one, Sir." Then Jesus said, "Neither do I condemn you; go, and sin no more." She bowed in gratitude and cried, thankful for His mercy and forgiveness. She became a steadfast follower of Jesus.

> Christ has shown that our neighbor does not mean merely one of the church or faith to which we belong. It has no reference to race, color, or class distinction. Our neighbor is every person who needs our help. Our neighbor is every soul who is wounded and bruised by the adversary. Our neighbor is everyone who is the property of God.
> —*The Desire of Ages*, 503

"The Light of Life"

At night during the Festival of Tabernacles, giant lamps were lit throughout Jerusalem, flooding the city with light. The lamps reminded the people of the pillar of fire that guided their ancestors through the desert and pointed forward to the coming of the Messiah. Jesus saw this as an opportunity to talk to people about spiritual lamps that would give spiritual light. Jesus called Himself "the Light of the world," which the leaders thought seemed arrogant.

The Pharisees asked Jesus who He was and why He taught what He did. He said, "I'm the one who has been speaking to you since the beginning of time. I only say what My Father has told Me to say, and everything I do is to please Him. If you believe in Me and do what is commanded in Scripture, you will know the truth and be free." If we sin and don't do what God wants us to do, we eventually become servants of sin. To prevent this, we must give our hearts to Jesus and ask Him to help us. Only a relationship with Jesus can set us free from that bondage.

The rabbis continued their attempts to draw out a statement or action from Jesus that would allow them to arrest Him. Try as they might, they failed to find a single sin. Jesus explained that, in contrast to their hostile reception of the Savior, Abraham had been happy to see Him. He told the rabbis that having a genetic connection to Abraham was not enough to make them heirs to the promises. They also had to have a heart of faith in the Messiah as Abraham had had. The rabbis mocked Him and said that He was too young to have known Abraham, who'd lived hundreds of years before. Jesus said, "Before Abraham was, I AM." Here, Jesus claimed to be God, and this enraged the religious leaders, who accused Him of blasphemy. Jesus told them He had given them plenty of evidence to show that He was God's Son, but they refused to see it. The crowd started picking up rocks to stone Him, but Jesus escaped.

Soon after this, the disciples saw a blind man and asked Jesus, "Master, why is this man blind? Did he sin against God, which caused him to become blind, or did his parents sin against God to cause this to happen?" Jesus said, "Neither one." He walked over to the man and took some of His saliva and dust from the ground to make a tiny bit of mud. Then He put some on the eyelids of the man and told him to get the pool of Siloam and wash off the mud. The man did as Jesus instructed, and his sight was restored. He looked like a different man. When the Pharisees found out he had been healed on the Sabbath, they accused Jesus of disobeying the Ten Commandments. When the man defended Jesus and answered their questions with divine wisdom, they mocked him and banned him from the temple. Jesus explained to the man that He was the Son of man, and that the Pharisees were spiritually blind and guilty of great wrong because they would not admit their sin.

The Divine Shepherd

Jesus always used illustrations from the lives of people to help them understand what He was saying. One time Jesus said, "I am the Good Shepherd and am willing to give

My life for My sheep. But a man who does not use the gate to go into the pen where the sheep are, but climbs over the back fence because he wants to steal a lamb or kill a sheep to take it home, is a thief and a robber." Jesus was trying to show the difference between His love for people and the self-serving pride of the Jewish leaders.

Sheep are the most helpless of animals, so easily attacked and killed. That's why a shepherd has to watch over his sheep day and night. He also has to take his sheep to areas with good grass and plenty of water. Shepherds give their sheep names, and when he calls them, they recognize his voice and come.

We are Jesus' sheep, and He is our Shepherd. He knows our name, where we live, and what our needs are. We mean more to Jesus than anything else. Jesus said to the people, "I not only have sheep in Israel but all over the world. Those who give themselves to Me, no matter what country they live in, they are Mine."

> The "one thing" that Martha needed was a calm, devotional spirit, a deeper anxiety for knowledge concerning the future, immortal life, and the graces necessary for spiritual advancement. She needed less anxiety for the things which pass away, and more for those things which endure forever.
> —*The Desire of Ages*, 525

The Last Journey From Galilee

Jesus knew that one day soon His ministry would close, but He continued His work. His disciples didn't want Him to continue to go back to Jerusalem, because they were afraid He would be arrested and killed. If, in order to save His own life, Jesus had decided not to go to Jerusalem, the world would have been lost.

During the last months before Jesus was killed, He spent a lot of time teaching and ministering in Perea. After He sent the Twelve out in pairs to reach lost souls, He ordained seventy more, taught and trained them, and sent them on a different mission, including reaching those in Samaria. They went to prepare the people in the cities where Jesus planned to visit.

Jesus told the people, "I'm standing at your heart's door and knocking to get in. If you open the door of your heart, I will come in and sit down and eat with you, but if you don't open the door, I will not force My way in." So each time Jesus knocks on our heart's door and we don't open it to let Him in, we become less and less inclined to do so. Jesus never forces anyone to choose Him, and His followers are also forbidden to force religious beliefs on others. We must testify of the great things He has done for us, but using force, shame, or guilt are not methods from God.

We must also recognize that Jesus defeated Satan at Calvary, so we should focus on Jesus' power and not worry about Satan and what he can do to us. The Holy Spirit can help us stay close to Jesus, so we should ask Him for help, because we can't do it on our own. We must also remember that our selfish natures are always ready to take credit for the good God accomplishes through us.

The Good Samaritan

True religion is not only about believing in God and being good, but also about doing good and helping others. Once, a Jewish lawyer asked Jesus how he could be saved. Jesus reminded him of the commandment to love God and love your neighbor as yourself. "Whom should I consider to be a neighbor?" asked the lawyer, who believed that Israelites were the only people worthy of kind treatment. So Jesus told him the story of a good Samaritan, a man from a group of people the Jews hated.

Once there was a Jewish man who was going from Jerusalem to Jericho, and on the way he was attacked by robbers. They beat him up, took everything he had, and left him there to die. A Jewish priest came by, looked at the man, and kept going. Then a Levite, a priest's assistant, came by, looked at the man, and kept going. They thought that helping the man would be a bother and an expense, and, if he died anyway, a total waste of time.

Then a Samaritan, someone the Jews hated, came along riding on a donkey, saw the man, and felt like he had to help. He got off his donkey, bandaged the man's wounds, put a robe on him, and helped him get on the donkey. Then he led the donkey to an inn where he could stop, check in, and take care of the man all night. By morning, the man was a little better, so the Samaritan asked the innkeeper to take care of him until he was well enough to go home. He also promised the innkeeper that he would pay whatever it cost to take care of the man.

Then Jesus looked at the Jewish lawyer and asked, "Which one of these three men was a real neighbor?" The lawyer said, "The one who stopped to help." The point Jesus was making is that everyone is our neighbor, no matter what race, religion, political persuasion, or national origin.

Not With Outward Show

The Pharisees demanded that Jesus tell them when the kingdom of God would come. They had in mind a literal kingdom, not a spiritual one. Jesus said to them, "The kingdom of God is not something that you can see. It's in your heart." The disciples also had been expecting Jesus to set up an earthly kingdom. It wasn't until after Jesus was crucified, was resurrected, and had ascended and the Holy Spirit came to help them preach the gospel that they fully realized that Jesus had been talking about a spiritual kingdom.

The disciples felt bad that they had let the Jewish expectation of an earthly kingdom influence their thinking. It will only be after Jesus comes back to the earth a second time that He will set up a physical kingdom here.

Blessing the Children

Jesus loved people, but especially little children. Songs of praise from innocent lips were music to His ears and refreshed His weary spirit. The disciples thought that Jesus' work was too important to be interrupted by children brought to Jesus by mothers who wanted Jesus to bless them. When Jesus saw the disciples telling the mothers not to bother Jesus, He said, "Let the mothers and their children come to Me. That's what the kingdom of God is all about." Then He took the children in His arms and blessed them. Jesus saw in these children future men and women who would always be loyal to Him.

No one really knows at what age children are converted, nor is it important for us to know. However, young ones are more open to spiritual truths than hardened adults. Jesus also has great sympathy for the work of mothers, who yearn for the salvation of their little ones. The Savior was also the ideal example of a good father; He spoke with authority but always in kindness and with grace. As children obey their parents because they love them, so we ought to obey Jesus because we love Him.

> The one who stands nearest to Christ will be he who on earth has drunk most deeply of the spirit of His self-sacrificing love,—love that "vaunteth not itself, is not puffed up, . . . seeketh not her own, is not easily provoked, thinketh no evil" (1 Corinthians 13:4, 5).
> —*The Desire of Ages*, 549

"One Thing Thou Lackest"

Once a wealthy and powerful young Jewish ruler came to Jesus and asked, "Good Master, what do I have to do to receive eternal life?" Jesus responded, "Why are you calling Me 'Good'? No one is good but God." Jesus said this because He knew that the young ruler had a high opinion of how good he was.

Then Jesus said to him, "Keep God's commandments, and you'll receive eternal life." The young ruler said, "I've kept the commandments all my life." Jesus said, "That's good. So now go and sell everything you have, and use your money to help the poor. Then come and follow Me." The young ruler was sad at the thought of giving up his money and power, so he turned and walked away. If we are not willing to give up everything we have for God, if we don't value Him over things, the ambitions of this world will gradually take over.

"Lazarus, Come Forth"

One of Jesus' best friends and most faithful followers was Lazarus. His love for Jesus was strong, and Jesus' love for him was the same. Lazarus had two sisters, Mary and Martha. Whenever Jesus went to their house, He felt welcome. It was a peaceful home, so Jesus was comfortable there. The whole family was very courteous. Martha was quick to entertain, but Mary was always interested in what Jesus had to say. Sometimes Martha complained to Jesus that her sister wouldn't help her with hostess duties. Jesus would say, "Spiritual things are more important than food."

One time while Jesus was out ministering to the people, Lazarus came down with a terrible sickness. The sisters sent word to Jesus about his condition. But Jesus didn't hurry to go heal him, which surprised the disciples. A couple of days later, Lazarus died. So the sisters sent word, "Lord, it's too late now. If only You had been here, our brother wouldn't have died." Then Jesus said to His disciples, "Let's go. Lazarus isn't dead, he's just sleeping." The disciples were surprised and said, "Lord, if he's sleeping, he's probably getting better."

> He turns no weeping, contrite one away. He does not tell to any all that He might reveal, but He bids every trembling soul take courage. Freely will He pardon all who come to Him for forgiveness and restoration.
> —*The Desire of Ages*, 568

Jesus waited a couple more days because the people believed a person isn't really dead until they've been dead for three days. Jesus wasn't indifferent to his friends' pain. He felt every heartbreak. But because He planned to raise Lazarus from the dead to glorify God, He waited so that there could be no mistake of the miracle in store. Now it was time to go comfort Mary and Martha.

When Jesus arrived in Bethany, He greeted Mary and Martha, then asked where Lazarus was buried. There, the sisters and all their friends and family, along with professional mourners, were weeping. Both from sympathy for their pain and knowing that some there would participate in putting Him to death, Jesus started to cry too.

Jesus said, "He'll come back to life."

Martha said, "Lord, we know that he will at the time of the resurrection."

Then Jesus said, "I am the Resurrection! Someone please move the huge stone covering the entrance to his burial cave."

The sisters objected and said, "No, Lord. Lazarus has been dead four days, and his body is deteriorating and smells."

When they relented and rolled away the stone, Jesus stood at the door of the cave and prayed, thanking God for hearing Him and giving life back to Lazarus. Then Jesus said with a loud voice, "Lazarus! Come out!" To the shock of those gathered,

Lazarus, still wrapped in his graveclothes, came out looking strong and healthy. The people couldn't believe it. Then Jesus said, "Unwrap him so he can be free from the tight graveclothes."

Priestly Plottings
The city of Bethany where Lazarus and his sisters lived was not very far from Jerusalem. The news of Lazarus's resurrection got to Jerusalem quickly, and from there it spread everywhere. Most of those who witnessed the resurrection now believed that Jesus truly was the Son of God.

When the Pharisees and Sadducees heard about the resurrection and how it had turned the allegiance of many to Jesus, they called a meeting to decide what to do. They had tried to turn the Romans against Him before, but that hadn't worked. Eventually, they decreed that anyone who believed in Jesus was no longer allowed to worship in the synagogue.

The Sanhedrin continued talking about what to do with Jesus. Then Caiaphas, a wicked high priest, spoke up and said, "There is nothing wrong for one man to die to save a nation." Caiaphas had gotten that idea from the neighboring heathen nations, which did not hesitate to kill one of their own citizens to save the country. Caiaphas's speech swayed the council and they agreed to kill Jesus as soon as they found a good opportunity. However, fearing that the people would riot if they killed Him, they decided to wait.

The Law of the New Kingdom
Soon it was time for the Passover, and Jesus decided to go to Jerusalem with His disciples. As they were walking along, Jesus said to them, "Everything written in the Scriptures about Me will happen. I will be arrested, beaten, and crucified. They will bury Me, but on the third day I will rise again." The disciples couldn't understand what He was talking about, because they had been preaching that a new kingdom was about to be set up.

John and his brother, James, were the first ones to follow Jesus. Their mother had ministered to Jesus and was looking forward to her sons having an honored place in the kingdom. Jesus asked the brothers if they were willing to suffer for Him, and they said, "We are!" Jesus said, "You will."

The other disciples thought James and John had scored special favor and became jealous. They all began arguing among themselves about who would be the greatest in the new kingdom. Jesus was telling them that the new kingdom would be built on different principles from earthly kingdoms, but they just didn't seem to understand. In His kingdom, Christ's followers must be willing to serve others, not to seek their own glory.

Zacchaeus

On the way to Jerusalem, Jesus traveled through Jericho. At that time of the year, Jerusalem was filled with Roman officials, soldiers, and tax collectors, who were collecting taxes for the Romans. The Jews hated these tax collectors, known as publicans.

Zacchaeus was one of these tax collectors, and he was very rich and really hated. He routinely asked people to pay more taxes than they owed and kept the extra for himself. He had heard John the Baptist preach repentance, and he was convicted that what he was doing was wrong. He felt the need to confess his sins to God and ask for forgiveness.

When Zacchaeus heard that Jesus would be passing through Jericho on His way to Jerusalem, he was determined to see Him. The roads were overcrowded, and he was a small man. So he decided to climb a tree to see Jesus. He sat up there scanning the crowd as it moved slowly along. Suddenly the crowd stopped, and down below, he saw Jesus. Jesus looked up at him and said, "Zacchaeus, come down. I want to go to your house and visit with you." Zacchaeus could hardly believe it. He climbed down and led Jesus to his house. The people didn't like that Jesus would go visit a man they considered to be a terrible sinner who collected taxes for the Romans.

As Jesus and Zacchaeus started to walk to the house, people nearby overheard him say, "Lord, I'm sorry for what I did. Please forgive me. I will give half of everything I have to the poor, and if I have taken more taxes than I should have from anyone, I will give him back four times the amount I overcharged him." When they got to the house, Jesus said, "Forgiveness and salvation have come to your house."

Followers of Jesus are to be completely honest in their business dealings. He calls us to treat those we employ and those we serve with utmost integrity. We must also confess and make right any unjust past dealings.

> To fall upon the Rock and be broken is to give up our self-righteousness and to go to Christ with the humility of a child, repenting of our transgressions, and believing in His forgiving love. And so also it is by faith and obedience that we build on Christ as our foundation.
>
> —*The Desire of Ages*, 599

The Feast at Simon's House

A Pharisee named Simon lived in Bethany where Lazarus lived, and he had become a follower of Jesus but had not yet accepted Him as his Savior. Jesus had healed him of leprosy, and he was so grateful to Him. On His way to Jerusalem for the Passover, Jesus stopped in Bethany to spend the Sabbath with Lazarus. The people following Him expected Lazarus to speak about his experience being dead, but there was nothing to tell, since the dead are not aware of their condition. Instead, he just kept telling them that Jesus was the Son of God and that they should listen to Him. The people wondered if Lazarus would go with Jesus to Jerusalem, but he decided not to go.

The Pharisees and priests called a meeting to discuss what to do if Jesus came to Jerusalem for the Passover. They decided not to arrest Him just yet because of the respect and admiration people had for Him, especially since the resurrection of Lazarus. They decided that when they did get a chance to kill Jesus, they should kill Lazarus, too, so there wouldn't be living proof that Jesus had power over death.

While this was going on, Simon the Pharisee decided to invite Jesus and His disciples to his house for a meal. Martha was there helping serve, while Mary was listening to Jesus. Out of gratitude to Jesus for what He had done for her, Mary had bought some expensive perfume to have on hand to anoint Jesus' body just in case He was killed. Then she heard people say He would be crowned king. She was so happy to hear this news that she quietly walked up to Jesus, sprinkled some perfume on His head and feet, then knelt, cried at His feet, and dried them with her long hair.

This display upset Judas, who was the treasurer for the disciples. He spoke up and said, "This was expensive perfume. It could have been sold and the money given to the poor." Judas didn't actually care about poor people. He embezzled much of the money in their accounts for his own use and would have done the same with the money from Mary's perfume.

Jesus thanked Mary for what she had done to honor Him and asked Judas, "Why would you say something like that? She did a good thing for Me." At this rebuke, Judas decided to get revenge, so he went directly to the priests and rulers and offered to betray Jesus to them.

Simon was also offended that Jesus would let Mary touch Him. Simon knew she was a sinner, because he had sinned with her. Through gentle words and a parable about two who were forgiven debts they could never hope to repay, Jesus softened his heart and Simon was able to see himself in a true light, as someone who needed a Savior every bit as much as Mary.

"Thy King Cometh"

Jesus knew that the time of His death was coming, and according to the prophecy of Zechariah centuries before, Jesus decided to travel into Jerusalem for the Passover riding on a young donkey. He asked two of His disciples to borrow a donkey with a colt; they found one, and the owner agreed to let the Lord use it. The disciples thought Jesus was preparing to announce Himself as king, so they told everyone they could find as they returned from their task. Excitement in the people reached a fever pitch. Jesus chose to ride the colt, which had never been ridden before. The disciples threw their robes and coats over the little donkey's back, and Jesus climbed on. This is what kings of old did when they announced their kingship, and everyone around shouted for joy and called Him their King. For the first time, Jesus allowed them to express this sentiment, even though He knew they didn't really understand what was happening.

People started shouting, "Here comes the King of the Jews! Hosanna to the Son of David!" Those He had healed shouted the loudest. Then the people took off their robes and spread them, along with leafy olive and palm tree branches, on the road ahead of Jesus. To the disciples, this was the crowning day of their lives.

As the procession reached the hill above the city, Jesus stopped to take in the sight of the temple, sparkling with the rays of the setting sun. All eyes were on Jesus. They expected Him to look happy, anticipating His coronation, but He looked sad. Then, as the Savior thought about His arrest, condemnation, and crucifixion, He burst into mournful cries, agonizing over the fate of those who had rejected Him.

A Doomed People

The Romans appreciated Jesus because of what He did to help people, so they didn't stop the procession when the Jewish leaders accused Him of planning a coup. Instead, the Romans accused the Jews of causing the disturbance. Jesus proceeded unhindered to the temple. He stayed there for a short time then went with His disciples to Bethany where Lazarus lived to have some peace and quiet and spend the night in prayer.

> A man may gather all he can for self; he may live and think and plan for self; but his life passes away, and he has nothing. The law of self-serving is the law of self-destruction.
> —*The Desire of Ages*, 624

Early the next morning, He and His disciples made their way back to Jerusalem to the temple. They hadn't had breakfast and were quite hungry. On the way they saw a large, leafy fig tree, and they expected to see figs, because fig trees generally fruit before the leaves grow. However, Jesus and His disciples were disappointed, because there was no fruit. Jesus cursed the fig tree and compared it to the Jewish nation, which put on a big religious show but did not reach out to help people or demonstrate humility and love.

Christ invites people to accept Him, reject sin, and be saved. He stands at the door of our hearts and knocks, again and again. Eventually, however, if we turn Him away enough times, He will stop knocking and leave us to inherit the consequences of our choices.

The Temple Cleansed Again

Jesus again went to the temple and, as He had three years before, He found it still defiled with cattle, animal vendors, money changers, and other unholy ruckus. All eyes were on Him, and His divinity was evident. A hush fell over the crowds, and Jesus spoke like a powerful trumpet: "Get all this unholy mess out of here!" Many of the same vendors who had been there three years before were still there, and again they were powerless to disobey His command. The vendors rushed to exit the holy space, and throngs of Jesus' followers pressed in to fill the space they'd left. Jesus healed and ministered to them all.

The priests and rulers asked Him, "Who gave You the authority to do this?" Jesus said, "Before I will answer your question, let me ask you one. By whose authority did John the Baptist preach: by man-made authority or by the authority of heaven?" The priests and rulers knew that if they said John preached by the authority of heaven, Jesus would say, "Then why didn't you do what he said?" And if they said John preached by his own authority, the people would turn against them. So they said, "We don't know."

Jesus told them several stories designed to illustrate their guilt in rejecting Him. He also reminded them that building Solomon's original temple required a cornerstone stronger than all the other stones. Workers tried all kinds of stones that had been cut in the quarry. Some didn't fit. Others fit but broke under the weight of the temple. Finally, they found a stone that had once been rejected and sat out in the elements, unused, for a long time. The large stone fit the space perfectly and held up the wall. Jesus compared that stone to Himself as the Stone on which people could build their lives.

> As you open your door to Christ's needy and suffering ones, you are welcoming unseen angels. You invite the companionship of heavenly beings. They bring a sacred atmosphere of joy and peace. They come with praises upon their lips, and an answering strain is heard in heaven.
> —*The Desire of Ages*, 639

Controversy

The priests and rulers quietly listened to what Jesus was teaching, but they were more determined than ever to find an excuse to arrest Him. So they sent some young men to spy on Him and trap Him with a question. They sent young spies to flatter Him, and then ask, "Is it right for us to pay taxes to the Romans?" If Jesus said it was not right, they would turn Him over to the Romans. If He had said it was right, the whole country would turn against Him, because they believed paying tax to the Romans was contrary to God's law. Jesus showed them a Roman coin and asked, "Whose face is on this coin?" They said, "Caesar's." So He said, "Give to Caesar what belongs to Caesar and give to God what belongs to Him." If they had been faithful to God in all things, including paying their tithes and offerings, the Romans would never have been allowed to occupy their country. This silenced their line of questioning.

Then the Sadducees followed with their own questions. They told the people that God created man a free moral agent and that He pays little attention and takes little interest in what he does. They believed in select scriptures, but rejected the idea of a resurrection or future existence. Jesus told them clearly that they were ignorant of the Scriptures and that without the resurrection, Scripture, which they claimed to believe, would be pointless.

Next, the Pharisees sent a lawyer to ask Jesus which of the Ten Commandments is most important. Jesus told them they were to first love God with all their hearts and then to love their fellow man and that all the other commands were built on these. Then Jesus asked the crowd a question about the relationship between David and Christ that was so profound no one could answer Him, so they stopped asking Him trick questions.

Woes on the Pharisees
The last day that Jesus taught in the temple, Jerusalem was packed with people. They saw Him meet challenge after challenge with dignity and couldn't understand why the priests and rulers were so against Him. These prideful leaders loved to be respected and to be called rabbi. Jesus reminded them that instead of thinking about being respected, they should be thinking about respecting God by obeying Him.

Later in the day, Jesus saw a poor widow slowly walk up to the offering box by the door of temple and drop in a few coins, which was all she had. What a contrast between her and the rich Pharisees, who liked to show off when they gave their offerings. Jesus called the attention of His disciples to the poor widow and said, "In God's sight, she gave more than all the Pharisees." It's not the amount we give to God or the great things we do for Him that He appreciates as much as the spirit in which we do what we do.

The extremes to which the Pharisees went with making rules was ridiculous. For example, while the Scriptures told the people to be careful what they ate for health reasons, the Pharisees told the people that they must even sift their drinking water and that failing to do so would be a sin. That's why Jesus said to them, "You blind guides! You sift your drinking water for a tiny gnat but swallow a camel full of man-made nonsense."

In the Outer Court
The Greeks had heard of Jesus' triumphal entry into Jerusalem and came to the temple to meet Him. They said to Philip, "Sir, we want to see Jesus." Philip told Andrew, and they went to find Jesus and told Him that some Greeks wanted to see Him. When Jesus heard this His face lit up, because the request represented the people from all over the world wanting to know Him. Jesus went to the outer court to meet the Greeks and

had a good conversation with them. He knew that the attitude of the Jews toward the Greeks and other people had to change.

During Jesus' conversation with the Greeks, a cloud appeared around Him. As He spoke, mournful but resolute, about His impending trial, a heavenly light flashed from the cloud and surrounded Jesus. From it, God spoke words of affirmation that everyone nearby heard. A few of the people thought it was the voice of an angel, but the Greeks knew that it was God letting them know that Jesus was the Son of God.

Jesus did not come to earth *just* to die to save humanity. He also demonstrated that God is love, not a harsh dictator like Satan claims. In spite of all the evidence He gave, many Jewish leaders still did not believe that Jesus was the promised Messiah. Others did believe but were afraid to admit it because of what the Pharisees might do to them.

> All true obedience comes from the heart. It was heart work with Christ. And if we consent, He will so identify Himself with our thoughts and aims, so blend our hearts and minds into conformity to His will, that when obeying Him we shall be but carrying out our own impulses.
> —*The Desire of Ages*, 668

On the Mount of Olives

While they were in the temple, Jesus had said, "The day is coming when this temple, which was rebuilt after King Nebuchadnezzar destroyed the first one, will also be destroyed. Not even one building stone will be left on another."

After Jesus and the disciples left the temple and headed up to the Mount of Olives, Peter, Andrew, James, and John asked Him when those things would happen. Jesus said, "What's more important for you to know is that you must be careful not to be deceived by men claiming to be Christ. There will be wars and rumors of wars, and all these things must happen before the end comes."

Jesus told them that before He comes, Christians will be persecuted, killed, and betrayed—even by family and friends. With unmistakable language, Jesus made it clear that all this would happen again and again until the end comes.

During the end time, there will be millions who will have given their hearts to Christ and millions more who just like talking about Him. Some will prepare for His coming, and others will live as they please, only to be taken by surprise when He appears in the clouds.

"The Least of These My Brethren"

Jesus had told His disciples they would be persecuted for their faith in Him, as would many other believers to come. Some would be driven from their homes and others would be arrested and imprisoned. All who put Jesus first, even above their family and friends, are true disciples of Christ. Like Jesus, they reach out to help others, especially the poor and suffering, and angels help them. In addition, many will be in heaven who didn't know Jesus but who embraced His principles of love and kindness and obeyed the evidence of God's laws found in nature.

Many consider it a great privilege to be able to visit the places where Jesus lived and walked. However, the most profound way to walk in His footsteps is by doing the good works He did—serving and helping those in need of physical, emotional, and spiritual healing. There are so many people who need help, and many more need to hear the gospel and the good news of what Jesus has done for them.

Jesus' followers need to spread the gospel and to plant the love of God in the hearts of others. All who truly love Jesus can act as one family. When we who profess Christianity fail to share the Savior's love and grace with others, it is a sign that we don't really love Him after all.

A Servant of Servants

During the Passover, Jesus and the disciples found a house in Jerusalem where they could eat the Passover meal together. As they sat down to eat, they noticed that Jesus looked very sad, as if something was troubling His mind. Then He took a cup of grape juice, prayed, and said, "Each one of you take a sip from this cup." Then He took the small loaf of bread, prayed, and said, "Each one take a small piece and then pass it on."

Silence filled the room and the disciples wondered what was on Jesus' mind. They kept thinking about what Jesus had said concerning His kingdom, wondering what part they would have in it, and imagining who would have the highest position there. When they first came in and were seated, Judas quickly sat next to Christ while John sat next to Jesus on the other side.

It was the custom that before men sat down to eat, a servant would wash the dirt off their feet for them. This time, no servants were there. Not one of them moved, not even to wash their own feet. Then Jesus got up, took a basin of water, and began washing the feet of the disciples, including the feet of Judas. Most of the disciples were stunned and humbled to think that the Son of God would do this. Judas was offended that Jesus was doing the

> How easily could the angels, beholding the shameful scene of the trial of Christ, have testified their indignation by consuming the adversaries of God! But they were not commanded to do this. He who could have doomed His enemies to death bore with their cruelty.
> —*The Desire of Ages*, 700, 703

work of a servant. He thought, *How could He be our King?* This humiliation confirmed his decision to turn Jesus over to the authorities.

When Jesus came to Peter to wash his feet, Peter said, "Lord, I will not let you wash my feet. I should wash Yours!" Jesus said, "If you don't let Me wash your feet, you can't have part in My kingdom, because in My kingdom everyone is willing to serve." Jesus made it clear that serving others doesn't detract from anyone's dignity or value. Just the opposite—when we take part in Christ's servant ministry, we reach heights impossible to achieve without humility.

"In Remembrance of Me"

At the Passover supper, Jesus instituted the Communion service to commemorate His death and our deliverance from Satan's control. The Jewish Passover commemorated Israel's deliverance from slavery in Egypt.

As the Passover supper began, Jesus said, "You are not all clean." The disciples wondered what He meant, but Judas understood that Jesus knew about his plan to turn him over to the religious leaders. During the meal, Jesus said, "One of you will betray Me." They all looked at one another wondering which one would do such a thing. Then each asked Jesus, "Is it me?" Judas was only half listening and didn't chime in as the others had. All eyes were on him. To break the tension, Judas asked the same question. Jesus dipped a piece of bread in some olive oil or sauce, handed it to Judas, and said to him, "You said it. Now whatever you're going to do, do it quickly." At that, Judas got up and left. The disciples assumed that Jesus had sent Judas on a money-related errand since he was their treasurer. Jesus had not chosen Judas to be one of His disciples because He knew that Judas would betray Him.

Judas only followed Jesus because he thought Jesus would be crowned king of Israel and give Judas a high-paying, high-power job. We should follow Jesus because we love Him and want to be like Him, not because we think there may be material benefits. He will give us the strength we need to follow Him if we ask Him for it. The Lord's Supper, known as the Communion service, is designed to remind us that Jesus died for us but is coming again soon.

"Let Not Your Heart Be Troubled"

Jesus knew that Judas had gone to betray Him and that during the night he would lead a mob to arrest Him. Jesus said to the disciples, "It won't be long now until I will leave you. You can't come with Me." The disciples wondered why they couldn't go where He was going.

Then Jesus said, "Don't worry. I am going to prepare a mansion for you, and I will come again to take you there." The disciples were more puzzled than ever.

Then Thomas spoke up and said, "Lord, we don't know where You're going, so how can we follow You?"

Jesus said, "I am the way to the Father."

Philip said, "Lord, please help us know the Father."

Jesus responded, "How is it possible that I have been with you for three years and yet you ask Me to show you the Father? Everything I've been doing, the Father has been doing, for the Father lives in Me." Then He told them how much the Father really did love them and that, after Jesus left, the Father would send the Holy Spirit to teach them and help them.

Then Jesus led the disciples in a hymn of praise and ended with prayer. As they walked toward the Mount of Olives, Peter said, "Lord, though others may leave You, I will not."

Jesus looked at him and said, "Don't be so self-confident. Before tomorrow morning you will deny knowing Me three times. But you will repent and be faithful to Me and even die for Me."

Jesus then reminded them that they were like the branches of a vine; without connection to the Source of life, they would wither and die. They, and we, must keep a constant connection with Him, our Vine, to live and produce fruit.

Gethsemane
It was dark outside but the moon was shining, so Jesus and the disciples made their way to the Garden of Gethsemane. As they walked along, Jesus began feeling sad. The disciples had never seen Him so down. It was even hard for Him to keep walking. Twice He swayed as if He was about to faint, and the disciples had to hold Him up.

When they got to the entrance of the garden, Jesus told the rest of His disciples to stay there and pray for Him while He, Peter, James, and John went in He asked these three to stay there and pray with Him. Then He went a little ahead, fell to His face on the ground, and prayed, "Oh, Father, please don't make Me suffer, but whatever You decide, may Your will be done." He prayed this heart-wrenching prayer three times, and was so exhausted from bearing all of man's sin that He was sweating blood and looked like He was dead. The Father, with whom Jesus had always had such close communion, had withdrawn. Jesus felt the absence profoundly, and with the darkness of all of mankind's sin crushing His soul, He was afraid that the separation would be forever. He struggled to His feet, went to the disciples, and found them fast asleep. He woke them up and said, "Couldn't you have stayed awake even an hour to pray for Me?" Then He went back to His separate spot to pray and wrestle with Satan even more.

Finally, seeing that Jesus was near death, one of heaven's leading angels pushed through the legion of satanic forces pressing around the Savior and showed Him how many people would be in heaven as a result of His sacrifice. This strengthened Jesus, and though He was still in pain, His mental anguish disappeared. The disciples, who had woken at the heavenly light, watched the angel take care of Jesus. Then, as if they were drunk, they fell asleep again.

With renewed strength, Jesus got up and woke His friends. He told them that Judas was on his way with Roman soldiers and temple police and priests to arrest Him. To the surprise of the disciples, He said, "Let's go meet them."

They did, and Jesus asked, "Who are you looking for?" They said, "Jesus of Nazareth!" Jesus said, "I am Jesus." When He said that, a mighty angel momentarily passed between Jesus and the mob, and they all, including Judas, fell over backward as if they were dead. When they got back up, Judas walked up to Jesus and kissed Him on the cheek. Jesus said, "You are betraying Me with a kiss?" Then the temple police rushed up and tied Jesus' hands together. When Peter saw this, it made him so angry that he pulled out his short sword and swung it at the closest man, slicing his ear off. Jesus freed His hands, reached out, touched the man's hanging ear, and healed it. Then He turned to Peter and said, "Put your sword away."

> Christ felt the anguish which the sinner will feel when mercy shall no longer plead for the guilty race. It was the sense of sin, bringing the Father's wrath upon Him as man's substitute, that made the cup He drank so bitter, and broke the heart of the Son of God.
> —*The Desire of Ages*, 753

Before Annas and the Court of Caiaphas

After they arrested Jesus, the mob took Him to Jerusalem to Annas, the retired high priest, for a preliminary trial. Annas brought two charges against Jesus—one, that He claimed to be the Son of God, and two, that He was rallying people against Rome. It was on the last charge that the Romans could step in and take over.

Annas examined Jesus but was unable to get Him to say anything illegal, so he sent Him to his son-in-law, Caiaphas, the ruling high priest and the head of the Sanhedrin. When the council assembled, Roman soldiers also attended because of the second charge. They wanted to see if Jesus would say the things He was accused of saying.

As Jesus stood humbly at his feet, Caiaphas thought Jesus seemed like God, that He was innocent and should be set free. Pride changed his mind, so he went ahead with the trial. False witnesses were brought in to testify against Jesus. They twisted Jesus' words about His own body being the temple of God and accused Him of planning to destroy the temple and build another one. Jesus calmly listened to all the false accusations against Him and said nothing. Finally, Caiaphas raised his hand and asked Jesus to answer under oath whether He was the Son of God. He said, "It is as you said. The Son of man will one day be sitting at God's right hand to judge the world." The idea of a future judgment scared Caiaphas, and, in a fit of rage inspired by Satan, he took hold of his royal robe and tore it in half. The council swiftly pronounced the death penalty on Jesus, but it was against the law to do it at night, so they to reconvene in the morning when all the members of the Sanhedrin would be present.

As the guards escorted Jesus to the guardroom that night, they passed through the courtyard full of people. Peter was warming himself by the fire, trying to blend into the crowd. Someone there looked at Peter and accused him of being a follower of Jesus. This happened three times, and each time Peter denied it more vehemently than the last. As the final tirade of denial slipped off his tongue, a rooster crowed. Peter heard it and remembered that Jesus had told him this would happen. Peter couldn't believe his own weakness, and he couldn't bear to be near Jesus anymore, so he ran away to the Garden of Gethsemane where Jesus had prayed. He fell on his knees, confessed his sins, and gave his heart to Christ all over again.

In the morning, the Sanhedrin gathered and Jesus was brought in to stand trial all over again. They asked Him if He was the Son of God and He said, "You asked Me this last night. Yes, I am the Son of God!" Then the council members said, "We heard Him say it, and for this He must die!" Then a wild satanic rage came over all the people, and they shouted, "He must die!" Even the priests forgot their dignity and began to shout and curse Him, and those nearby spit in His face and rushed at Him. Only by the force of the Roman soldiers in attendance was the mob prevented from murdering Him on the spot.

Judas

Judas had the potential to do so much good for God. His problem began with his love for money. Judas had seen Jesus heal the sick, the lame, and the blind and cast out devils. He had wished that by connecting himself with Jesus he could do the same.

The disciples welcomed him and liked having him as one of them. But Judas never did give his heart fully to Christ, and he had begun pointing out the flaws of each disciple. Peter was impetuous, John could not be trusted, Matthew was being too honest, and so on. Judas flattered himself that he was the important one. It was true that the disciples were not flawless, but they were trying with all their hearts to follow Jesus.

From time to time, Judas would express doubts about Jesus. He would quote Scripture that had no connection with what Christ was teaching, but at least it would give others the impression that he was a sincere disciple. Judas was upset when Jesus told the rich young ruler to give away all his money to the poor and the young ruler turned away, because to have someone rich like that in the inner circle might have benefited Judas somehow.

Unfortunately, Judas had opened his heart to Satan, which allowed him to control Judas's thinking more and more. That led him to betray Jesus. Judas didn't think Jesus would be crucified, and as he watched the proceedings of the trial and heard the conviction, the guilt and fear of condemnation was too much. He stood up and screamed, "He's innocent!" Then he went up front and threw down the thirty pieces of silver the rulers had paid him for betraying Jesus, and he went out and hanged himself.

In Pilate's Judgment Hall
After the Sanhedrin condemned Jesus, they decided to take Jesus to Pilate, the Roman governor, to confirm their judgment, because the Jews had no right to do it. The trial of Jesus had taken place during the night, so Pilate had to get up before morning to meet their demands. He wasn't very happy about being awakened before dawn. Pilate assumed that the prisoner must be extra bad if the Jewish leaders wanted him executed, but when he looked at Jesus, Pilate noticed He didn't look like a criminal. There was no anger, hate, or defiance on His face.

Who was this Man that the Jews had brought to him so early in the morning? So Pilate asked the Jews, "What has this Man done?" The Jews said, "If He wasn't a troublemaker, we would not have brought Him to you." Pilate wasn't satisfied with such an answer. Pilate usually signed death warrants in a hurry, but there was something about Jesus that made him hesitate. He said to the Jews, "You judge Him according to your laws." They said, "It's against Roman law for us to execute people." Then they lied and said, "He refuses to pay taxes to Caesar and says that He's King of the Jews."

Jesus was standing behind Pilate and heard all this but didn't say a word. Pilate was amazed. So he pulled Jesus aside and asked, "Do You claim to be King of the Jews?" Jesus answered, "Are you asking Me this because you want to know or because you heard others say this about Me?" Pilate said, "Why should I care? I'm not a Jew." Then Jesus said, "I am a king, but not a king of this world." Pilate was confused. Then he turned and said to the Jews, "I find nothing wrong with this Man." Then the Jews told him that they would report him to Caesar if he didn't condemn Jesus.

To take the heat off himself, Pilate decided to turn Jesus over to Herod, who was governor of Galilee, where Jesus was from. Herod, the one who had ordered John the Baptist's head on a platter, happened to be in Jerusalem. Herod was glad to see Jesus; he had heard of Jesus' miracles and wanted to see some for himself. Herod told Jesus to perform some miracles and he would let Him go, which upset the Jews, who had seen His miracles and knew His power. But Jesus said nothing and did nothing, which made Herod angry. He turned Jesus over to the soldiers, who abused Jesus in every way they could. Roman soldiers intervened again, and Herod sent Jesus back to Pilate.

Pilate decided to have Jesus whipped until His back was ripped open and bleeding and then let Him go. Then he had Jesus stand before the Jews, hoping they would be satisfied, but they weren't. Pilate didn't think it would come to this.

During the night an angel had visited Pilate's wife and given her a dream about Jesus and who He really was. In the dream she saw and heard all that her husband had been going through since early morning. She heard her husband say that he found no fault in Jesus but then condemn Him. She saw how the soldiers abused Him, saw the Crucifixion, and heard Jesus cry out, "It is finished." She immediately sent a note to her husband, telling him about her dream and telling him not to have anything more to do with the demand of the Jews to execute Jesus.

Then Pilate had an idea to shift the blame from himself. He ordered his soldiers to get the prisoner Barabbas, a killer and a murderer whom the Jews hated, and in order to let the Jews decide which man should be set free, Jesus or Barabbas. To Pilate's surprise, the Jews chose Barabbas, which meant that Jesus would be executed. Pilate looked at Jesus and asked Him to forgive him for letting things go this far. Then he asked for a basin of water and washed his hands in front of the Jews, declaring that he was not accepting responsibility for Jesus' death.

The crowd then began to abuse Jesus. They covered His lacerated back with a purple robe, symbolizing royalty, and put a crown made of sharp thorns on His head, which they smashed repeatedly into His temples. They yelled at Him and mocked Him and said all kinds of cruel things. Satan spurred them on, hoping Christ would finally break and abort the mission.

> Christ is not there. Look not to the empty sepulcher. Mourn not as those who are hopeless and helpless. Jesus lives, and because He lives, we shall live also.—*The Desire of Ages*, 794

Calvary

The news of Jesus' condemnation spread throughout Jerusalem and crowds of people came to watch the Crucifixion. Then Jesus was taken from Pilate's court and the cross intended for Barabbas was put on Jesus' shoulders. Barabbas's two criminal friends were also to be crucified.

Jesus was too weak to carry the cross. He hadn't eaten since the Passover meal and had wrestled all night with Satan in the Garden of Gethsemane. He had also lost a lot of blood from the whipping. He took a few steps with the cross on his back and collapsed. The soldiers tried to find someone to carry the cross for Him, but the Jews refused because they would be unclean and unable to celebrate Passover. Just then, a foreigner named Simon saw what was going on and offered a look of compassion. That was the opportunity the guards needed. They pulled Simon from the crowd and transferred the cross to his back.

Along the road to Calvary, the place where they would crucify Jesus, were lots of people who had been healed by Jesus or who had loved ones healed by Jesus. When Jesus saw the women crying, His heart went out to them. He said, "Don't cry for Me; cry for your people and for Jerusalem."

When they got to Calvary, they stripped Jesus and the other two men naked and stretched them on their crosses. The two criminals struggled with the soldiers, but Jesus made no such resistance. As the soldiers were nailing His hands and feet, He prayed for them, "Father, forgive them; they're just doing what they're told to do, and they don't understand what it means."

As soon as Jesus was nailed to the cross, it was lifted up and dropped in the small hole prepared for it to keep it upright. This was extremely painful. Over Jesus' head Pilate had the soldiers nail a sign that read, "The King of the Jews." The priests objected and asked Pilate to take it down or change it. Pilate was so angry with them that he said, "I wrote what I wrote."

Jesus' mother, Mary, was at there and the emotional pain she suffered from seeing her Son hanging on the cross was too much and she almost collapsed. John had to hold her up. Then Jesus looked at John and said, "John, this is your mother. Take care of her." Then He looked at His mother and said, "Mother, this is your son. He will take care of you."

One of the criminals being crucified looked at Jesus and started cursing Him and shouted, "If You are the Son of God, why don't You save Yourself and us?" The other criminal replied, "Don't you have any respect for God? We're getting what we deserve, but this Man hasn't done anything wrong." Then he turned to Jesus and said, "Lord, forgive me for what I've done, and don't forget me when You set up Your kingdom." Jesus looked at him and said, "You're forgiven, and you will be with Me when I set up my kingdom."

Jesus had been hanging on the cross for hours when suddenly the sun went dark at midday and a dark cloud around the cross hid the presence of God and the holy angels. Onlookers fell to the earth, facedown. Lightning flashed around. The ground rumbled. The earth quaked violently, tossing the people into piles, creating panic and confusion. Rocks on the mountains split and rolled down below. Graves opened and dead people fell out of them.

Jesus knew that at any moment He would die. He cried out, "Father, I place Myself into Your hands. It is finished!" At that, His heart gave out and He bowed His head and died. At that moment, back in the temple, the priest was about to do the evening sacrifice. As he lifted the knife to kill the lamb, the curtain separating the Most Holy Place from the rest of the temple ripped in half from top to bottom. The priest dropped the knife in fear, and the lamb escaped to freedom. The ultimate sacrifice had been made. The price for sin had been paid once and for all by the Lamb of God.

"It Is Finished"

When the angels saw that Jesus had died, they knew that the controversy with Lucifer, which had begun in heaven and had been going on for more than four thousand years, was finally settled.

God could have destroyed Satan when he disobeyed in heaven, but the angels and the whole universe had to see what kind of angel he really was. From the time Jesus was born until he died on Calvary, there was no rest from the temptations that Satan brought against Him.

After the Jews arrested Jesus, He had been taken to trial seven times—twice before the priests, twice before the Sanhedrin, twice before Pilate, and once before Herod. Satan had been behind it all. Any last hints of sympathy the universe had for Lucifer as a fallen angel evaporated when Christ cried, "It is finished" with His last breath.

Even though Satan knows he has lost the war, he will continue fighting to doom as many people as possible until the end of the earth's history. When that day comes, everyone's allegiance to God and His law will have been tested. When the controversy between Christ and Satan started in heaven, the angels and the other unfallen worlds didn't fully understand everything involved. But when they realized that by Jesus' death on the cross sin and death were finally defeated, they rejoiced.

> It is our work to look to Christ and follow Him. We shall see mistakes in the lives of others, and defects in their character. Humanity is encompassed with infirmity. But in Christ we shall find perfection. Beholding Him, we shall become transformed.
> —*The Desire of Ages*, 816

In Joseph's Tomb

The long day of shame and torture was finally over. The setting sun announced the coming of the Sabbath, and according to Jewish custom, Jesus had to be taken down from the cross and be buried before the Sabbath.

Joseph of Arimathea and Nicodemus were members of the Sanhedrin who believed Jesus was the Messiah. They determined that Jesus should be given an honorable burial, not the burial of a criminal. So they went and asked Pilate for permission to release Jesus' body from the cross and bury it. Pilate was surprised that Jesus had died so quickly, after just about six hours; death by crucifixion generally took longer, sometimes even days. Pilate agreed, so the two returned to Calvary to help the women and the disciples prepare His body and bury Him. Joseph had purchased a tomb near Calvary for himself, and he decided to give it to Jesus. This was a great relief to the disciples, especially John, because they didn't want their Master's body buried in the grave for criminals.

Gently, they straightened Jesus' bent arms and legs, dressed Him with expensive fragrance, wrapped His body in burial clothes, and laid Him in Joseph's tomb. The women who loved Jesus were there, watched Him being buried, and saw the men roll a huge stone in front of the entrance to the tomb to close it up. There, Jesus rested on the Sabbath. His followers also went home to rest, but they kept thinking about Jesus, their Master, Friend, and Savior. What would the future hold without Him?

In the meantime, the priests had gone to Pilate and asked him for soldiers to guard the tomb so the disciples wouldn't steal Jesus' body and claim that He rose from the dead. Pilate agreed and sent a couple of soldiers to secure the stone with cords and put a Roman seal on it. He also stationed one hundred soldiers there to guard the tomb.

"The Lord Is Risen"

The dark early hours of the first day of the week were slowly passing. The Roman guards were still there keeping watch. The tomb was surrounded by evil angels trying to keep Jesus in the tomb, but good angels were also there waiting to welcome Jesus back to life.

As the day dawned, there was a powerful earthquake and the angel Gabriel descended with lightning flashing ahead of him. The guards shook for fear and fell to the ground as if they were dead. Gabriel rolled the huge stone from the entrance to the tomb as if it were a pebble and cried out, "Jesus, Son of God. Your Father calls You!" Then Jesus walked out of the tomb by His own divine power and said, "I am the Resurrection and the Life!" All the angels who were there bowed to the Son of God, worshiped Him, and sang a magnificent chorus of praise.

As soon as they regained their senses, the guards ran, stumbling to tell Pilate what happened. They also told everyone they met along the way. When the priests heard about this, they bribed the soldiers to say that the disciples had stolen Jesus' body while the guards slept, and Pilate went along with that ridiculous lie.

When Jesus emerged from the grave, He also opened the tombs of many others who had been killed for following Him. Those brought back to life provided more evidence of His resurrection through their testimonies.

"Why Weepest Thou?"

Early Sunday morning, the women who had watched Jesus die and be buried on Friday began making their way from all over the city to the tomb to put fragrance on His body. Along the way, they shared with one another the things Jesus had done during His ministry. Then they asked one another, "Who's going to roll away the huge stone at the entrance of the tomb so we can put these ointments on His body?"

Mary Magdalene arrived first, saw the huge stone rolled away, and ran back to tell the disciples. As the others began arriving, they saw a light shining around the tomb and a young man wearing clothes of light sitting nearby. The mighty angel Gabriel had taken on a human form to avoid scaring the women, though it didn't really work. He spoke gently, "Don't be scared. Jesus is not here. He has come back to life as He promised. Take a look for yourselves, then go tell everyone!"

When Peter and John were told about the stone being rolled away, they raced there to see for themselves. Yes, it had been rolled away, so they looked inside and saw that Jesus' body was gone. The graveclothes were still there, but they were not just thrown in a heap like grave robbers would have treated them; they had been neatly folded and laid aside by Jesus Himself. After all, He is the God of order and perfection.

Mary Magdalene had followed Peter and John back to the grave and, seeing it still empty, began to cry. As she came out, she heard Someone say, "Woman, why are you crying?" She thought it was the gardener, who might have moved the body of Jesus to another grave site.

Then Jesus said, "Mary!" She immediately recognized His voice and said, "Master! Is that You?" She reached out as if to hug Him, but Jesus said, "Don't hold on to Me, Mary; I have not yet ascended to My Father, who is also your Father. Go and tell the disciples, especially Peter, that I will meet everyone in Galilee." The women left to deliver His message. Even so, the disciples' grief and lack of understanding were so strong that they didn't believe the reports of the women who had seen the Savior face to face.

Meanwhile, Jesus visited the Father in heaven to get confirmation that His sacrifice had been accepted as redemption for mankind, and then He returned to the world to share His power and glory with His followers.

The Walk to Emmaus

Sunday afternoon, two of Jesus' disciples were walking home from Jerusalem to Emmaus, about eight miles away. They kept talking about Jesus, His crucifixion and burial, and the reports of His resurrection. Sadness and gloom hung over them, and they cried. Was Jesus the promised Messiah or not?

Jesus appeared behind them, caught up with them, and asked, "What are you two men talking about?" They thought He was a stranger, so they told Him about Jesus, the promised Messiah, how He was arrested and crucified and buried, and how His body

> With joy unutterable, rulers and principalities and powers acknowledge the supremacy of the Prince of life. The angel host prostrate themselves before Him, while the glad shout fills all the courts of heaven, "Worthy is the Lamb that was slain to receive power, and riches, and wisdom, and strength, and honor, and glory, and blessing." Revelation 5:12.
>
> —*The Desire of Ages*, 834

had disappeared. Jesus asked them, "Do you believe what the prophets have written about the Son of God, that He could come, be crucified, and rise from the dead?" Then He spelled out the history of Christ's redemptive mission from the beginning of time. As they listened they got excited.

The sun was beginning to set as they got close to home, and it looked like Jesus was going to go on. Jesus never presumes to force Himself on anyone; we must be intentional about inviting Him in. Fortunately, the disciples urged Him to stay overnight because it was supper time and they wanted to talk more, though they were still blind to their Guest's identity. When supper was ready, they asked Jesus to offer the blessing. As He spread His hands to pray, the disciples saw the nail scars in His hands, and exclaimed, "Jesus!" They leaped up to fall at His feet and worship Him when suddenly He disappeared.

No longer tired or hungry, they decide immediately to run back to Jerusalem to tell the other disciples that Jesus was really alive. It was dark, but they scrambled back to Jerusalem, climbing over rocks and boulders, slipping and sliding, losing their path and finding it again. All this time Jesus was alongside, protecting them from unseen dangers in the dark, just like He does for us today.

"Peace Be Unto You"

When they got to Jerusalem, they went where the disciples were staying and knocked on the door, but no one answered. Then they knocked again and announced who they were, and the door opened. Jesus went in with them, unseen. Then the door was closed and locked again, because they were sure the Jews were looking for them.

Everyone inside was excited because Jesus had appeared to Simon. Then the two who had just arrived from Emmaus told their story. As they finished, Jesus appeared and said, "Peace to all of you! Don't be afraid; I'm not a ghost. A spirit does not have flesh and bones like I have. Come and touch Me." When He asked for some food and began to eat, the disciples realized He was real, and their fear turned into joy.

Thomas wasn't with the others that night, and he didn't believe their story. He said, "Unless I can personally see Him and touch Him, I won't believe what you're telling me." A week later, Thomas was with them in the upper room when Jesus appeared. He said to Thomas, "Come here and touch Me and look at the scars in My hands and feet." Thomas recognized Jesus, threw himself at His feet, and cried out, "My Lord and my God!" Jesus said, "Thomas, because you have seen Me, you believe, but people who have not seen Me and believe anyway are truly blessed."

Many people look high and low for reasons to doubt the power of Jesus. Satan will always create things that seem to contradict Scripture, so we must be willing to believe by faith that's built by evidence from the Bible and from people's testimonies.

By the Sea Once More

Jesus had told the disciples that He would meet them in Galilee, so as soon as the Passover week was over, seven of the disciples left Jerusalem and made their way there. When they arrived, Peter suggested they go fishing to earn money for food and clothes. They fished all night but caught nothing. As they were coming back to shore the next morning, they saw Someone standing on the beach. He called out, "Did you catch anything?" Peter shouted back, "No!" The Man called back, "Before you come in, throw your nets out on the right side of the boat and you'll find the fish!" They obeyed and caught so many fish that the weight nearly broke their nets.

John recognized this was the Lord and said, "It's Jesus!" Peter leaped into the water and swam to shore to greet Him. On the shore, there was a small fire burning with some cooked fish and bread. Realizing that his companions were still struggling with the heavy load of fish, Peter quickly swam back to help pull the massive bounty to shore.

Jesus invited the disciples to sit for a bite to eat. He knew they were hungry after fishing all night. As they were eating, Jesus looked at Peter and said, "Peter, do you love Me?" Peter said, "Yes, Lord, I do." Then He asked him again, and Peter said, "Lord, You know that I do." When they finished eating, Jesus asked Peter a third time, "Peter, are you sure you love Me?" Peter said, "Lord, You know my heart. You know that I love you." Jesus had asked Peter three times whether he loved Him, because He wanted the other disciples to hear it so they would trust Peter again. At each affirmation, Jesus replied to Peter, "If you love Me, then feed My lambs." Here Jesus was assigning to Peter the job of nurturing new believers, a task for which the newly matured disciple was now equipped after his own failure and repentance.

Then Peter turned to John and asked Jesus, "Master, what about John? What do you want him to do for you?" Jesus said, "Don't worry about him; just keep your eyes on Me."

Go Teach All Nations

Before Christ ascended to heaven, He said to His disciples, "I have all the power of heaven to give to you. Now go preach the gospel and tell everyone everywhere about Me." Jesus was placing His work in the hands of His disciples and followers. From Jerusalem they were to spread out and go to the whole world. Jesus had also agreed to meet more believers in Galilee, and about five hundred of them came. The disciples went around talking to the people, telling them all they knew about Jesus. Then Jesus, with His face shining like God, suddenly appeared, and the people worshiped Him.

If the disciples and the believers were to preach to others, they first needed to get along with one another. So after Jesus went back to heaven, they put all their differences aside and got together to pray as He had told them to. For ten days they prayed for the Holy Spirit to come help them share the gospel with people at home and abroad.

On the tenth day, as they prayed, a powerful wind blew through the whole house and little flames appeared above the heads of the disciples and all Jesus' followers who were gathered. They were filled with the Holy Spirit. Then Peter got up, went outside, and began to speak to the people and all the foreigners who were there. They could each hear him in their own language. This was the beginning of people in every nation hearing the gospel.

"To My Father, and Your Father"
His work completed, it was finally time for Jesus to go back to heaven. He decided to do so from the Mount of Olives, overlooking Jerusalem. The disciples followed Him, and they talked again about the lessons they had learned and the task that lay ahead. When they reached the top, He stopped. The disciples gathered around Him, and He stretched out His hands as if He was ready to bless them again. He promised that He would always be with them, and slowly, He began to rise up toward heaven as if unseen hands were lifting Him. The amazed disciples watched as Jesus ascended higher and higher and finally disappeared in the clouds. They could hear the angels singing, welcoming their Master home.

As Jesus led the heavenly procession toward the city of God, accompanied by those who had been restored to life at His resurrection, the angels who were with Him called out, "Open the gates, and let the King of Glory come in!" The angels at the gates called back with knowing joy, "Who is this King of glory?" To which came the reply, "The Lord, mighty and strong, He is the King of glory!" Again the angels at the gates called out, "Who did you say we should open the gates for?" The response: "The Lord, the King of Glory!"

The gates opened, and the angels and representatives from other worlds and every heavenly creature were there, ready to welcome Jesus with great celebration. But first, He must see the Father and be welcomed by Him. Jesus said, "Father, I have done Your will, and now I'm home!"

The Father's arms embraced the Son and declared that Love won the ultimate war. Then all heaven burst into joyful praise and worship for the triumph and return of the Prince of Life, the beloved Lamb of God.

THE
DISCIPLES

Insights From
The Acts of the Apostles

God's Purpose for His Church

Jesus established His church with His own blood, so disloyalty to the church—God's faithful people—is disloyalty to Jesus. Throughout this world's history, Satan has attacked the church relentlessly. Christians have been tortured and killed for their faith, in ancient times and in the modern era.

As small as the church is in comparison to the population of the world, it is close to the heart of God. He loves to reveal His grace and power through its members as they help and bless others. Everyone who has Christ in his or her heart is a worker for God, and spiritual life flows out from them.

The Training of the Twelve

To begin His church's work, Jesus ordained His disciples for ministry. He did not choose disciples from the Jewish religious elite, but from the humble fishermen and others who had open hearts ready to listen to Him. "Come, follow Me," was not a command but an invitation. God knew these men would preach the gospel and witness for His Son. For

> Enfeebled and defective as it may appear, the church is the one object upon which God bestows in a special sense His supreme regard. It is the theater of His grace, in which He delights to reveal His power to transform hearts.
> —*The Acts of the Apostles*, 12

three and a half years, Jesus gave His disciples on-the-job training for the type of ministry He wanted His followers to do—helping, healing, restoring, and, when hearts were open, teaching.

Jesus wanted His disciples to break down the prejudice that the Jews had against others. He accepted everyone and healed people regardless of who they were or where they had come from. This is what His church is all about, and it has no skin color barriers, political lines, or geographical borders.

Among the disciples there were personality differences. Comparing mild John with powerful Peter would be one example; and then there was Thomas, who struggled to have faith, and Judas, who always thought about money. Jesus wanted to create unity among them to be one in thought and action and one in heart and mind.

As Christ's ministry was closing, He also wanted to prepare His disciples for what was coming. He knew that He would be arrested, beaten, and crucified and that their faith in Him would be tested. So He said to them, "I have come into this world for your sake, and when I go back to the Father, I will continue to love you and work for you." He also told them that the Holy Spirit would come and take His place among them. Then He prayed, "Dear Father, bless these men and all those who will believe on Me through them."

> As in the typical service the high priest laid aside his pontifical robes and officiated in the white linen dress of an ordinary priest; so Christ laid aside His royal robes and garbed Himself with humanity and offered sacrifice, Himself the priest, Himself the victim.
> —*The Acts of the Apostles*, 33

The Great Commission

After the Crucifixion, the disciples remembered how Judas had betrayed Jesus. He had told the priests and rulers where to find Jesus; he hoped that Jesus would defend Himself, set Himself up as King, and give Judas an important position of power. That's not what happened, and when Jesus was arrested and crucified, Judas hanged himself.

When Jesus fully revealed to the disciples the plan of salvation, including His death and resurrection, the men had been so confused about their rank and how that played into Israel's release from Roman control that they completely missed the message and were unprepared for Jesus' crucifixion. They didn't understand that He would rise again. In despair, the disciples went to the upper room of their house and locked the door, scared that the Jewish leaders would come after them too.

It was in this room that Jesus came to them after He rose from the dead on the third day. Now in hindsight, they were able to fully understand how Jesus had fulfilled the ancient prophecies from Scripture. Finally, their faith grew deep roots. The Messiah spent days explaining their commission. He asked them to preach the gospel to the Jews first to give them another chance to accept Him as the Messiah.

Jesus told the disciples that ministry would be difficult, but He promised that the Holy Spirit would take His place with them to support their labor. He reminded them that they were not to preach the gospel by arguing with people but to preach it with hearts and words filled with kindness and love. After forty days, Jesus led the disciples to Bethany, gathered them around, stretched His hands over them, and slowly ascended into the heavens.

Pentecost

The disciples went back to Jerusalem and waited for the Holy Spirit to come, as Jesus had instructed. The women and Jesus' mother and brothers also joined them. There they also selected Matthias to take Judas's place. While they waited for the Spirit, they prayed, confessed, and reminisced. They wished they had not argued among themselves about who would be the greatest in God's kingdom, and they asked one another and God for forgiveness.

As they were praying, suddenly a powerful, roaring wind blew like a freight train into the open house where they were staying. Then what looked like two-pronged tongues of fire appeared over the heads of the people there, and they were each filled with the Holy Spirit. People from countries all over were in Jerusalem. When they heard the mighty rushing wind and the commotion that followed, they came to see what was happening. When the believers spoke to the people, those from other countries could hear them speak in their own language. This is one of the ways God helped them spread the gospel to all the surrounding nations.

> The Lord is more willing to give the Holy Spirit to those who serve Him than parents are to give good gifts to their children. For the daily baptism of the Spirit every worker should offer his petition to God.
> —*The Acts of the Apostles*, 50

Some of the people thought the disciples and others were drunk. Peter stood up and told them that the prophet Joel had foretold that the Holy Spirit would be given to men and women, young and old. He also told them that just as Christ rose from the dead, those who died believing in Jesus will be resurrected when He comes back.

When the people, especially those who had been part of putting Jesus to death, heard all this, they said, "What should we do?" Peter said, "Repent and be baptized and you, too, will be forgiven and receive the power of the Holy Spirit." That day three thousand people responded and were baptized in the name of the Father, the Son, and the Holy Spirit.

The Gift of the Spirit

The gift of the Holy Spirit is not limited by race or age. All who accept Christ as their personal Savior will receive the Holy Spirit to help them reflect Jesus. Believers, especially missionaries, should pray every day for the Holy Spirit.

Claiming to be filled with the Holy Spirit doesn't make it true, especially when the claim is accompanied by an unpredictable spiritual frenzy. To be a true Christian means to surrender heart, mind, and will to God every day and, with the help of the Holy Spirit, to keep God's commandments and fulfill the Great Commission.

Those who don't seek the Holy Spirit daily and do what they can for God are giving Satan a chance to get their attention and lead them into sin. Believers must not sit around waiting for a dramatic spiritual revelation to come on them before putting their faith into action. A constant connection with God is critical for spiritual survival and growth.

> Those whose hearts are filled with the love of Christ will follow the example of Him who for our sake became poor, that through His poverty we might be made rich. Money, time, influence—all the gifts they have received from God's hand, they will value only as a means of advancing the work of the gospel.
> —*The Acts of the Apostles*, 71

At the Temple Gate

One day Peter and John went to the temple to pray. When they got there they saw a crippled man begging at the entrance. Peter stopped and said to him, "We don't have any money to give you, but what we have we will give you. In the name of Jesus, stand up and walk!" Then he took the man's hand to help him up. Power began to flow through the man's body and he leaped up and ran into the temple to praise God. The people around were shocked. Peter turned to them and said, "This power didn't come from us, but from Jesus who was crucified and then raised from the dead." Then he invited the people to repent and give their hearts to Jesus.

The priests and leaders heard that the disciples were preaching about Jesus and winning many people to Him. They decided it needed to be stopped or their leadership would be jeopardy, so they arrested Peter and John and put them in prison. The next day they were brought before the Sanhedrin to be tried. When Peter was given a chance to speak, he said, "The crippled man who was healed, was healed by the power of Jesus Christ. You killed Him, God brought Him back to life, and through Him we are saved."

Confused and embarrassed, the court ordered Peter and John to be taken back to prison to give the Jewish leaders time to decide what should be done. Meanwhile, the other disciples prayed to God with all their hearts for them to be released. The council knew the people would revolt if they tried to punish Peter and John harshly, because the evidence was in their favor. Instead, they told the disciples to stop preaching about Jesus and let them go. Peter said, "Whatever God says, we will do."

A Warning Against Hypocrisy
After their release, the disciples went back to preaching, and people responded. Some who became Christians had been rejected by their families and friends and needed financial help. To support them, the believers brought donations to the disciples to distribute.

One couple, Ananias and Sapphira, decided to sell some property and donate the money to help fellow believers in need. However, the more they thought about giving away all that money, the less they wanted to do it. So that the believers would think they were good people, they decided to donate a little and secretly keep the rest. When Ananias came with the money, Peter asked, "Is this the amount you got from the sale of your property?" Ananias said, "Yes." Then Peter said, "The property was yours to do with it what you wanted. You promised God you would give all of it, then you changed your mind and decided to keep some of it for yourself. Yet you lied and told me that this is all of it." When Ananias realized that Peter knew he was lying and that soon the whole church would know, he went into shock and fell over and died.

About three hours later, Sapphira came looking for her husband and lied about the profits from the sale. Peter said, "Why did the two of you decide to lie to God? He knows everything." When Sapphira realized that Peter knew about their dishonesty, so she, too, went into shock and fell over and died. The men who had buried her husband also took her body and buried it.

God leaves us free to decide what offering to give, but once we promise to give something and then don't, or only give part of it, that's lying to God, which has consequences. People may no longer immediately drop dead because they lied to God, but He is no less disgusted by fraud than He was in Bible times, and the punishment will ultimately be the same.

> When for the truth's sake the believer stands at the bar of earthly tribunals, Christ stands by his side. When he is confined within prison walls, Christ manifests Himself to him and cheers his heart with His love. When he suffers death for Christ's sake, the Saviour says to him, They may kill the body, but they cannot hurt the soul.
> —*The Acts of the Apostles*, 85

Before the Sanhedrin

In Jerusalem, various ideas were circulating about who Jesus really was. So the disciples decided to preach more fervently about Christ, who He was, and His death and resurrection. Every day the number of believers increased. The disciples also worked miracles, and people would bring the sick and dying to be healed. The Holy Spirit gave the disciples courage to continue preaching no matter what.

This really upset the Pharisees and Sadducees because they were losing their influence with the people. Like madmen, their singular focus became stopping the disciples from preaching. Soon Peter and John were imprisoned again, but during the night an angel came, opened the prison doors, guided them out, and told them to go preach in the temple.

The high priest thought that Peter and John were still in prison and sent for them. The officers arrived at the prison and found the prison doors still locked but realized Peter and John were gone. When the high priest learned the two men were in the temple preaching, he ordered the captain and his officers to bring them before the Sanhedrin.

When they arrived, the high priest said, "Didn't we order the two of you to stop preaching?" Peter answered, "We must obey God first, then men." The Jewish leaders were so angry that they decided to kill Peter and John without further trial. However, one council member spoke up and said, "Gentlemen, we need to be careful what we do to these men. If what they are preaching is from God, we can't stop it no matter what we do." The members of the council saw wisdom in his words, so after giving the two disciples a severe beating, they let them go. Peter and John experienced a little of what Jesus had gone through.

The Seven Deacons

As the church grew, the disciples realized they needed more help managing the needs of the church and the believers. The Jews helped the widows and the needy among their own people, but did not help those who had become Christians.

As the church grew, so did the burden on the disciples. To help, the Holy Spirit directed the disciples to appoint seven deacons to help look after the details of the church so the disciples could focus on spreading the gospel.

God values order. He expects the work of the church to be carried forward with thoroughness and organization, both on a local level and around the world. He has a part for every child, woman, and man to play and gifts His people with abilities that, if employed faithfully, will build the church and glorify Him.

The First Christian Martyr

Stephen, the leader of the seven deacons, was very committed to Jesus. He was also a powerful preacher, and many people gave their hearts to Christ after hearing him speak. The priests and rulers hated Stephen and decided to silence him one way or another.

The leaders met with Stephen and demanded that he stop preaching. When that failed, they brought him before the Sanhedrin for questioning. There, false witnesses accused Stephen of blasphemy and threatening the temple. Stephen responded that the temple was not as important as having God in their hearts, which threw the leaders into a rabid frenzy. They grabbed him and dragged him out of the city to stone him.

As the rocks flew, Stephen knelt down, looked up, and with a strong voice called out, "I see heaven open and Jesus standing on the right hand of God! Lord, don't hold this against them." Then he fell down and died.

After this, Saul, one of Stephen's lead accusers, was elected to the Sanhedrin, which gave him the authority to do anything to silence those preaching about Jesus.

The Gospel in Samaria
Saul put as many believers as he could find into prison. The persecution got so bad that many of Jesus' followers decided to leave Jerusalem and live elsewhere. Philip, one of the deacons, moved to Samaria. His preaching there was so successful that he had to send for help.

One day the Lord asked him to go to the road south of Jerusalem to meet a man from Ethiopia who was headed home after going to Jerusalem to worship God. Philip saw a chariot coming with a man sitting in it, reading. As the chariot came near, Philip called out to ask the man what he was reading. The man stopped the chariot and asked Philip to come sit with him. He was reading from Isaiah and didn't know who Isaiah was talking about. So Philip explained that Isaiah was talking about Jesus and told him about Jesus' life and death and what it meant. The Ethiopian listened carefully and decided to give his heart to Jesus. As they rode along and talked, they saw a pond and the Ethiopian asked Philip, "Look, there is water. Why can't I be baptized?" Philip said, "If you believe with all your heart that Jesus is your Savior, you can."

The Ethiopian stopped his chariot, and he and Philip went down into the water, where Philip baptized him. As the Ethiopian got back in his chariot to head home, the Holy Spirit picked up Philip and took him to the city of Azotus. He preached there and every city along the route to Caesarea.

The spread of the gospel is not only the responsibility of ministers. Every Christian, without exception, has a responsibility to serve others and to spread the good news about Jesus. A consecrated believer with a missionary spirit can do a lot to spread the gospel and the love of God.

From Persecutor to Disciple

When the believers in Jerusalem scattered and moved to other cities because of the persecution, the Sanhedrin decided to find them and bring them back to Jerusalem to face trial. The council assigned Saul to apprehend Christians in Damascus, so he gathered some men and went.

When the group was just outside the city, a light from heaven as bright as the sun suddenly surrounded them. Saul and his company were nearly blinded, and they fell facedown on the ground. Then they heard a voice ask, "Saul, why are you persecuting Me?" Saul answered, "Who are You?" The Voice said, "I am Jesus, whom you are persecuting by doing harm to My people." Shocked, Saul asked Jesus what He wanted him to do. Jesus told Saul to go into the city and wait for more instructions.

Saul's companions had seen the light and heard the Voice, but only Saul saw Jesus. Saul was immediately converted and convinced that Jesus was the promised Messiah. When the light faded, Saul was blind. His men took him into Damascus to the house of a man named Judas, who took care of him. Saul fasted and prayed for three days, confessed his sins, and gave his heart to Jesus.

Then, in a vision, Jesus told a disciple named Ananias to go see Saul and touch him to restore his sight. Ananias had heard about how Saul had persecuted Christians and was afraid to go, but he obeyed in spite of his fear. When he got there, he introduced himself, placed his hands on Saul's head, and prayed that his vision would be restored and that he would receive the Holy Spirit. Saul's sight returned immediately and he asked to be baptized. After his baptism, Saul changed his name to Paul.

> When the mind of man is brought into communion with the mind of God, the finite with the Infinite, the effect on body and mind and soul is beyond estimate. In such communion is found the highest education. It is God's own method of development. "Acquaint now thyself with Him"(Job 22:21), is His message to mankind.
> —*The Acts of the Apostles*, 126

Days of Preparation

After Paul's baptism, he stayed in Damascus with the believers a little while, then he went to the synagogue to preach about Jesus. When the Jews in Jerusalem heard that Saul had become a Christian, they were stunned. The Jews in Damascus got so angry with Paul that an angel told him to leave because it wasn't safe to stay.

Paul escaped to the Arabian wilderness to study and pray. He was there about three years, and Jesus communed with him during that time. When he returned to Damascus to preach, the Jews got angry again and decided to kill him. They shut the city gates and stationed guards there day and night, hoping to catch him. The believers helped Paul escape by lowering him over the wall in a basket.

From there, Paul went to Jerusalem to meet the disciples, especially Peter. The disciples were afraid of him, because they remembered how he had persecuted the believers. However, Barnabas explained that Jesus had appeared to Saul, that he was converted and baptized and was now called Paul. At that, they welcomed him.

Paul was determined to show his former colleagues in the Sanhedrin the error of their ways. They had hardened their hearts against the truth, and not only did they reject the message, they determined to kill the messenger. During a vision in the temple, an angel told Paul to leave the city. Paul didn't want to leave Jerusalem; he wanted to be brave for Jesus. When the disciples heard about his vision, they insisted that Paul obey and leave. He went to his hometown of Tarsus, and, as a result, the Jewish leaders settled down and Christians in Jerusalem got a little reprieve from persecution.

A Seeker for Truth

As Christianity spread geographically, the apostle Peter decided to go to Lydda to see how the believers there were doing. While he was there, they told him about a man who was paralyzed and had been confined to his bed for eight years. He went to see the man, prayed for him, and said, "Jesus will heal you. Get out of bed, stand up, and walk," and the man did. When the people saw this, they were amazed and opened their hearts to what Peter had to say about Jesus.

In the nearby city of Joppa lived a lady named Dorcas, who was known and loved for helping the poor and needy get food and clothes. Unexpectedly, she got sick and died. The believers sent for Peter. When he got there and saw everyone crying, he knelt beside her bed, prayed, and asked God to heal her. Then he looked at her and said, "Dorcas, get up," and she did.

Not far away lived a Roman captain named Cornelius. Through his contacts with the Jews, he learned about the God of heaven and began worshiping Him. He also did a lot to help poor people. One day an angel appeared to him while he was praying and told him to send some men to Joppa to get Peter. The angel told him exactly where Peter was staying and even the occupation of the man who owned the house. God knows the details of our lives!

Cornelius sent two of his servants and a soldier to find Peter and bring him back. In the meantime, the same angel visited Peter in a dream. He saw a big sheet full of all kinds of animals being lowered from heaven. A voice said, "Kill and eat." Peter said, "All these animals are unclean and God has told us not to eat them." This happened three times. Peter, like the other Jews, considered the Romans unclean and didn't want anything to do with them. The Voice told Peter not to call unclean what God said was clean, which showed Peter that the message of Jesus must go beyond the Jews to the Gentiles, whom the Jews considered unclean.

Cornelius's representatives arrived and asked for Peter. The Holy Spirit told Peter, "There are three men downstairs asking for you. Go meet them and then go with them," and he obeyed. Peter chose six believers to go along as witnesses, and they left the next morning. When they got to Cornelius's house, he welcomed Peter by bowing to him. Peter lifted him back up and said, "I'm just an ordinary man, so please don't bow to me."

Cornelius explained to Peter what the angel had said, and Peter shared with the captain and his family and friends the good news of the gospel. As they were talking about Jesus, the Holy Spirit came on them as He had on the disciples and filled them all, Jews and Gentiles alike. Peter saw that God had blessed them, so he commanded that the new believers be baptized.

When Peter got back to Jerusalem, he told the disciples about it. They said, "You mean you baptized Romans?" Peter said, "How could I not, after the Holy Spirit came on them and told me to baptize them?" Finally, the disciples realized their prejudices were wrong as they began to understand God's plan of salvation more fully.

> It would be well to remember that every true child of God has the co-operation of heavenly beings. Invisible armies of light and power attend the meek and lowly ones who believe and claim the promises of God.
> —*The Acts of the Apostles*, 154

Delivered From Prison

About this time, King Herod Agrippa wanted to please the Jews, so he arrested the disciple James, a leader of the church, put him in prison, and had him beheaded. After that, he arrested Peter and decided to execute him publicly as a warning to other believers once the Passover festival mobs departed.

The believers were heavily grieving over James and couldn't imagine losing Peter too. They prayed earnestly for Peter. Herod had ordered sixteen soldiers to guard Peter's cell in shifts around the clock. Each shift was to have two guards in the cell with Peter, with his wrists chained to theirs.

The night before Peter's execution, an angel came into Peter's cell and woke him. The chains fell off Peter's wrists while the two guards continued sleeping. Peter stood up quietly, went over to the cell door, and it swung open. The guards stood there like statues and didn't move. Then Peter followed the angel through two more bolted, chained, guarded doors, which both swung open silently. The guards all stood like statues, unaware of the movement.

Outside the prison, the angel disappeared and Peter realized he was free. He made his way to the house where the disciples and some other believers were staying. They were praying aloud for him, so when he knocked they couldn't hear it. A young girl named Rhoda heard a knock, so she went to the door and asked, "Who's there?" Peter answered, and she got so excited that she forgot to open the door. She ran back and told the others that Peter was at the door. They said, "You must be dreaming! Peter's in prison." Peter kept knocking, so they went to the door, opened it, and let him in. Peter hushed their excitement, explained what had happened, and then left to visit other believers. He knew that soldiers would look for him there. When Herod learned Peter was out of prison, he blamed the guards and had them executed.

Not long after that, Herod went to Caesarea for a festival. While he was there, he had a very painful heart attack and died. He knew God was judging him for beheading James, plotting to kill Peter, and unjustly executing the guards. News of Peter's escape and Herod's death caused many people to turn to God.

The Gospel Message in Antioch

Because the Jewish leaders in Jerusalem were relentless in their persecution, most of the disciples left and went to preach in other cities, such as Phoenicia and Cyprus. Barnabas went to the international resort city of Antioch to preach. The work there was so successful that Barnabas needed help, so he went to Tarsus to get Paul to help him. For a whole year, they worked together. It was in Antioch that the believers were first called Christians, a name given them by God because Christ was the central theme of their preaching and prayers.

When Paul saw what was happening in Antioch, he was convicted that the Lord was calling him to preach in other Gentile cities too. Paul and Barnabas had clearly been called by God, but they had not yet been officially ordained for ministry by the organized church. So God instructed those who had been ordained to ordain the two of them, which they did. This gave them the public authority to baptize people and organize new churches.

Heralds of the Gospel

Paul and Barnabas started their missionary adventure by going to Seleucia and then on to the island of Cyprus. Barnabas took his relative, John Mark, with them.

The governor of Paphos, Sergius Paulus, had heard about the gospel and wanted to know more. A sorcerer by the name of Elymas wanted to keep him from meeting with Paul. Satan was working through him to stop the preaching of the gospel. Paul rebuked Elymas and prayed that he would be blinded for a while to warn him of the danger of interfering with the gospel work. When the governor saw this miracle, he accepted the gospel and gave his heart to Christ. After some time at Cyprus, the Holy Spirit told Paul and Barnabas to work separately because of their different gifts.

From there, Paul and his companions went to Perga in Pamphylia. The trip was a hard one and there were all kinds of dangers along the way. They got tired and hungry and cold, but they didn't think about themselves; they were concerned about those who needed to know Jesus. John Mark couldn't tolerate the hardships of mission work anymore and went home. Paul was upset that young Mark gave up, but later they again became friends and worked together.

Paul and Barnabas went back to Antioch. One Sabbath they attended a Jewish synagogue. After reading from the Scriptures, the man in charge of the synagogue invited Paul and Barnabas to address the congregation. Thankful for the opportunity to address fellow Jews, Paul stood up and reminded them of their deliverance from Egypt, the kingship of David, and what John the Baptist had said about Jesus. Then he explained that Jesus had come as promised and had been killed and resurrected as the prophecies foretold. Paul then invited them to repent and accept Jesus as their Savior. Many did.

When the service was over, the visiting Gentiles begged Paul and Barnabas to preach to them the next Sabbath. Word got out about the event, and nearly the whole city turned out to hear Paul preach. Paul told the Gentiles that they, too, were the children of God and that Jesus had come to save them also. This, of course, angered the unbelieving Jews, but Paul made it clear that their own rejection of the message of Christ was the reason God had broken the barrier between them and the Gentiles.

Eventually, the unbelieving Jews stirred up the people of Antioch against Paul and Barnabas and forced them out of the city. The new converts were sad that their mentors were gone, but they faithfully carried on the work by sharing the story of salvation with people throughout the city and everywhere else they could.

Preaching Among the Heathen
From Antioch, Paul and Barnabas went to Iconium. They began their work in the Jewish synagogues and had success reaching Jews and Gentiles alike. The unbelieving Jews, angered by their fading influence, frequently arrested the disciples on charges of creating chaos and insurrection. The judges always let them go because their testimony was so clear and powerful. Paul and Barnabas kept preaching the gospel, and soon the city was divided. The leaders of Jews were so angry they planned to stone Paul and Barnabas, so the men decided it was best to leave the city and return after the uproar had quieted.

Paul and company traveled from Iconium to Lystra, where they began preaching because there was no synagogue. The people were superstitious heathens, many of whom worshiped Jupiter, so the disciples began by telling them about the God of heaven, who created all the beautiful things of nature, including the stars. Then they told the people about Jesus and about His life and ministry, and they ended with His rejection, crucifixion, burial, and resurrection.

One day while Paul was talking to the people about Jesus, he saw a crippled man sitting on the ground watching him. Paul's heart went out to the man, and he walked over and asked him to stand up. Suddenly, the man's legs got strong and he stood up and jumped for joy. When the people saw this, they said, "The gods have come to visit us!" To show their gratitude, they decided to get some animals to sacrifice to Paul and Barnabas. Paul finally convinced the people that he and Barnabas were not gods but just ordinary men serving God.

Some of the unbelieving Jews from Jerusalem and Antioch followed Paul and Barnabas from town to town for the sole purpose of sabotaging their work. After Paul stopped the people from sacrificing animals to him, their wounded pride left them open to these men's evil suggestions. Some the people turned against Paul, stoned him, dragged his limp body out of the city, and dumped it. Barnabas couldn't stop it. When the mob left, a group of believers walked up to Paul, looked at his bruised and bloodied body and thought he was dead. Then Paul lifted his head, stood up slowly, and praised God.

After Paul recovered from the ordeal, he and Barnabas went to Derbe, and God blessed their work there. As they talked about the believers in the cities they had recently been to, they decided to go back to see how they were doing and to strengthen their faith despite the danger. They also made sure those churches were properly organized. Everywhere they went, Paul and Barnabas trained others to continue their work.

> Those who labor for souls must attain to a deeper, fuller, clearer knowledge of God than can be gained by ordinary effort. They must throw all their energies into the work of the Master. They are engaged in a high and holy calling, and if they gain souls for their hire they must lay firm hold upon God, daily receiving grace and power from the Source of all blessing.
>
> —*The Acts of the Apostles*, 205

Jew and Gentile
Then Paul and Barnabas went back to Antioch where they began their missionary journey and told the believers there where they had been and what God had done. By now the Gentile converts outnumbered Jewish converts. Arguments over whether

circumcision, sacrifices, dietary restrictions, and so on were required of the Gentile believers were so contentious that the church was at risk of splitting.

Church leaders finally decided to call Paul and Barnabas to a meeting in Jerusalem to help solve the debate. Peter spoke to all the Christian leaders there. He reminded them about his experience with Cornelius, the Roman captain and how the Holy Spirit had come upon all the Gentiles and Jews alike at his home. After the church leaders discussed it, James, who was the head of the church, said, "My decision is we don't bother these new converts with the laws of Jewish ceremonies, such as the requirement for circumcision. God's Ten Commandments are enough."

The elders agreed they would send a letter to the Gentile converts teaching them that some of their customs, such as fornication and blood consumption, were not compatible with the tenets of Christianity. The conclusions didn't please all of the Jews, but the official discussion ended.

Exalting the Cross

When Paul and Barnabas and the delegation of new believers got back to Antioch, they told the other believers that the church leaders in Jerusalem had decided not to require circumcision. Then Paul suggested to Barnabas that they visit the newly baptized members in other places to see how they were doing. Barnabas wanted to take Mark with them again. Paul refused, thinking Mark was too weak and uncommitted, so Barnabas decided to sail with Mark to Cyrus. Paul took Silas and together they went to visit the new converts, beginning with Syria and Cilicia then on to Derbe and Lystra.

When Paul and Silas arrived in Lystra, they found the members there still strong in the faith in spite of the opposition. Paul met a young believer named Timothy in Lystra. Paul was impressed with his commitment to Christ and decided to train him to be a missionary. Timothy's father was a Greek, but his mother and grandmother were Jews who deeply loved God. His home life had been good; he loved the Scriptures; he was faithful and trustworthy. Plus he could speak well. Paul loved him as if he were his own son and asked him to join their ministry.

As they traveled from place to place, Paul taught Timothy how to be a successful worker and not act on impulse and to think things through. His responsibility was not only to win souls but also to make sure the new converts would keep growing spiritually.

In the Regions Beyond

The Lord gave Paul a vision of a Macedonian man saying, "Come over here and help us!" So Paul, Silas, and Timothy went to Macedonia, which was part of Greece. In the city of Philippi, they went to a river on Sabbath to pray and rest. Some women were doing laundry there. One of the women was Lydia. She heard the men praying and opened her heart to the Lord. She listened to what Paul had to say and gave her heart to Christ, and soon she and her family were baptized. Then she invited Paul, Silas, and Timothy to stay at her house.

In that city, a woman possessed by the devil kept harassing Paul by following him around and shrieking that he was bringing a message from God. This made people think Paul might have had the same spirit, so they stayed away. Paul and the others endured it for a while, but one day Paul confronted the woman and commanded the evil spirit to come out of her. There was an immediate change. Her mind was free, and she became a Christian.

The men, who were making money by charging people a fee to get the woman's fortune-telling readings, were angry about her conversion, as were others in the city who made money from the work of evil spirits. They told the authorities that Paul and the men with him were Jews who had come to the city to cause trouble. The officials arrested Paul and Silas, tore off their clothes, and had them whipped. Then they put them in prison and fastened their feet between two blocks of wood. Paul and Silas were in a lot of pain, but, during the night while the other prisoners were cursing and swearing, they began singing and praising the Lord. The guards and the other prisoners wondered who these men were who could be tortured and yet still sing.

As the magistrates learned more details about the apostles' work in town and saw the woman who had been freed from the demonic spirits, it became clear that Paul and Silas's treatment had been rash and unjust. During the night there was a tremendous earthquake, the whole prison shook, the prison doors opened, and the chains and clamps on Paul and Silas fell off.

When the jailer saw that the prison doors had opened, he assumed that all the prisoners had escaped and that he would be held responsible and executed. He pulled out his sword to kill himself when Paul called out, "Wait! Don't! All the prisoners are here!" The jailer was shocked, dropped his sword, and ran inside. He told Paul and Silas that he was sorry about the way they had been treated and asked what he had to do to be saved. The jailer took the men to his house, cared for their terrible wounds, and fed them. That night, his entire family was baptized in a nearby pool.

Paul and Silas were Roman citizens, and it was against the law to beat a Roman citizen without first giving him a fair trial. The magistrates publicly admitted that what they did was wrong and let Paul and Silas free. News spread about what had happened at the prison, and the people couldn't wait to hear Paul preach. Many became Christians, and Paul established a church in Philippi.

Thessalonica

When Paul and Silas left Philippi, they went to Thessalonica. The Jews allowed them to speak in the synagogue, and Paul told them all that had happened to them, giving God the glory. For three Sabbaths, he unfolded the story of his early life, his commitment to the Jewish faith, his experience on the road to Damascus, and his conversion. He pointed them to the Old Testament prophecies about Jesus and how each one—Jesus' birth, death on Calvary, resurrection, ascension, and promised return—was fulfilled. Many of the Greeks who were there believed, including some prominent women, but only a few Jews. The other Jews turned against Paul and Silas and joined other men in the city accusing Christians of trying to set up another king in place of Caesar.

The city was in an uproar and the authorities went looking for Paul and Silas. They had been staying at the home of Jason, a new believer, but when the mob arrived, they weren't there. The magistrates arrested Jason for harboring Paul and Silas but later released him. The believers sneaked Paul and Silas out of the city during the night, and they went to Berea.

Berea and Athens

The Jews in Berea were willing to listen to Paul and Silas. Then they studied the Scriptures earnestly to substantiate their messages, and many accepted Jesus. Many Greeks became believers as well. Unfortunately, some of the Jews from Thessalonica, who were against Paul and Silas, followed them from town to town to cause trouble. For his safety, Paul left Berea and went to Athens.

Athens was the Greek capital and a center of heathenism. The people were intelligent and highly educated. Everywhere there were statues of their gods, Greek heroes, works of art, magnificent buildings, and beautiful temples. Paul knew that, in spite of being filled with beauty, the city was spiritually desolate. He sent some of the Berean believers back to Berea with a message that Silas and Timothy should join him at once.

While waiting for his companions, Paul spent time debating with the Jews in the synagogues and conversing with philosophers and others in the marketplaces. The leaders in the city heard that a discussion was going on in the marketplaces. They assumed he was an uneducated religious zealot but found that, in fact, he spoke with logic, philosophy, and learned wisdom. Because they found him respectable, they

> In every effort to reach the higher classes, the worker for God needs strong faith. Appearances may seem forbidding, but in the darkest hour there is light above. The strength of those who love and serve God will be renewed day by day.
> —*The Acts of the Apostles*, 242

invited Paul to a sacred place called Mars Hill where Athenians traditionally held discussions about religion.

Poets, artists, teachers, and philosophers attended. Paul inspired them with stories about God's power and glory. After seeing an altar engraved with the phrase, "To the Unknown God," he said, "Let me tell you about the God you say you don't know." He told them about the God of heaven, who created everything—even human beings. He told them about Jesus' life, death, and resurrection. When he got to the subject of the Resurrection, the people laughed at him and closed their hearts. The Athenians were proud of their human education and would not humble themselves by rejecting what they already believed. Thus Paul's work in Athens ended, and only a few there believed.

Corinth
From Athens Paul went to the city of Corinth, one of the world's leading commercial centers. Among the Jews who lived there were Aquila and Priscilla. When they met Paul, they invited him to stay with them. Idolatry was prominent in the city, and Venus, the goddess of love, was the resident's favorite diety. Paul realized that preaching the gospel in Corinth would require a different approach than in Athens; he would preach Christ alone. He decided to go to the synagogue and preach to the Jews first as he had in other cities. However, they didn't like his message and became hostile. Paul said to them, "Your blood is on your own hands. I'll go and preach to the Greeks."

About this time, Silas and Timothy arrived to help Paul preach the gospel. Their hearts were aglow with the love of Jesus as they remembered that He had said, "If I be lifted up, I will draw all men unto Me." The unbelieving Jews from Jerusalem, who had moved to Corinth, remembered the miracles of Jesus but told people that He did them through the power of evil spirits. They said the same thing about Paul's miracles.

Discouraged, Paul decided to leave Corinth, but the Lord appeared to him in vision and said, "Stay here. I'll watch over you to make sure that no one hurts you because there are still a lot of people in this city who will give their hearts to Me." Encouraged,

> The enemy often persuades men to believe that it is God who is guiding them, when in reality they are following only human impulse. But if we watch carefully, and take counsel with our brethren, we shall be given an understanding of the Lord's will; for the promise is, "The meek will He guide in judgment: and the meek will He teach His way" Psalm 25:9.
> —*The Acts of the Apostles*, 279

Paul stayed, preached, visited the sick, and helped the poor, and, as a result, many people turned from their idols to Jesus. The unbelieving Jews were determined to stop him, so they took him to the governor of Achaia and accused Paul of breaking the law. The governor saw through their lies and let Paul go. The apostle stayed in the city a while longer to strengthen the new believers.

> The sap of the vine, ascending from the root, is diffused to the branches, sustaining growth and producing blossoms and fruit. So the life-giving power of the Holy Spirit, proceeding from the Saviour, pervades the soul, renews the motives and affections, and brings even the thoughts into obedience to the will of God, enabling the receiver to bear the precious fruit of holy deeds.
> —*The Acts of the Apostles*, 284

The Thessalonian Letters

When Silas and Timothy came to see Paul, they gave him good news about the faith of the believers in Thessalonica who were standing firm for Christ. This really encouraged Paul, and he decided to write them a letter. In it he expressed his gratitude for their steadfast faith and told them he and the other believers were praying for them every day.

He reminded them that when he first preached to them, his motive was not to honor them but to honor God and to bring them to Jesus. Then he taught them that when people die, they don't go to heaven, but sleep in their graves until Jesus comes. Then they will be resurrected and taken to heaven. This provided great comfort because they feared that only believers who were still alive when Jesus comes would go to heaven. He told them not to forget the signs of Jesus' coming.

Paul, Silas, and Timothy had organized the church in Thessalonica with pastors, elders, and deacons, but some believers had begun to criticize the church, spread their own religious theories, and refused to cooperate. This was a real problem. Paul told the believers to respect those who had been chosen as church leaders and to love and respect each other. He reminded them that every day they were praying for them asking the Lord to bless them and help their church to grow.

In his second letter to the Thessalonians, Paul again expressed his gratitude for their faith and their love for Jesus. Then he tried to correct any misunderstanding they had about the return of Jesus. Paul warned them about the future and urged them to hold on to Scripture no matter what as false teachings would come into the church before the return of Christ. He also pleaded with them to hold on to what they had been taught and work for Jesus while patiently waiting for Jesus to come back. Then he concluded his letter with a prayer that the grace of the Lord Jesus Christ would be with them forever.

Apollos at Corinth

Paul's next missionary stop was Ephesus, but his stay there was short because he had to go to Jerusalem. Aquila and Priscilla, who had moved from Rome to Corinth where they had met Paul, came to Ephesus with him and stayed there because Paul had promised to continue his work.

There was a Jew born in Alexandria, Egypt, named Apollos. He really knew the Scriptures and was a good speaker. Apollos came to Ephesus and, while there, he met Aquila and Priscilla. They shared the gospel with him, and he became a powerful defender of the Christian faith. He preached to the Jews and showed them from Scripture that Jesus was the promised Messiah.

Apollos decided to continue his ministry in some of the places where Paul had preached. The believers in Ephesus gave him a letter of recommendation, and he went to Corinth. The believers there thought that he was a better preacher than Paul. When Paul first came to Corinth, he had presented the gospel in very simple language because the people had had no prior knowledge of Christian principles—thus comparing Apollos and Paul wasn't really fair. They were good friends, and their messages were in perfect harmony.

The Holy Spirit gives different people different gifts and responsibilities. God calls some people to be evangelists and to sow spiritual seeds, and others to be pastors and to water the seeds and help them grow. The Holy Spirit also gives some people the ability to be church leaders and wants the church to support them.

Ephesus

While Paul was in Jerusalem, he had not forgotten to keep his promise to return to Ephesus. When he got there, he met twelve men who had been disciples of John the Baptist but who knew only a little about Jesus. They were very sincere, so Paul asked if they had been baptized.

They said, "Yes, by John the Baptist."

Paul asked, "Did he baptize you in the name of the Father, the Son, and the Holy Spirit?"

They said, "What do you mean? We haven't even heard about the Holy Spirit."

Then Paul asked, "In whose name were you baptized?"

They said, "It must have been in the name of John the Baptist."

Paul told them about Jesus' birth, mission, life, death, resurrection, and ascension, and about the promise of the Holy Spirit. These men were grateful to know all this and accepted Jesus as their Savior. Then Paul laid his hands on them and baptized them, and they received the Holy Spirit. They were each given the gift of speaking in other languages, which made them uniquely qualified to go as missionaries around Asia Minor.

Many in Ephesus worshiped Diana of the Ephesians. Her temple was home to an idol they believed had fallen from heaven. Paul worked many healing miracles while in Ephesus. This caught people's attention because they had not seen such miracles before—even from their sorcerers. Paul always worked his miracles in the name of Jesus, which turned their minds away from the goddess Diana.

Certain unbelieving Jews tried to work miracles like Paul did by using the name of Jesus. Once, they heard of a man who was possessed by a demon, and they went to his house and said to the demon, "In the name of Jesus, the one who Paul preaches, get out, and leave this man alone."

The evil spirit said, "Jesus I know, and Paul I know, but who are you?" Then the demon jumped on them and beat them up, and the men fled, bleeding. Christ's name is sacred, and those who use it without knowing Him are putting themselves at grave risk.

Those who had not yet let go of their practice of magic and superstition listened to Paul's preaching, heard about the men fighting the demon, and became convinced that those things were of Satan. They brought all their magic-related books and tools together and burned them, demonstrating their maturing faith in Jesus. The news of Paul's ministry spread everywhere, and what happened in Ephesus was never forgotten.

> The surrender must be complete. Every weak, doubting, struggling soul who yields fully to the Lord is placed in direct touch with agencies that enable him to overcome. Heaven is near to him, and he has the support and help of angels of mercy in every time of trial and need.
>
> —*The Acts of the Apostles*, 299

Days of Toil and Trial

Paul labored in Ephesus for three years and built a thriving church with Jewish and Gentile members. The gospel spread throughout that whole area. Then Paul decided to go on another mission trip and said to himself, "I've been to a lot of places, but I feel God is telling me to go to Rome."

Just before he left Ephesus, there was a festival to the goddess Diana. It was believed that her image had fallen from heaven. A silversmith in town, named Demetrius, made little silver images of Diana and sold them, and he and his friends were getting rich. Paul told the people that Diana's image had not fallen from heaven, and that they should not to treat these little images with reverence. This cost Demetrius business, which infuriated him.

Eventually the whole city was in an uproar, and people were looking for Paul. Believers, who had heard about the plan to eliminate him, hurried Paul out of the city to a safe place. His time to die had not yet come. Because the mob couldn't find Paul, they grabbed Gaius and Aristarchus, the companions of Paul, and took them to the amphitheater to kill them. Paul was hiding not far from there, and when he heard about this, he wanted to go to the amphitheater to defend them. However, the other believers wouldn't let him go because they knew he would be killed.

The crowd in the amphitheater started shouting, "Great is Diana of the Ephesians! Great is Diana of the Ephesians!" and carried on this way for two hours. Finally exhausted, the crowd settled down and a city official announced, "People of Ephesus, don't shout so much; everyone knows that Diana is our goddess. Even if Demetrius is losing business, and the pagan priests are not getting paid as much, there is no reason to kill these innocent men."

When the uproar finally stopped and the mob disbanded, Paul called together his friends, prayed for them, and left for Greece. Paul loved these new believers and spent many sleepless nights praying for them.

A Message of Warning and Entreaty

During the last part of his stay in Ephesus, Paul dictated a letter to the Corinthian church. He had worked there for a year and a half and had carefully taught them what it means to be a Christian. In his letter, he urged them to be faithful to their baptismal vows. If they weren't, they would be tempted to go back to worshiping idols.

> The conversion of sinners and their sanctification through the truth is the strongest proof a minister can have that God has called him to the ministry. The evidence of his apostleship is written upon the hearts of those converted, and is witnessed to by their renewed lives. Christ is formed within, the hope of glory.
> —*The Acts of the Apostles*, 328

While he was in Corinth, Paul inspired the believers to totally commit to godly living. Now that he was gone, the believers had slipped. Pride, immorality, and idol worship had weakened their commitment to Christ. In addition, false teachers were telling them not to pay attention to what Paul had taught them. The Corinthians wrote a letter to Paul asking him for advice on some of the issues they faced, but they didn't mention the loss of commitment to Christ, sins, or the division that had come into the church.

When Paul finally heard about all these problems, he felt sick over it. He cried and prayed, asking God what to do. He would have gone back to Corinth, but that was still too risky, so he sent Titus to get the work started and planned to go himself as soon as it was safe. He also wrote a very strong, clear letter, answering their questions and warning them that their sins would lead them away from Christ.

The believers had also been trying to settle their squabbles by taking each other to court. Paul told them to settle their differences among themselves and let their pastors and church leaders help them instead of going to court.

Called to Reach a Higher Standard

Paul tried to impress the believers with the importance of spiritual self-discipline and used an example from the athletic competitions in Corinth. The most popular sport was foot racing. Young men from all ranks of society took part. Contestants disciplined themselves and trained hard to win. Commoners, nobility, and public officials all followed the races.

The rules for the competition were strict and judges' decisions were final. If a runner broke the rules, even if he came in first, he did not receive a trophy. However, if he did everything right and won, he won the trophy and the applause of the people, which was so loud that it echoed back from the surrounding hills.

Paul used these games as an example of the spiritual race for Christians. We also must employ self-discipline and strength, focus on Christ, and follow God's rules without collapsing or quitting. The trophy is eternal life.

> He who teaches the word must himself live in conscious, hourly communion with God through prayer and a study of His word, for here is the source of strength. Communion with God will impart to the minister's efforts a power greater than the influence of his preaching. Of this power he must not allow himself to be deprived.
>
> —*The Acts of the Apostles*, 362

The Message Heeded

From Ephesus, Paul set out on another mission trip. He stopped at Troas and preached the gospel there with some success. He didn't stay there long, though, because he was thinking about the new believers in other areas, who needed to be encouraged. He stopped next in Philippi and met with Timothy. Titus joined them there and brought good news from Corinth—the believers there were doing well. They had accepted the counsel in Paul's first letter, repented, and refocused on Christ.

At this news, Paul dictated another letter to the Corinthians expressing his joy about their faithfulness to Christ. He explained that he had agonized over speaking so firmly in his first letter, fearing that the believers would be disheartened or reject the message. Then he said to them, "Believers are like priceless treasures. Their bodies belong to God and should be treated that way. They were changed by the power of Christ."

In this second letter to the Corinthians, Paul focused on Christ as the Son of God, who for our sake humbled Himself, obeyed His Father, went to the cross, and died for us. Then he added, "Here is where you see love. God loved us so much that He gave His Son to die for us."

A Liberal Church

In his second letter, Paul reminded the members in Corinth to support their pastor. Farmers care for their working animals, so why shouldn't a church care for its pastor? God asks Christians to bring their tithe to the church to support those in ministry. In addition, we should give offerings to spread the gospel, help take care of the church expenses, and relieve the suffering of the poor.

People usually don't think twice about spending money on themselves and their own homes. Yet they fear that paying tithe or offerings would leave them too little to live well. However, those who have Christ in their hearts think about God first and always consider what they can do to help others. The spirit of giving is the spirit of heaven because God loved the world so much that He gave His Son to die for us. The spirit of selfishness is the spirit of Satan. He is the one who thought first about himself and caused all the original trouble in heaven.

> An important lesson for every minister of Christ to learn is that of adapting his labors to the condition of those whom he seeks to benefit. Tenderness, patience, decision, and firmness are alike needful; but these are to be exercised with proper discrimination. To deal wisely with different classes of minds, under varied circumstances and conditions, is a work requiring wisdom and judgment enlightened and sanctified by the Spirit of God.—*The Acts of the Apostles*, 385, 386

Every act of self-sacrifice makes us more like Jesus. First, though, we need to give our hearts to Him because no amount of self-sacrifice can buy an unbeliever's way into heaven.

Laboring Under Difficulties

All through his ministry, Paul supported himself by making tents. It was the tradition of the Jews to train their children to work with their hands, so Paul was used to doing it. In Thessalonica, he met some who refused to work with their hands. After Paul led them to Christ, he reminded them that Jesus worked with His hands in a carpentry shop, so they shouldn't think of working with their hands as demeaning.

When Paul first went to Corinth, he met Aquila and Priscilla, who also made tents. They had come from Rome when Claudius Caesar ordered all Jews to leave the city. The upper-class people in Corinth didn't like seeing Paul work with his hands, but he told them, among other benefits, doing so gave him contact with the working class. Sometimes Paul would work late into the night, not only to support himself but also to help support Timothy, Titus, and others who were active in ministry. He would even go hungry and give his food to the poor.

A Consecrated Ministry

Christ gave us a perfect example of unselfish ministry. He passed this on to His disciples and to pastors and ministers today, who also represent Christ. If for any reason they lose their spiritual sensitivity, God will hold them responsible. If they are true coworkers with Christ, they will have a deep sense of their sacred work. They will understand fully that spiritual strength comes from Christ and not from them.

Pastors' work doesn't end with the sermon. They should spend time with the people in their homes, pray with them, and do whatever they can to help them. When they become acquainted with people and their needs, they can tailor their ministry to make it more effective. Christ will always be by the pastor's side.

When Christ was here, He went from house to house healing the sick, comforting mourners, bringing peace into the family, and taking children in his arms and blessing them. Pastors should do what Christ did. They can't pastor effectively and be involved in some other kind of work or business with the goal of getting rich. Pastors should focus on ministry because, to do it well, it requires all the energies they have.

Paul put all his energy into ministry, helping people, winning souls, and helping new believers grow spiritually. He also intentionally mentored other future ministers, such as Barnabas, Timothy, Titus, and Luke. In the same way, pastors today should not try to do everything themselves. Instead, they should share the burdens of ministry with those who show potential as future ministers, thus training them.

Salvation to the Jews

Paul finally got back to Corinth. The believers had become strong in the faith; they loved Paul and were glad to see him again. He enjoyed worshiping and fellowshiping with them, and his spirit was able to rest and renew among friends. This restoration allowed him to think about future missionary journeys. He really wanted to take the gospel to Rome. There was a small church there already, so Paul wrote a letter to them in which he outlined his purpose for coming and the principles of the gospel. He also explained the meaning of justification by faith, which has blessed Christians for every generation since. Those who accept Christ as their Savior become sons and daughters of God, whether they're Jews or Gentiles.

Paul was especially burdened for the Jews and prayed for them constantly. Even though the Jewish leaders in Jerusalem had rejected Christ, God did not reject the whole nation. The people had stumbled and fallen spiritually, and God was using Paul to pick them up. Paul reminded them Christ offered them salvation, but that He also offered the same to the Gentiles and the rest of the world.

As the gospel travels around the world, the Jewish people are not to be forgotten. They may know the Scriptures, but they also need to know Jesus as their Savior.

Apostasy in Galatia

While he was working in Corinth, Paul became concerned about the churches that he had established in Galatia because some were mingling Jewish traditions with the gospel and forcing them on the Gentile believers. The churches were at risk of collapsing. Brokenhearted, Paul wrote to the churches telling them to reject such teachings. He said that even if an angel from heaven appeared and preached a different gospel, they should not accept it.

> A neglect to appreciate and improve the provisions of divine grace has deprived the church of many a blessing. How often would the Lord have prolonged the work of some faithful minister, had his labors been appreciated!
> —*The Acts of the Apostles*, 417

Every minister preaching the gospel and teaching people should do so with kindness and patience, but should not neglect to say what's right and wrong. There should be no wavering from the truth. If we love Jesus, failing to keep His commandments is not an option. Satan would love for us to think it doesn't matter. However, our relationship with God is based on respect and obedience, just like a good relationship in a family.

We must also beware of false teachings that adjust the gospel a little here and there and allow us to choose which commandments to keep and which to ignore. Paul took a firm stand on Scripture and reminded believers to do the same.

Paul's Last Journey to Jerusalem

It was time for the Passover festival in Jerusalem and Paul decided to go before leaving on his mission trip to Rome. This would give him a chance to meet Jews from all over the world and to distribute the offering the Gentile churches gave to help poor Jewish believers. This would also help build a bond with the church and its leadership in Jerusalem.

Paul went to Troas to catch a ship to Palestine. When he was ready to board, he learned about a plot to kill him. So instead of getting on the boat, he decided to go to another port before boarding. Paul, Luke, and a number of representatives from the various churches set out. Paul and Luke stopped in Philippi for a week to celebrate the Passover, and the others went on to Troas. Paul really loved the believers there, so he decided to call an evening meeting to say goodbye to all of them. Paul ended up preaching and teaching until almost midnight.

While Paul was speaking, a young man named Eutychus was sitting in an open window listening to Paul. Here he fell asleep, lost his balance, and fell three stories to his death. This was a terrible shock to everyone, and they wept for him. Paul gathered the young man in his arms and offered an earnest prayer to God to please restore the young man's life, and God did. At this, the people began praising God.

Paul was in a hurry to get to Jerusalem before Pentecost, but while they were docked at Miletus, he sent a message to Ephesus for the church leaders to come meet him. When they arrived, Paul told them that he wouldn't see them again. He encouraged and blessed them and warned them to guard the church from predators. Then they prayed and cried together, and the people walked to the ship with Paul.

When they got to Caesarea, they got off and stayed at Philip the evangelist's house. He had four daughters who also preached, prophesied, and evangelized. While there, a prophet named Agabus came to see Paul, reached out and took Paul's belt, wrapped it around his own hands and feet, and said, "The man who owns this belt will be arrested when he gets to Jerusalem." When the people in the house heard that, they begged Paul not to go. Paul felt God was calling him to go there; they couldn't convince him to stay away.

Paul a Prisoner

When they got to Jerusalem, Paul went to see James, who was the head of the church. All the elders were there too. He and the representatives from the Gentile churches gave a report of the work abroad and presented the freewill offerings they had brought with them from the Gentile churches to help the poor Jewish believers. James and the elders thanked them for their kindness and loyalty to the church, but Paul could tell that even then, some still considered the Gentiles unworthy.

Then the elders told Paul that the Jewish believers in Jerusalem had heard that, as Paul converted people in other lands, he taught them, including the Jews, that the ceremonial laws, such as circumcision, were no longer necessary. In an attempt to reinforce Paul's Jewish heritage and avoid the wrath of those who held onto their prejudice against the Gentiles, the elders asked him to take an oath and do a purification ritual at the temple to show that he was a Jew at heart. He hesitated, finally agreeing only because it might hurt his ministry among the Gentiles. However, God had not given His approval for this concession. In addition, it was not a good time for Paul to be at the temple because it was full of visitors from all over the world, many of whom hated Paul.

At the temple, some Jews from Asia pointed their fingers at Paul and cried, "Hey! This is the man who goes everywhere telling people that they don't have to keep the traditions of the Jews! He even brought Gentiles into our temple!" This was a false charge, but one punishable by death. They grabbed Paul, started beating him, and were ready to kill him. When the Roman captain in charge of keeping order heard about a riot in the temple, he took some soldiers there. He saw what was happening and assumed Paul must be an Egyptian who had been causing trouble in the city. He stopped the beating, arrested Paul, and took him to the Roman castle, while a mob followed them, shouting.

When they got to the steps leading up to the castle, Paul said to the captain in Greek, "Would you let me say something to these people?" The captain was surprised that an Egyptian could speak Greek. Paul said, "I'm not an Egyptian; I am a Jew and a Roman citizen." The agreed to let him talk to the crowd. Then Paul spoke to the mob in Hebrew. They quieted down and listened. He told them that he was born a Jew and shared some details about his life. When Paul told them about his conversion and his work among the Gentiles, they became furious and tore their robes and shouted, "Away with this man and kill him!" At that, the captain took Paul into the castle to the Roman magistrate and said, "This man claims to be a Roman citizen." The magistrate said to Paul, "I had to purchase my citizenship! And you say you were born a Roman citizen?" Paul assured him that he was, which made the magistrate nervous because it was required to treat Roman citizens with respect, and he had not.

The next day the magistrate called together the Jewish council because he wanted to know what they had against Paul. As Paul stood in front of the Sanhedrin, he answered their questions and then said, "For years I have been living before God with a clear conscience." When they heard that, the high priest told one of the guards to slap Paul across the mouth. Then Paul said to the high priest, "You're not supposed to treat me this way before I'm convicted."

> All who in that evil day would fearlessly serve God according to the dictates of conscience, will need courage, firmness, and a knowledge of God and His word; for those who are true to God will be persecuted, their motives will be impugned, their best efforts misinterpreted, and their names cast out as evil.
> —*The Acts of the Apostles*, 431

Someone said to Paul, "You shouldn't tell the high priest what to do."

Paul apologized, "I'm sorry, I didn't know that the judge was also the high priest." Then he added, "I was educated a Pharisee, and one of the reasons I was brought here to stand trial is because I believe in Jesus and the resurrection of the dead." When the council heard this, they took sides among themselves because the Sadducees did not believe in the resurrection of the dead. As the trial devolved into chaos, the Roman captain decided to take Paul back to the castle.

That night the Lord said to Paul, "Just like you stood up for Me in Jerusalem, you will get to stand up for Me in Rome." Paul always wanted to go to Rome but didn't realize he would be going there as a prisoner.

More than forty of the Jews who hated Paul went to the priests and elders and said, "We have taken an oath not to eat or drink anything until we have killed Paul. Please ask the captain to bring Paul back to the council for questioning and, on the way, we'll kill him." The priests and elders agreed to the scheme. Paul's nephew heard about the plan and went to the castle to tell the Roman officers about it. In the middle of that same night, the magistrate ordered the captain to select nearly five hundred soldiers to escort Paul to Caesarea to see Felix, the Roman governor. In a letter, the magistrate explained to Felix what had happened. The governor read the letter and decided to personally interview Paul if members of the Jewish council would come to Caesarea to tell their side of the story.

The Trial at Caesarea

Five days later, members of the Jewish council arrived with their lawyer Tertullus. Tertullus began by flattering the governor and accusing Paul of breaking the Jewish law. He didn't realize that Roman judges don't appreciate taking time in court to be flattered.

Tertullus quickly charged Paul with crimes that would lead to his execution. Then he added that the Roman officer had stormed into the temple and taken Paul to the castle without letting the Jews judge him. Felix asked Paul for his response. He thanked the governor for the chance to defend himself, then made a clear and believable defense. Because Felix didn't want to upset the Jewish leaders, he decided to hold his judgment until Lysias, the Roman officer who had arrested Paul, could testify. Meanwhile, Paul was kept in prison, although with quite a bit of freedom.

Soon after this, Felix and his Jewish wife, Drusilla, sent for Paul. They wanted to hear more about Christ. Paul viewed this as an opportunity given by God, and he spoke very clearly about God's character, God's law, and Jesus' sacrifice, which paid the price for man's sin. Drusilla hardened her heart, but Felix was convicted of his past sins and became scared. However, instead of repenting, he sent Paul away so he wouldn't have to think about it.

For the next two years, Paul remained in prison. Felix was called to Rome to answer charges against his practices as governor. When he got there, he was removed from office and Porcius Festus was appointed governor in his place.

Paul Appeals to Caesar

Festus, the new governor, took his responsibility seriously. While visiting Jerusalem, the high priest asked Festus to bring Paul back for trail, but Festus read their intentions. He told them that it was not the practice of Rome to sentence a citizen to die before facing his accusers at a legal trial. He told the Jews to send a delegation to Caesarea to hold the trial there according to Roman law.

Grudgingly, the Jewish leaders went to Caesarea for the trial, this time without a lawyer. Festus sat as judge, and Paul was brought in. The Jews leveled many charges against Paul, none of which they could prove. Festus sensed that the real question about Paul had to do with the Jewish traditions and not anything criminal. However, he also realized that if he didn't sentence Paul to death or to life in prison, the Jews would create problems for him. Festus then asked Paul if he would be willing to go to Jerusalem to stand trial.

Paul knew he wouldn't get a fair trial there, so he said, "I am a Roman citizen, so I appeal to Caesar to be judged in Rome." Festus was surprised but couldn't deny Paul's appeal because after all he was a Roman citizen. Festus said, "You have appealed to Caesar, so to Caesar you will go!"

> He had no fears for himself; he knew that God would preserve him to witness at Rome for the truth of Christ. But his heart yearned with pity for the poor souls around him, sinful, degraded, and unprepared to die.
> —*The Acts of the Apostles*, 442

"Almost Thou Persuadest Me"

While they waited for a ship to transport Paul to Caesar, King Agrippa II and his wife, Bernice, came to Caesarea to congratulate Festus on his governorship. Festus mentioned that he had a prisoner whom the Jews wanted brought to Jerusalem to stand trial but that he couldn't find any merit in their charges. King Agrippa was fascinated by the story and asked to see Paul.

Paul began by telling King Agrippa about Jesus, His life, death, and resurrection, and that He was the world's Redeemer. He also told the king Jesus had appeared to him on the Damascus road, and he had accepted Him as his Savior and decided to be a missionary for Him. Everyone sat spellbound as they listened to Paul's stories.

Then Festus spoke up and said, "Paul you have lost your mind; too much learning has affected your thinking."

Paul replied, "Sir, I have not lost my mind. I'm telling you the truth." Then he turned to the king and said, "You believe, don't you, King Agrippa?"

The king said, "You've almost convinced me to be a Christian."

Paul said, "I wish you were, then everyone here would be as devoted to Christ as I am."

Then the king said to Festus, "This man has done nothing wrong to deserve imprisonment, much less death. If he had not appealed to Caesar, he could have been released." With that, Paul was returned to prison.

The Voyage and Shipwreck

Finally, Paul's ship was ready to sail. A Roman captain named Julius was in charge of his transport. Paul was not in good health, so the captain allowed Luke, a physician, and Aristarchus, another believer, to come along and take care of Paul. The trip began uneventfully. Their first stop was Sidon, then Myra. Headwinds were strong and their little boat struggled, so in Myra, the Roman captain found a large ship going to Italy and transferred to it. They started out and got as far as Fair Havens.

There they waited there for favorable winds so they could sail on. They knew that cold weather would soon come, the winds would change, and winter sailing would be impossible. Should they go on or not? The sailors and soldiers on board discussed their options; Julius, who respected Paul, asked him for his opinion. Paul told them that it was not a good idea to sail on because they would run into a terrible storm, the ship would be damaged, and lives could be lost. However, Fair Havens wasn't a great city, and the sailors and soldiers insisted they head for Phenice.

Once they reached open water, a strong wind came up and a storm blew in. The sailors prepared for the worst. They pulled the big life boat they had in tow onto the deck of the ship so it wouldn't be torn away by the strong waves. The storm lasted all night and into the next day. Then the ship developed a leak and began sucking in water. The crew and passengers worked as hard as they could to pump the water out to save the ship. The storm raged without stopping for two weeks, and the crew and passengers began to despair.

Paul was unwell and also suffered under all the stress, but he stood on the deck and spoke words of hope to the crew and passengers. He had prayed that God would spare

> Christianity makes a strong bond of union between master and slave, king and subject, the gospel minister and the degraded sinner who has found in Christ cleansing from sin. They have been washed in the same blood, quickened by the same Spirit; and they are made one in Christ Jesus.
> —*The Acts of the Apostles*, 460

their lives, and God promised to do so. He also encouraged them to rest for a bit and eat to regain their strength. There was a lull in the storm, and the sailors could tell that they were nearing land. The soldiers on board were afraid that they would lose control of the prisoners as they tried to get to land, and Roman law allowed them to kill the prisoners in this situation. However, out of respect for Paul, Julius commanded that everyone should swim for their lives. The ship had already been damaged by the heavy waves and some of its boards had been shaken off and were floating in the water. Those who couldn't swim could hold on to the boards and drift to the beach. When they got to shore, the captain took count and not one prisoner, soldier, or sailor was missing.

The people on the island of Malta were glad to help the castaways. They built a fire to dry out and keep warm. The crew and the prisoners were so grateful that they helped by picking up sticks and pieces of wood to keep the fire going. As Paul approached the fire with an armful of sticks, a poisonous snake among the sticks bit him and hung on to his hand. Paul quickly shook it off into the fire. Everyone expected that Paul would die, but when it didn't, they thought he must be a god and treated him with great respect.

Publius, the island's chief, invited Paul and Luke to come stay at his house a few days. His father was sick with a high fever and the family expected him to die. Paul went to the man's bedside, prayed and put his hands on him, and he was healed. When word got out, others on the island brought their sick to Paul, and they were all healed too. The people were so grateful that they gave Paul and Luke many gifts and supplies for their journey.

In Rome

When the weather got a little better and ships started sailing again, there was an Alexandrian ship that had wintered at Melita with plans to sail to Italy. Julius arranged for them to sail on it. They finally arrived at Puteoli on the coast of Italy. A few Christians lived there, and they knew about Paul from the Roman epistle he had written. They certainly had not expected to see him as a prisoner, but they asked Julius if Paul could stay and visit with them for a week.

On the eighth day, Julius, Paul, and the other prisoners and soldiers set off to Rome, one hundred forty miles from the harbor where they had landed. Finally they got to Appii Forum, forty miles from Rome. Many along the way mocked Paul, the old gray-haired prisoner.

Suddenly, a man jumped from the crowd, ran up to Paul, threw his arms around him, and cried with rejoicing. One after another, believers repeated the scene because they recognized him as the one who had preached to them at Corinth, Philippi, and Ephesus. The soldiers were impatient with the delay, but because they respected Paul, they didn't have the heart to stop such a joyful reunion. To be welcomed this way cheered Paul's heart and gave him courage.

When they finally got to Rome, Julius turned Paul over to the captain of the emperor's guard and gave him a good report about Paul. He also provided a letter from Festus. Because of these good references, Paul was allowed to live in a rented house with a soldier guarding him rather than rotting in a prison.

Three days after arriving, Paul called together the leading Jews in Rome. He explained the reason for his imprisonment; they had heard nothing about it. Then they asked to hear more about the gospel, and they set a date and gathered. This time Paul gave them details about his life and ministry and presented the gospel. He testified about all he had seen and done, and, in the end, some believed and others did not. For two years, Paul preached about Jesus to everyone in his house and everyone who came to visit. He also spent time writing letters to the churches he had planted. He trained new missionaries and sent them out to reach new cities. His influence was greater than if he had been traveling from place to place himself.

Among those who came to visit Paul was a pagan slave named Onesimus. He had offended his master and ran away. He realized what he had done was wrong and gave his heart to Christ. Then he did all he could to help Paul spread the gospel. Paul embraced him as a brother but said he needed to go back to his master, Philemon, and make things right. Paul wrote a letter to Philemon telling him about the wonderful change in Onesimus's life and asked him to forgive his slave and accept him as a son. Paul also promised to pay back whatever Onesimus owed Philemon and reminded him about the responsibility of Christians to forgive wrongs. When Philemon read the letter, he forgave Onesimus. Though not its intended result, Paul's letter to Philemon outlined Christian principles that revealed the un-Christian nature of slavery as a system.

Caesar's Household

As a general rule, the gospel spread faster among the lower class than among the upper class. However, even while Paul was a prisoner, the news of the gospel reached people of all classes, all the way to Caesar's palace. Members of the emperor's household became Christians and were living out their faith boldly, even though they were surrounded by many temptations.

Those who have given their hearts to Christ will always find opportunities to say a word for Jesus. They don't let circumstances keep them from sharing their faith. They are able to resist temptations and criticism because of the power they receive through prayer and studying Scripture. Meeting life's challenges with the Holy Spirit's power develops the Christian character.

Written From Rome

Early on in his ministry, God gave Paul a vision of heaven. The impressions made on him stayed with him throughout his life. The letters he wrote to the churches contained some of what he had seen, but he wasn't allowed to tell them everything. Even so, he encouraged them to be faithful to Jesus and reminded them that he was always praying for them.

Paul was especially concerned about the Colossian and Laodicean believers, who were surrounded by a heathen culture not conducive to Christian living. He urged them to be careful and not to be deceived by philosophy and false doctrines, which could destroy their faith. These same risks exist today in the teachings of Godless macroevolution, spiritualism, and even the pursuit of wealth and pleasure. Christians shouldn't sit back and relax, content that they know Christ. They must always be on guard against sinful temptations, including bad habits and hereditary tendencies.

Paul wrote a letter to the Philippian believers reminding them that God began a good work in them, and He would continue to grow and refine their faith until Jesus comes back. He reminded them that every believer must try their best to live according to God's commands, but that success in that mission is entirely dependent on God's help and surrendering to Him daily. Finally, Paul reminded the believers that, regardless of their circumstances, they must rejoice in their salvation and keep their eyes on Jesus. The same applies today.

At Liberty

When Paul arrived in Rome, the captain assigned to him was a just and honest man. He let Paul have visitors and do gospel work. This went on for about two years. Then the captain was replaced by a guard who wasn't good and kind.

Emperor Nero's second wife had converted to Judaism, and the Jews used her to gain an advantage to get at Paul. However, Emperor Nero, a terribly wicked and cruel leader, declared Paul innocent of the charges and ordered that he be set free. Soon after, Paul left Rome.

Paul was already gone when a terrible fire broke out in Rome and nearly half of the city was destroyed. The rumors implied that Nero himself had started the fire so he

> The true minister of God will not shun hardship or responsibility. From the Source that never fails those who sincerely seek for divine power, he draws strength that enables him to meet and overcome temptation, and to perform the duties that God places upon him. The nature of the grace that he receives, enlarges his capacity to know God and His Son.
> —*The Acts of the Apostles*, 501

could rebuild a bigger and better Rome. To divert the attention from himself, he made a show of helping the poor and needy and blamed the Christians for starting the fire. As a result, thousands of Christians were killed.

Paul immediately began using his freedom to visit and fortify churches in the faith. His aim was to strengthen members against false teachings and to build greater unity between the Greek and Eastern churches. Given his age and failing health, Paul felt that he was likely doing his last work for God, so he gave it all the zeal he could.

The Final Arrest
The Jews, angry that Paul had been released, decided to start a rumor that he was responsible for burning Rome. Their evil plan worked, and Paul was again arrested and returned to prison in Rome. Instead of a comfortable home, they locked him in a dungeon.

Only Luke was still there to help him. Paul had sent Titus to Dalmatia and Tychicus to Ephesus. Most of his friends and coworkers had left Rome or been killed during the persecution. A few others couldn't bear being associated with Rome's most hated prisoner. Being confined to a gloomy, damp, dungeon wasn't good for Paul. A warm-hearted member of the Ephesian church named Onesiphorus visited Paul, which gave him great comfort. Through Onesiphorus and Luke, Paul could still communicate with the churches.

In his last letter to Timothy, Paul said, "May the Lord bless Onesiphorus and his family because he was not ashamed to be my friend. He brought me comfort and refreshed my heart and soul." Although Paul was a brave man and had endured a lot of hardships in his life, he did appreciate receiving love and sympathy.

Paul Before Nero
Eventually, Paul was pulled out of the dungeon and taken to Nero's court for trial. Among the Greeks and Romans it was customary for a prisoner to have a lawyer, but no one was willing to stand for Paul. In his second and final letter to Timothy, Paul told him what happened. "No one stood with me; I had to defend myself. I pray that God will not hold those accountable who could have spoken on my behalf but didn't."

Paul began his defense by telling the emperor about the cause to which he had devoted his life. As he listened, he thought about the day of judgment, and he shook with fear, knowing he had done so much evil in his life. Here, God was giving the deplorable Nero one last chance to repent. He ignored the call, however, and the door closed again. With that, he ordered Paul back to the dungeon.

Not long afterward, a messenger came and told Nero that a huge enemy army was approaching the city. Nero ran from the city to hide a few miles away. When he heard the horsemen coming, rather than being captured and tortured by his enemies, Nero killed himself.

Paul's Last Letter

Back in the damp gloomy dungeon, Paul thought of Timothy at Ephesus and sent him a letter asking him to come visit soon. Paul knew that it would take months for Timothy to get the letter and then travel to Rome, and he was afraid he might be executed before then. He wrote, "To Timothy, my beloved son in Christ, grace, mercy, and peace, from God the Father and Jesus Christ our Lord. I thank God that I am able to write you. I still pray for you day and night."

Throughout his years of service, Paul had never wavered in his allegiance to Christ and the Scriptures. In his letter to Timothy, he urged him to be faithful to Christ and the Scriptures and stay away from false teachings and theological arguments.

Timothy had a mild and warm personality, and Paul worried that he might not be forceful in calling out sin. As a soldier of Christ, he must put on the spiritual armor of truth, take the shield of faith, wear the helmet of salvation, and carry with him the sword of the Holy Spirit, which is the Word of God.

Young pastors should follow the example of ministers who, like Paul, are totally committed to Jesus and doing His work. They should be getting ready to take the place of older ministers and to carry on the work they had done. Paul concludes his letter to Timothy by telling him not to hesitate to come see him in spite of the needs of the churches because he has already asked Tychicus to go take Timothy's place.

> The love of Christ is not a fitful feeling, but a living principle, which is to be made manifest as an abiding power in the heart. If the character and deportment of the shepherd is an exemplification of the truth he advocates, the Lord will set the seal of His approval to the work. The shepherd and the flock will become one, united by their common hope in Christ.
> —*The Acts of the Apostles*, 516

Condemned to Die

During Paul's trial before Nero, the emperor had been so impressed by what Paul had said that he hesitated to have him killed and, instead, sent him back to the dungeon. Eventually, all of this was brushed aside, and Nero ordered him to be executed. Because it was illegal to torture Roman citizens, Paul was to be beheaded. A few of his friends were allowed to be there. Like Jesus, Paul forgave his executioners because they were just doing what they were told to do.

As Paul stood at the place of execution, he didn't look at the large sword of the executioner, but looked up into the blue sky and focused on heaven, the throne of God, and the resurrection. He said to himself, "It's my time to die, and I am ready. I have fought a good fight and finished what God asked me to do. I have kept the faith, and, like all believers, God has a crown of righteousness ready with my name on it."

A Faithful Under-Shepherd

Acts doesn't say much about the apostle Peter's work. After Peter denied Christ and repented, Jesus told Peter to, "Feed My sheep." Throughout his ministry, that's what Peter did. After the outpouring of the Holy Spirit on the day of Pentecost, Peter worked even harder and shared the gospel with both Jews and Gentiles. Later in his ministry, he wrote letters to the churches to strengthen their faith and urged them to look forward to the coming of Christ.

> Our Saviour is always ready to hear and answer the prayer of the contrite heart, and grace and peace are multiplied to His faithful ones. Gladly He grants them the blessings they need in their struggle against the evils that beset them.
> —*The Acts of the Apostles*, 532

Peter encouraged the believers not to waste mental and physical energies on the things of this world. They should not forget that Jesus came and gave His life for us so that we might have eternal life. Because of this, we should show our love for what He has done for us by studying His Word and obeying Him. Without Him, we would be nothing more than grass that sprouts, grows, dies, and disintegrates.

Peter also said that we should be good citizens and obey the government as long as it doesn't go against what Jesus said. We should be servants of God, respect people, love our fellow church members, and be grateful for the gospel. Believers should dress modestly and not spend money on fancy accessories to attract attention to ourselves. Instead, we should wear a gentle, Christlike spirit and use our resources and talents to advance the gospel.

Then Peter reminded the church elders of their responsibilities as undershepherds of God. They are to feed the people spiritual food and do so willingly, not as masters but as servants. They should not focus only on preaching but should also spend time with people in their homes and pray for them and their families. In addition, ministers should set an example for others by caring for the poor and the needy.

Steadfast Unto the End

In his second letter, Peter teaches believers how to build their Christian character. He stresses that they should begin with faith, then, by the power of the Holy Spirit, add virtue, knowledge, temperance, patience, kindness, and love that serves others. These are like steps on a staircase, which we take one at a time; as we get closer and closer to Christ, we become more and more like Him.

On our own, we don't have the strength to climb the staircase. Every day, we need to pray, asking Jesus to help us. Every day, Jesus will give us the grace and strength we need to get through. Peter used his own vast experience to encourage members to grow in grace and deepen their relationship with Christ.

Peter realized that one day he would have to give his life for Christ. He told the members that he would not always be with them and spent his time teaching them how to mature in the faith without him. He knew that false teachers would try to deceive people by mixing truth with error. Believers needed to be careful and hold on to the truth as taught in Scripture.

Like Paul, Peter closed his ministry in Rome where Nero arrested him and sentenced him to death. These two veteran apostles worked to spread the gospel for many years, although they never worked together. Unlike Paul, who was a Roman citizen, Peter was a foreigner. Because of this, Peter was beaten, scourged, and condemned to die by crucifixion. He remembered that Christ had said, "Peter, while you are young, you can go wherever you want to go. But when you get old, they will arrest you, put you in prison, nail you to a cross, and place it where you would never want to be placed." Peter didn't feel worthy to die in the same way Jesus did, so he asked his executioners to crucify him upside down. They agreed, and that's how Peter died.

> It is no part of Christ's mission to compel men to receive Him. It is Satan, and men actuated by his spirit, who seek to compel the conscience.
> —*The Acts of the Apostles*, 541

John the Beloved

The disciple John loved Jesus very much, more than any other disciple, and Jesus responded to his love the same way. When the disciples heard that Jesus had been resurrected, he and Peter ran to the tomb to see for themselves, and John was so excited that he outran Peter.

John did not naturally have such a loving character. He and his brother James were prideful and aggressive. They even wanted to force people to accept Jesus as the promised Messiah. Jesus reprimanded the two brothers for their uncontrolled tempers. He explained that only love will attract true believers; coercion doesn't work.

The longer these brothers were with Christ, the more they changed. They began to show the same love for people that Jesus had. More than anything, John wanted to be like Jesus. He fully placed himself in the Savior's grace, and people could see the change in his life.

> Jesus does not present to His followers the hope of attaining earthly glory and riches, of living a life free from trial. Instead He calls upon them to follow Him in the path of self-denial and reproach.
> —*The Acts of the Apostles*, 576

A Faithful Witness

After Jesus returned to heaven and the Holy Spirit was poured out on the disciples, John became a powerful, earnest preacher, speaking to the people in simple, beautifully phrased words. The believers responded, loved Jesus more, and nurtured each other.

Gradually, though, things began to change. The believers started complaining and criticizing each other. They put more emphasis on ceremonies and appearances and took their eyes off Jesus. John wrote a letter to the churches saying, "Let us love one another, because true love comes from God, which we have seen when God gave His Son to die for us. He requires that we love one another. If you hate another believer, you are not in Christ."

When members lose their love for Jesus and look for faults in each other, it is a bigger danger to the church than outside influences. Others will say, "Look at these people, they claim that Christ is Love, but they can't even get along with each other." Love for Jesus and love for one another is a wonderful gift that God can give us. We can't do it ourselves. We need to give our lives to Jesus every day because only He can give us a heart of love. If salvation depended on us and our efforts, we could never be saved. We can't hold on to Jesus, He must hold on to us. By placing our hands in the hands of Jesus, He will hold on to us and never let go unless we choose to pull away.

Some who claim to be Christians believe that they don't have to keep all of God's commandments. Others believe that keeping the commandments is enough, even though they don't really believe in Jesus or have a relationship with Him. Some even believed that Jesus was nothing more than a good man. John also warned that love does not excuse continuing in sin. John wrote, "If we confess our sins, God is willing to forgive us our sins, and cleanse us from all unrighteousness."

Transformed by Grace

The apostle John was a true example of a changed life. What Jesus taught him, he took to heart, and the love of Jesus became more and more evident in his life. The contrast between John and Judas is stark. John fought against his sinful inclinations, while Judas nurtured them.

A relationship with Jesus is not just based on one decision, but rather a lifetime of daily, hourly commitment. Like any human relationship, such as marriage, commitment to Christ must be cultivated. As long as Satan is at work, he will tempt us to go our own way and ignore what we know is right.

One way to strengthen our relationship with Jesus is through prayer. We need to pray for the Holy Spirit to help us to love Jesus and to become more and more like Him. We need to ask for faith to believe and for courage in spiritual things. A quiet place of prayer early in the morning is an ideal way to start the day.

Some people don't grow spiritually because they interpret the Scriptures to suit themselves so they can do what they want to do. Instead, we need to surrender our heart, our will, and our intellect to Jesus, recognizing that we belong to Him because He gave His life for us.

Patmos

During the first fifty years of the church, opposition and persecution were always an issue. Even so, the apostles steadfastly maintained their faith. John lived a long time and saw many things happen in his life, including the destruction of Jerusalem and the temple by the Romans years after Jesus had ascended.

Because of John' faithfulness to Christ and his influence with the people, the Jews were determined to get rid of him. They had him arrested and taken to Rome to stand trial. He was accused of all kinds of things, none of which were true, and Emperor Domitian sentenced him to death by being thrown into a pool of boiling oil. However, as He had with the three Hebrews in the fiery furnace generations before, Jesus protected John, and he wasn't hurt. The same men who threw him into the oil pulled him back out, and Domitian was so angry that he sentenced John to life in prison on the barren, rocky island of Patmos, where the government exiled criminals.

There John enjoyed the quiet of nature and intimate fellowship with the heavenly host. Jesus unfolded the future of mankind to John, and from those scenes, John wrote

> The opening labors of the Christian church were attended by hardship and bitter grief. In their work the disciples constantly encountered privation, calumny, and persecution; but they counted not their lives dear unto themselves and rejoiced that they were called to suffer for Christ. Irresolution, indecision, weakness of purpose, found no place in their efforts.
>
> —*The Acts of the Apostles*, 595

the book of Revelation. When faithful believers age and no longer have the physical strength to work actively for God, He still uses them to share wisdom, testimony, and council to others. Young people should look at the commitment of old people like John and be inspired to be faithful to the Lord.

The Revelation

In the Book of Revelation, the church of Ephesus symbolizes the early Christian church. Jesus said about Ephesus, "I know your patience and labor of love, and that you can't stand those who say they are Christians when they are not. But you have stood firm and not given up." The members in Ephesus loved Jesus and did what they could for Him and others. They took the gospel to all the inhabited parts of the earth, and many people were converted.

Sadly, as time passed the believers' zeal grew weaker and some even forgot about the gospel. The early adopters were getting old and dying off, false doctrines crept in, and many younger members left the church. It was during this time that John was imprisoned on Patmos.

One Sabbath, John sought a quiet place among the cliffs and rocks on the island where he could be alone and worship the Lord. Suddenly, he heard a voice behind him say, "I am the Alpha and the Omega, the first and the last." He turned to see who was talking to him and saw Jesus. He didn't look as He had when He was on the earth. Instead, He was glorified with a brightness as powerful as the sun. When John saw Jesus, he fell at His feet as if he were dead. Jesus gently rested His hand on John and said, "Don't be afraid. Listen to what I have to say." Then Jesus gave John a vision and told him to write down what he saw. Scene after scene unfolded and John saw the history of the world from the beginning to the end of time and all the way into heaven. These visions were designed to guide and comfort the churches from John's day until the end of time.

Emperor Domitian was assassinated in AD 96. His replacement, Emperor Nerva, was said to have released all Domitian's Patmos prisoners, and that John returned to Ephesus to live out the rest of his life. There he was able to write his books, including what he saw in vision, known as the book of Revelation. John wrote, "Blessed is he who reads the words of this prophecy. But if anyone adds something to what is written or twists the words, God will take his name out of the Book of Life." The book of Daniel in the Old Testament is a companion book to the book of Revelation in the New Testament; together they give a united prophecy and its fulfillment.

In vision, John saw seven periods of history of the church, which are called the seven churches. John saw Jesus walking among these seven churches throughout history. Sometimes they had to be encouraged and sometimes disciplined, but no matter what, Christ always loved the church. His love and tenderness was blended with justice, always upholding what was right.

God's people will always be a small percentage of the world's population. The numbers don't matter so much because God's presence makes it a safe place.

One of the most hopeful scenes for the Christian is John's vision of the earth made new and the Holy City, New Jerusalem, coming down from heaven to the earth as a beautiful bride dressed for a wedding. There, God's people will join with the angels to sing the praises of Jesus forever and ever.

The Church Triumphant
John, under the direction of the Holy Spirit, wrote about the future of the church. The church is built on the foundation of Scripture with Jesus Christ as the cornerstone, and it will stand forever. John was the only original disciple who didn't die a violent, martyr's death. He was probably nearing one hundred years old when he died. Centuries of persecution followed and many Christians were killed, but many more took their places, and the church continued to grow.

The apostles and early believers laid the foundation for the church, which is God's spiritual temple. As Christians share the gospel with people around the world, the church will continue to grow. John wrote, "I saw a great multitude which no man could number from all nations, races, languages and people dressed in white robes standing before God saying, 'Salvation comes from God on His throne and from the Lamb forever and ever!' "

One day God will wipe away the tears from our eyes, and there will be no more death, sorrow, crying, or pain, because sin will be no more.

THE
GREAT WAR

Insights From
The Great Controversy

The Destruction of Jerusalem
When Jesus was here carrying out His ministry, one day He looked down from the top of the Mount of Olives near Jerusalem. Everything looked peaceful. As the sun set, its rays flooded the city and made the temple sparkle like fresh snow. People were coming to Jerusalem to celebrate the Passover, so the streets were flooded with people. As He made His way down the mountain and approached the city, He was overcome with sorrow and began to cry. This is where He would be crucified, die, and be buried. He didn't cry because of what would happen to Him but because of what would happen to the city and its people. The Father had sent His Son to save them, but they had turned against Him. When Jews arrested Jesus and turned Him over to Pilate to be crucified, God's special blessings on Israel ended.

Jesus saw in Jerusalem a symbol of the world, and the brokenness of the human race made Him cry bitter tears. The Majesty of Heaven in tears? What a terrible sight! All heaven was shocked when they saw the Son of God in tears. It was clear how God and His Son are really hurt when people sin. Had the disciples fully understood what lay ahead after Jesus' crucifixion—the invasion of Jerusalem by the Romans and the destruction of the temple—they would have been overwhelmed with horror.

How thankful and grateful we should be for the protection we have against Satan. It is the power of God and His Son that keeps us from being controlled by him. What would happen to us if Satan had full control? Time after time, Christ gave the Jews opportunities to accept Him. Even as the Roman armies gathered at Jerusalem's gate, God held the invading forces so the Christian's could escape the city. Any Jews who would could join them. At the end of time, God's protection will be withdrawn from those who don't obey Him, and there will be no turning back for those who have chosen to walk away from the Lord of Life.

> God does not stand toward the sinner as an executioner of the sentence against transgression; but He leaves the rejectors of His mercy to themselves, to reap that which they have sown. Every ray of light rejected, every warning despised or unheeded, every passion indulged, every transgression of the law of God, is a seed sown which yields its unfailing harvest. The Spirit of God, persistently resisted, is at last withdrawn from the sinner, and then there is left no power to control the evil passions of the soul, and no protection from the malice and enmity of Satan.
> —*The Great Controversy*, 36

Persecution in the First Century

When Jesus talked to the disciples about the fall of Jerusalem, He also told them about what would happen to them and His followers after He left. The Romans were concerned about the growing number of Christians and decided to do something about it.

Persecution began, and believers were stripped of their possessions and driven from their homes. They were laughed at, arrested, beaten, and thrown into prison. Others were thrown to wild beasts in the large stadiums of Rome as multitudes watched, enjoying the show. Jews and Romans accused Christians of causing crime everywhere and of bringing down the anger of the gods, causing earthquakes and disasters.

Many believers were arrested and burned at the stake, but as the flames leaped around them, their songs of triumph ascended to heaven. Others hid in the wilderness, in the mountains, in caves, or in retreats tunneled into the hills. This is where many of them lived and where they had to bury their dead. Through it all, the believers kept their faith. In spite of the persecution, many more gave their hearts to Christ, and the number of Christians grew.

Eventually, Satan realized he could not stop the church by physical threat or violence, so he changed his tactic. Instead of killing believers, he decided to work from inside the church itself. With this, the era of persecution stopped. Instead, Satan brought pagans into the church who accepted part of the Christian faith but not all of it. This was not a good time for the church. Many believers compromised their faith to save their lives. The church became corrupted with all kinds of unchristian practices, including worshiping the statues of Jesus, Mary, and the apostles.

An Era of Spiritual Darkness

More and more heathen practices and paganism found their way into the Christian church. Pomp and pageantry replaced simple faith. This gradually led to the development of the Roman Catholic Church. Its leader was called Lord God the Pope and deemed infallible. It seems the believers forgot that Jesus said, "You must worship the Lord your God only." The teachings of the pope were not in harmony with Scripture, and in order to hide that fact and to keep people ignorant of God's teachings, for hundreds of years the church forbid owning, reading, or distributing the Bible.

This period of spiritual darkness allowed the Catholic Church's doctrines to gain a foothold. Idol worship mixed with Bible figures, and people began worshiping images of Christian figures, such as the early apostles, rather than the Lord of those apostles. The Church removed the second Commandment about not worshiping images, then split the tenth to make it look like nothing had changed. Then, Satan caused the church to repurpose the heathen "day of the sun" as a day to celebrate Christ's resurrection. Because the Jews had made the Sabbath a burdensome day, and Christians were eager to separate themselves from the Jews, Sunday gradually replaced God's Sabbath under the emperor Constantine's direction.

The Roman Catholic Church continued to spread around the world, and its membership became larger than the Christian church. With its headquarters in Rome, the church eventually became a small independent country with its own government and ambassadors. In the sixth century, the Catholic church began 1,260 years of terrible oppression against Christians as prophecy had foretold in Daniel 7 and Revelation 13. During this period, known as the Dark Ages, the church persecuted those who refused to accept its teachings and held on to the Christian faith as taught in Scripture. As a result, thousands were persecuted and killed for their faith.

As the power and abuses of the church grew, so did their doctrinal errors. One of these damaging doctrines was the concept of purgatory. The church taught that those who died and were not qualified to go directly to heaven had to go first to purgatory—a place where tormenting fire would cleanse the soul from impurity to qualify it for heaven. Others included the doctrine of indulgences, the blasphemous claim that the priests could create Jesus' actual body and blood during the communion service, and finally the Inquisition.

The Waldenses

In spite of the papacy's persecution, the truth could not be stopped. All through the years there were men and women who held on to Christ and the Bible, including the Sabbath, as the rule of faith. The names of those faithful people are written in the books of heaven.

The true faith spread to England and from there to Scotland and Ireland. The papacy demanded, under great penalty, that these believers declare their allegiance to the Roman Catholic Church. These were no idle threats. War, fighting, intrigue, and deception prevailed until the churches in England were destroyed or its members submitted to the pope.

In lands beyond the control of Rome, such as Africa and Asia, there were Christians who remained totally free from the influence the papacy. In Europe, the Waldenses committed themselves to the Scriptures and resisted the teachings of the papacy. They refused to acknowledge the pope as the head of the church or give in to the authority of the Catholic Church. They held on to the freedom to worship God according to the dictates of conscience, which included the right to keep the Bible Sabbath.

The Waldenses had a translation of the Bible that they could read. They memorized large portions of the Bible and taught their children to do the same just in case their Bibles were taken away from them. In this way, they could share the truths of the Bible with others wherever they went without carrying their Bibles with them. They lived in the mountains and farmed every piece of land they could. Sometimes they hid in caves and, by the light of torches, wrote out portions of Scriptures to give to others.

The Waldenses schooled their children at home and taught them from early ages to obey, work hard, and think with wisdom. They prepared their young people to attend the universities in France and Italy. These young men and women took portions of Scripture with them, hiding them however they could and shared them with those who expressed an interest. Some university students were converted as they saw the difference between the teachings of the Catholic Church and what the Bible said.

The young men among the Waldenses who wanted to be pastors were required to take the necessary training and then serve for three years in a mission field before taking charge of a church back home. They usually went out in pairs or teamed with an experienced mentor. When they returned home, they eagerly shared their experience with excitement, joy, humility, and gratitude.

The Waldenses' determination to be faithful to the Scriptures offended the papacy. The church sent men to destroy their crops and burn down their homes. When they fled, they were hunted like animals. The moral characters of these peaceful, happy people were above reproach. Their only offense was that they did not worship according to the dictates of the Catholic Church. For this, they were condemned as heretics.

John Wycliffe

Before Luther and the Reformation, there were very few Bibles available to the people because the Scriptures had been translated into Latin, which most common people couldn't read. Yet God was watching over His Word and would not let it be totally destroyed. Throughout Europe, people were searching for the truth as for some hidden treasure. When they did find Bibles they could read and understand, they studied with intense interest and were willing to accept the truth no matter what the cost.

John Wycliffe was an English scholar known for his piety and preaching talents. In college, he started studying the Bible and found there answers to many of life's questions. He began to see the difference between what the Bible said and what the Roman Catholic Church was teaching. For many years, students at the universities had been deceived by the teachings of the priests and friars, so many parents refused to send their children there, which created a void of educated citizens.

Wycliffe also continued to uphold the right of England to govern itself without interference from Rome or the pope. Because the king respected him, he was appointed as England's royal ambassador. While in the Netherlands, he spent a couple of years with representatives of the pope and clergy from other countries and learned what was happening behind the scenes. When he returned to England, he determined to preach with greater zeal than ever before.

The pope began to feel threatened by Wycliffe's messages, and he sent letters to the king of England and to the university where Wycliffe taught, demanding that action be taken against him. If necessary, he should be arrested and thrown into prison or burned at the stake. God intervened to save him. The reigning pope died and two

> The effort to grasp the great truths of revelation imparts freshness and vigor to all the faculties. It expands the mind, sharpens the perceptions, and ripens the judgment. The study of the Bible will ennoble every thought, feeling, and aspiration as no other study can. It gives stability of purpose, patience, courage, and fortitude; it refines the character and sanctifies the soul. An earnest, reverent study of the Scriptures, bringing the mind of the student in direct contact with the infinite mind, would give to the world men of stronger and more active intellect, as well as of nobler principle, than has ever resulted from the ablest training that human philosophy affords.
>
> —*The Great Controversy*, 94

enemy popes were elected in his place. Their fight against each other weakened the Catholic Church's position and redirected its leaders away from Wycliffe.

As a professor at the University of Oxford, Wycliffe continued to preach the Word of God. Soon the students began calling him "The Gospel Doctor." Wycliffe felt called to translate the Bible into English so that its messages of truth would be accessible to everyone. Unexpectedly, he got sick and had to stop teaching and preaching. It looked like he would die. Thinking the teacher would recant his words condemning them, the friars came to visit him. Wycliffe asked his attendant to help him sit up in bed so he could speak to them. "I am not going to die from this sickness. I will get better, and I will continue to preach against the false teachings of the Catholic Church." When the priests who were there heard this, they left in shock.

Wycliffe did recover, and he used his time to work on translating the Bible into English. Printing presses had not yet been invented, so copies had to be written by hand. The demand was so great that the copyists couldn't keep up. The preachers Wycliffe had trained circulated the Bibles that were available, and soon half of the people in England became Protestant Christians.

Wycliffe's enemies determined as never before to silence him. Twice times he was called to stand trial, and each time he successfully defended himself and was let go. When he was brought to court a third time, he said, "Who do you think you're dealing with? An old man standing at the edge of a grave? No! Truth is stronger than death and will overcome all wickedness." Then he turned and walked out of the courtroom, and no one tried to stop him.

Eventually he was called to appear in the court before Pope Urban VI. However, his health was failing and he was unable to make the trip, so he sent a letter in his place. Not long after, Wycliffe was preparing to serve communion at his church, and he had a stroke and soon died. Wycliffe's work continued to influence Christianity for generations upon generations. The young men he trained preached the truth with even greater zeal. Even some nobles, including the king's wife, were converted. This led to great persecution for believers in England, and many were martyred.

Huss and Jerome

In Bohemia, Christians had a copy of the Bible in their language, and they worshiped in public. This upset the pope, who declared that God prefers to be worshiped in unknown tongues and decreed that the Bible should be off-limits. Many of the Waldenses and Albigenses had come to Bohemia (now known as the Czech Republic) from France and Italy, and they worked secretly for centuries to preserve the truth. They were persecuted heavily.

When John Huss was still young, his father died. His mother taught him to love God. John attended his local school and then went to the university in Prague. His mother decided to go with him. As they got near the city, she knelt beside her son and prayed, asking God to be with him and bless his life. Little did she realize how God would answer that prayer.

At the university, John was an excellent student and his gentle, winning personality made everyone love him. After completing college, he entered the priesthood and soon became a professor and then an administrator of the university. He was the pride of his country and respected everywhere. Eventually, he was assigned as the preacher at the Bethlehem Chapel in Prague.

A young friend of Huss named Jerome, also a citizen of Prague, visited England and brought back with him a copy of Wycliffe's writings. This material helped Huss understand the gospel more clearly. It also exposed the true nature of the Catholic Church. Huss shared these insights with his students, and when they went back home to Germany, they shared the truth with their families and friends. And the truth spread.

Word about this reached Rome and the pope asked Huss to come explain himself. The king and queen of Bohemia asked the pope to allow Huss to stay in Prague and communicate by proxy. The pope refused. Instead, he had a trial without Huss present, then condemned both Huss and the whole city of Prague. By this verdict, he cut the city off from the church. No one could marry in the church or be buried in church cemeteries. These ceremonies held significant spiritual consequences in the Roman Catholic religion, which caused many to reject Huss. Yet he did not stop preaching against the abuses of power within the Roman Catholic Church. To let the situation in Prague cool off, Huss went to share the truth in surrounding countries. Eventually, he returned home to the Bethlehem Chapel, and Jerome joined him in working for reform.

The Roman Church's three rival popes and Huss were called to a meeting in Constance. Huss knew his life was in danger, so as he left Prague, he asked his friends to pray for him. When he got there, he was arrested and thrown into a damp and dirty prison, even though the emperor had given him an order of protection.

Finally, Huss was brought before the council, and when he refused to recant his testimony, they condemned him to death by being burned at the stake. As he stood, stripped of his priestly robes and tied to the stake with the fire burning his body, Huss began singing, "Jesus, have mercy on me." He continued singing until his voice was silenced by death. When his body was totally consumed, they gathered his ashes and dumped them into the river that flowed into the sea. His ashes, like the truths he had preached, were carried to the world.

Huss's friend Jerome was also soon arrested and imprisoned and tortured in a dungeon. Months later, the council gave him the choice to give up his faith or die at the stake. He decided to say that he, Wycliffe, and Huss had been wrong and to acknowledge the Catholic Church's infallibility to avoid being burned alive. Back in prison, this decision tormented his soul, and after many more months of imprisonment, he took back his testimony and spoke in favor of Wycliffe, Huss, and the truth. With this, he was condemned to die at the stake like his friend, and, like Huss, Jerome burned with a song in his heart and a prayer on his lips.

The death of these two holy men made their message spread even faster. The pope and the Roman emperor tried hard to wipe them out, sending army after army to exterminate the Hussites. Each time, the Roman forces were sharply defeated, sometimes by invisible supernatural means. Eventually, Bohemia formed a treaty with Rome, though Rome misapplied its policies and the true believers were again subjected to severe persecution.

> The spirit of the world is no more in harmony with the spirit of Christ today than in earlier times, and those who preach the word of God in its purity will be received with no greater favor now than then. The forms of opposition to the truth may change, the enmity may be less open because it is more subtle; but the same antagonism still exists and will be manifested to the end of time.
> —*The Great Controversy*, 144

Luther's Separation From Rome

In Germany, the time had finally come for Martin Luther to lead people to the truth in Scripture, which began the Reformation. He grew up in a humble German home in poverty. His father was a miner and worked very hard so his son could go to school and become a lawyer. Instead, Luther decided to become a priest, which disappointed his father.

His parents loved God and did all they could to train their children properly and prayed for them every day. At school, Luther was treated harshly and even received beatings. Sometimes he was so hungry that he went from door to door singing and begging for food.

At eighteen, Luther went to the University of Erfurt. Things were better there. His parents were more financially stable, so they helped him. He also had friends who uplifted his spirits. His life of self-discipline and dependence on God helped him become an excellent student and prepared him for future challenges. Every day he prayed that God would help him, which He did. Luther would often say, "Prayer is the better half of study."

One day while examining books in the university library, he discovered a Latin Bible. He didn't know such a thing existed, and as he turned the pages and read some of it, his passion for Christ was kindled. It was this desire to have a closer walk with God that then led him to join a monastery.

In the monastery, he had to do the lowest chores and still had to go from house to house begging for food. In every spare moment, he studied the Bible, even depriving himself of time to eat and sleep. Above all his other studies, Luther loved studying the Bible. The monastery had a Bible chained to the wall where he would often go to read. The more he read, the more he felt like a dirty sinner, and he threw himself into earning forgiveness.

Staupitz, a God-fearing man, helped Luther understand the Scriptures more deeply. He encouraged him to look away from himself and the eternal punishment that awaits sinners and to turn to Jesus as his Savior. When Luther did this, he finally experienced peace.

Then Luther was ordained a priest and was called from the monastery to be a professor at the University of Wittenberg. There he studied the Scriptures in their original languages and began lecturing from the Bible.

Luther decided to visit Rome, journeying there on foot. Germany is a long way from Rome, but he started and stayed overnight at different monasteries along the way. When he got to Italy, he was amazed at how well the monks lived. He saw their fancy apartments, the ornate robes they were wearing, and the abundance of food on their tables. He contrasted all this with his own life of self-denial and hardship when he was in the monastery at home.

When Luther finally saw Rome in the distance with the seven hills surrounding the city, he fell to the ground, overcome with emotion for the home of the church he loved. However, as he visited the churches, monasteries, and other places in the city, he was shocked at the indecent jokes and sinfulness of the priests, monks, and citizens alike.

There was a staircase in the city that was said to be the stairs on which Jesus descended as He left Pilate's judgment hall to be crucified. The Church claimed it had been miraculously transported to Rome from Jerusalem. The pope promised special forgiveness and blessings to anyone who climbed this staircase on his knees. One day, Luther decided to do this. Part way up, he heard a loud voice say, "Believers live life by faith and not by their own works!" He stopped, stood up, and left. His view of the Roman Catholic Church would never be the same after that.

When he got back to the University of Wittenberg, Luther received his Doctor of Divinity degree. He could now devote all his time to Bible study. He taught and preached that people should embrace only doctrines supported by Scripture, which went against everything the papal system taught.

About this time, a church official named Tetzel came into town selling certificates of forgiveness of sins, known as indulgences. Luther was still a papist and a priest, and when the people came to him with their certificates for absolution, he refused to accept them. He told the people they needed to repent and change their lives, and that forgiveness cannot be bought with money. Some of the people took their certificates back to Tetzel and demanded their money back. In turn, he called them heretics and said that he had received orders from Rome to kill all heretics.

Luther decided to come out boldly on behalf of the truth. He began preaching passionately about repentance, forgiveness, and God's grace. The day before the festival of All Saints, when people would flock to the castle church for confession, Luther nailed a written protest against the practice of buying forgiveness on the church door for everyone to read. It contained ninety-five reason why indulgences were, in fact, a sinful extortion crafted by the church and not by God. In just a few days, Luther's protest had spread by word of mouth all over Germany and beyond. As he thought about what he had done, one man against Rome, he became overwhelmed. Many who had pledged their support disappeared in their cowardice.

The pope declared Luther a heretic and ordered him to come to Rome to defend himself against a charge of heresy. Luther's friends knew what would happen to him if he went to Rome, so they asked that the trial be held in Germany. The pope agreed to send a cardinal to Augsburg as his representative, though his instruction was to capture and execute Luther. However, Luther received a protection order from the emperor.

The cardinal met with Luther several times. He demanded that Luther renounce his teachings. The Reformer defended what he preached with Scripture while the pope's representative defended the Church by Catholic traditions. Luther saw that he was not getting anywhere with the representative, so Luther got permission to put his defense in writing. At their next meeting, Luther again gave a testimony backed by the Bible. When the pope's representative saw that he had failed to accomplish what he was sent to do, he became so angry that he began hurling threats and insults at Luther. Before dawn the next morning, Luther and his friends left the city to return to Wittenberg.

Frederick, the governor of Saxony, secretly rejoiced over Luther's success and saw a new interest in the Scriptures sweep over Germany. More students eager to learn from Luther came to the University of Wittenberg. From here, the truth spread to Switzerland, Holland, France, Spain, Belgium, Italy, and England.

Luther worried that if the Scriptures did not become primary among the subjects taught at the universities, the schools and their students would eventually become corrupt. This initiated a powerful reform on the universities in the country, but it made the pope and the Catholic Church leaders so angry that Luther and all his followers were given sixty days to change their minds or they would be cut off from the church. This tactic had worked over the centuries to bring other rulers and their countries into line.

When Luther received a copy of the pope's letter, he called together students, professors, and citizens of all ranks to burn the letter in their presence. He said, "They have burned my books, so I will burn this letter." After this, Luther decided to separate himself completely from the Catholic Church because its teachings did not follow Scripture. The pope then sent another letter excommunicating the Reformer and all who believed what he taught.

Luther Before the Diet

A new emperor, Charles V, came to the throne of Germany. Representatives from the pope came to congratulate him and to verify that he would take a stand against Luther and the Reformation. However, the governor of Saxony asked him not to agree to that until unbiased judges had heard Luther's case. He decided to evaluate Luther's teachings at the upcoming national council, and Luther agreed to go even though his health was failing.

The pope's representative who had failed to apprehend Luther at Augsburg appeared before the council and opened Rome's case against Luther. Because the Reformer wasn't yet there, the cardinal's eloquent speech swayed the council members. However, one of them, Duke George of Saxony, who didn't care much for Luther, stood up and spoke passionately against the abuses of the papal system. At that point, the council demanded that the emperor set in motion reforms for the broken system, and they insisted that Luther speak.

Together with three of his friends, Luther made his way to the assembly meeting—called a *diet*—at Worms, Germany. In spite of many warnings about his safety, he went on. When he got to the gates of the city, a huge crowd welcomed him.

> We shall not be approved of God in looking to the example of our fathers to determine our duty instead of searching the word of truth for ourselves. Our responsibility is greater than was that of our ancestors. We are accountable for the light which they received, and which was handed down as an inheritance for us, and we are accountable also for the additional light which is now shining upon us from the word of God.—*The Great Controversy*, 164

The next day, an officer brought Luther to the council. As he was about to come in, an old general, a hero of many battles, said to him, "You are now going to fight for truth, greater than I and my men have fought in battle. Don't be afraid; God is with you."

Luther went in and stood before the emperor on his throne, surrounded by the most honored of the empire. Luther was visibly nervous at the thought of having to speak before such an important assembly with thousands of spectators. One of the princes noticed this and whispered to him, "Don't be scared; stand for the truth."

An officer of the court pointed to Luther's books and asked him two questions: Did he admit that these books were his, and would he be willing to change his mind about what he said. Luther agreed that the books were his, but needed more time to think about the second question. His response convinced the court that he was a reasonable man, and they asked him to return the next day with his answer.

That evening in his room, Luther prayed and wept, overcome with his own unworthiness for the task ahead. He wrestled all night with God, begging Him to help him defend the truth. He placed his left hand on his Bible, raised his right hand to heaven, and took an oath to remain faithful to Scripture. The next day, when he returned to the council, he appeared calm and confident as he stood before the emperor.

He said, "Most honored emperor and princes, I stand before you today to answer the question you asked me yesterday. All my books are not about the same thing. In some, I talk about faith and good works, in others about the abuses of the papacy, and in others about wicked people." Luther had spoken in German, and the council asked him to repeat everything he said in Latin.

The spokesman for the assembly was not satisfied with Luther's answer and demanded that he say whether or not he had changed his mind about the Catholic Church. Luther said, "Since I am required to answer in plain and simple language, let me say that I will not submit my faith to the Catholic Church. My conscience has been captured by the Word of God. I cannot and will not change. Here I stand! God help me!" The assembly was surprised at such a firm answer, and the emperor, moved with admiration, said, "This monk speaks with a strong heart and unshaken courage." Many of the German princes there were proud of Luther.

The council and many of its members continued to urge Luther to take back the things he'd said against the Roman Catholic Church, the pope, and the abuses within

> So in the days of the Great Reformation. The leading Reformers were men from humble life—men who were most free of any of their time from pride of rank and from the influence of bigotry and priestcraft. It is God's plan to employ humble instruments to accomplish great results. Then the glory will not be given to men, but to Him who works through them to will and to do of His own good pleasure.
> —*The Great Controversy*, 171

the papal system. He continued to refuse, citing the dangers of denying Scripture. He said, "The gospel cannot be compromised. My life may be in the hands of men, but my faith is in the hand of God."

The Roman cardinal finally convinced the young emperor to let Luther's conviction as a heretic stand. Though he promised to allow Luther safe passage back home, he changed his mind and commanded that he was to be arrested. In addition, those who supported him were also to be arrested and all their possessions taken away. To protect Luther, Frederick, the governor of Saxony, had Luther arrested on his way home and taken to a safe place that even he didn't know. Luther was safe in the remote mountain castle of Wartburg. He took advantage of the peace and quiet there to write day and night. He wrote many tracts and translated the Bible into German.

The Swiss Reformer

In Switzerland, Ulric Zwingli was the one promoting commitment to Scripture. He was born in the Alps and was about the same age as Luther. As he was growing up, his grandmother told him stories from the Bible. He was very bright, and his father wanted him to continue his education, so at the age of thirteen, they sent him to one of the well-known schools in Bern. While there, the monks tried to persuade him to join one of the monasteries, believing the appeal of a popular young scholar would increase their revenue. His father got word about the scheming monks' intentions and told Ulric to come home without delay. He obeyed and shortly transferred to a school in Basel.

Zwingli's ancient languages professor, Wittembach, had studied Scripture and shared his insights with his students. The truth about Jesus set the stage for Zwingli's future. After graduating, he became a priest. His first church was not far from his beautiful home valley. He continued studying the Scriptures and praying that the Holy Spirit would help him to understand what it said. The doctrines he preached did not come from Luther but from his own research and study.

Zwingli then became a pastor at the convent in Einsiedeln. While he moved in, he saw a statue of the Virgin Mary that was believed to have the power to work miracles and forgive sins. People came there from all over, including other countries, to pray to the statue. Zwingli told them that God is everywhere and that Christ died on the cross and paid for their sins, so their long pilgrimages and acts of sorrow for sin were not necessary. Some of these pilgrims didn't appreciate knowing that their rituals were unnecessary. It was easier to listen to the priests and to buy forgiveness with works than to change their lives and stop sinning. However, others welcomed what Zwingli said and went back home to share the good news with family and friends. As a result of Zwingli's work, fewer pilgrims came to visit his convent, resulting in fewer offerings and less income for him. But he didn't mind because the truth was more important.

After three years in the convent, Zwingli was called to serve at the cathedral in

Zürich. The priests there told him to do everything he could to increase money coming into the church, especially from the poor and sick, and not to bother much with ministering to people who weren't wealthy or powerful. Zwingli told them, "I am committed to preaching the whole gospel, especially the life of Christ, what He has done for us, and that salvation is free and cannot be bought." The church dignitaries didn't like that because it would cost them money, but Zwingli would not change. He continued telling people that the Bible was the supreme authority, not the pope, and his message was spreading like wildfire.

People from all walks of life, from scholars to peasants, listened to him, and their numbers increased. Many went home from church praising God, saying, "This is our Moses, to lead us out of the errors of the Catholic Church and into the truth."

That's when Satan really began to work. Eventually, the religious leaders started to openly oppose Zwingli's teachings, and Rome began to push the doctrine of forgiveness in exchange for money. An Italian Franciscan monk named Samson was in charge of the sale of indulgences in Switzerland. When he approached Zwingli's territory, he found that Zwingli's preaching against the practice had been so effective that he left without selling a single thing.

About this time, the plague swept through the country, and the reform made progress as people came face to face with death and realized that their religious forms held little meaning. Zwingli also became ill to the point of death, but he recovered and began preaching more powerfully than ever. The people flocked to hear this man of God preach Bible truths. This disruption alarmed the papists. They sent three representatives to the council at Zürich to accuse Zwingli of heresy and inciting insurrection against the church. The council decided not to punish Zwingli, so Rome scheduled another trial at Baden, which Zwingli did not attend. Two other representatives of the Reformation went in his place. Students delivered transcriptions of the meetings to Zwingli undercover, and he returned arguments for the Reformers to use.

The meeting continued for eighteen days, and at the end, the assembly condemned Zwingli and the Reformers. However, witnesses were swayed by the Reformers' powerful testimonies, and the cities of Bern and Basel took their stand for Zwingli and what he taught. This caused wars to break out between the different sections of Switzerland, and during one of them, Zwingli was killed.

Progress of Reform in Germany

Meanwhile in Germany, Luther's disappearance on the way home from the city of Worms caused the wildest rumors. Some believed that he was murdered, so they took an oath to avenge his death. Finally, the news reached them that he was safe, but officially a prisoner in the Wartburg castle. This both calmed them and sparked more interest in his case, which gave the Reformation momentum.

However, Satan was not sleeping. Soon, some men claiming to be prophets with divine revelations from heaven announced that they had come to carry on what Luther had started. One said he had been taught by the angel Gabriel. Many students at the universities were deceived. Many quit school and stopped studying the Bible. The Reformers didn't know what to do. When the papal priests saw this, they gained courage and said, "One last struggle, and we will win."

Luther, safe in the castle at Wartburg, heard about the new threat and was distressed. In a letter to Frederick, he told the emperor that he was going home to Wittenberg to take care of the problems.

When the news reached the people that Luther was back and would preach again, thousands came to hear him. Standing behind the pulpit, he spoke disapproving of the violent measures some were using trying to overthrow the presence and influence of the papacy in Germany. He said, "We must leave the matter in God's hands. If we were to use force, what would we gain? God can do more through His Word than we can through force."

Every day for a week, Luther preached from Scripture. Finally, God's word broke the hysterical spell over the people, and the false prophets left Wittenberg. For several years, the radicals remained in check before returning in force.

A man named Thomas Münzer was one of the most active fanatics. He taught that taking the Bible alone as authority was like the papal system, and that religious things must be given by God through impressions to certain special men, such as himself. Others blamed Luther and the Reformation for the fanatics' behavior. Luther had to defend the truth, which he did by holding up the Scriptures as an unquestionable authority.

People rejoiced when Luther finally finished and distributed his German translation of the New Testament. The Catholic priests did their best to stop its circulation, but it didn't work. Inspired by the warm reception of the New Testament, Luther began translating the Old Testament into German and published it in parts as fast as he could. People of every type and background read the Scriptures eagerly. Teachers in the village schools read them to their students. The Bible changed the hearts and minds of people. Women, children, and uneducated people knew more about the Bible than did the priests and Catholic scholars.

> To protect liberty of conscience is the duty of the state, and this is the limit of its authority in matters of religion. Every secular government that attempts to regulate or enforce religious observances by civil authority is sacrificing the very principle for which the evangelical Christian so nobly struggled.
> —*The Great Controversy*, 201

The attendance in the Catholic churches began to drop, and the priests appealed to the government to do something. Soon, persecution broke out against those who believed in Scripture, and thousands were killed, but the truth continued to spread in spite of the risks.

Protest of the Princes
The Christian princes in Germany attended a meeting in Spires in 1529. At the meeting, organized to address the issue of heresy against the Catholic Church, the priests insisted that the territories that had embraced the Reformation must fall into line with Rome. However, the princes, called Protestants because they protested against Rome telling people what to believe, weren't willing to turn their backs on God. Eventually, the council adopted a proposal that, if the Protestants would stop proselytizing, they could keep their faith, but it would not be allowed to take hold anywhere else. On faith, the princes boldly rejected this proposal.

> In our time there is a wide departure from their [the Scriptures] doctrines and precepts, and there is need of a return to the great Protestant principle—the Bible, and the Bible only, as the rule of faith and duty.—*The Great Controversy*, 204, 205

The government saw the different areas in Germany where Protestants lived as a threat to the unity of the country. The Reformers acknowledged an Authority higher than the country, yet they promised to be good citizens to maintain peace and security. Had the Reformers consented to compromise their faith in order to keep peace with the government, they would have been untrue to God and to themselves. The Reformation would have eventually failed.

A year later, the emperor Charles V called a meeting where the evangelical princes could further present their case. In the meantime, Frederick of Saxony, who was Luther's friend and protector, died, and his brother John took over. He, too, supported the Reformation.

The meeting at Augsburg was intended to settle the issue once and for all. The princes decided to bring a written statement of their faith, including scriptural support, to the meeting. They asked Luther and his associates to write it, which they did. Luther traveled with them part way and strengthened their faith by singing the hymn he wrote, "A mighty fortress is our God, a bulwark never failing."

At the meeting, the emperor sat on his throne, surrounded by princes and other dignitaries. The Protestants stood before the emperor and read their statement. This turned out to be one of the greatest days of the Reformation. A papist bishop at the meeting admitted that all the evidence was truth from Scripture and that the Catholic traditions' authority came from man and not the Bible. Many of the yet unconverted princes who heard the testimony accepted the truth.

While Luther was not allowed to attend the meeting, he was overjoyed at how it turned out. However, when it was suggested that the Protestant territories form a military alliance to defend the faith, he warned them against using government force to defend religion. He believed that every person must choose a position on the Bible and be willing to hold to it, even at the risk of his own life.

The power of the Reformation came from prayer. During the meeting at Augsburg, Luther had devoted three hours a day to pray. In the privacy of his room, he poured out his prayers to God in adoration, praise, and hope and talked to Him as to a friend.

The French Reformation

In France, before Luther's name had become synonymous with the Reformation, an old papist professor at the University of Paris named Lefèvre began studying the Bible to learn more about the saints. In Scripture, he found a very different picture of the saints, God, and faith than that which he'd learned from the Catholic Church. As he studied, he shared his findings with his students. One young student named William Farel, who had been a devout Catholic, eagerly accepted that salvation was by God's grace and not by our own works. He joined others and together they spread the truth throughout France. Even the sister of the king of France accepted the Reformed faith.

In the meantime, Lefèvre began translating the New Testament into French. His translation was published about the same time as was Luther's German Bible. No expense was spared to spread the Scriptures among the people who were glad to have copies in their own language. People everywhere praised the Lord for such a treasure. Instead of going to the bars to drink after work, they would assemble in each other's homes for study and prayer. Every day the number of converts increased.

The rapid expansion of the gospel infuriated the papists, and soon persecution broke out in Paris. Many Reformers were tormented and killed. The news of this happening in France shocked the believers in Germany, but even so, the truth continued to spread.

In one of the universities in Paris, a young man named John Calvin, who was the pride of the school, heard about the teachings of the Reformers and compared them with the teachings of the Catholic Church. One day, his cousin, a Reformer, explained that there are only two kinds of religion: one made by man, one made by God.

One day, Calvin visited the city square and saw a Reformer being burned at the stake. He was struck by the peaceful expression on the man's face. Calvin decided to study the Scriptures more deeply, and as he did so, he found that Jesus and gave his heart to Him. He quietly abandoned his plan to become a priest and devoted himself to sharing the gospel. He left Paris to take the truth to other cities. Princess Margaret, who loved the gospel, did all she could to protect young Calvin as he shared about the grace of Christ in people's homes.

After a while, Calvin went back to Paris, where he shared the truth from house to house. Then, when the king was out of town, Princess Margaret invited Calvin and other Reformers to speak at the palace every day. She invited people of every rank, including political leaders, nobles, lawyers, and business owners. Thousands crammed into the small chapel. Seeing the success of the endeavor, the king also opened a couple of churches in the city to continue the meetings. For two years, the palace hosted the sharing of the gospel message, and a revival spread throughout the city.

However, the papacy was not idle. They played to the people's superstitions and fears and turned many against the gospel. When it looked like it no longer served him, King Francis closed the churches. When Calvin was in Paris, studying and preparing himself for a larger ministry, the Catholics made plans to arrest him and burn him at the stake. His friends heard about it and rushed to Calvin's apartment to warn him. Just then they heard a knock on the door. A few friends went outside to talk to the officers who had come to arrest him while others helped him escape through a back window. He made his way out of the city where he found a farmer who was a friend of the Reformation. To disguise himself, Calvin put on his friend's farm clothes and carried a hoe. Then he headed south to the area controlled by Princess Margaret. He stayed there to study for a couple of months before moving on to Poitiers, a few hundred miles southwest of Paris. There, he preached in the privacy of homes to anyone who wanted to listen. When the crowds got too big, they found a cave in a gorge outside the city to establish the church.

Eventually, Calvin returned to Paris, but, finding every door closed, he traveled on to Germany. It's good that he left when he did, because the French Reformers became too eager for the movement in France keep pace with the Reformation in Germany and Switzerland. So one night, they posted signs all over France, including on the king's private door, condemning the Catholic Church. This enraged the king, and instead of advancing the faith, it brought condemnation on the Protestant believers. He vowed to execute all Lutherans. A Judas, willing to trade his faith to avoid the stake, agreed to identify every Lutheran believer. They went from house to house, dragging out entire families and burning them at the stake in the following days. With this, France rejected Christ and began its Reign of Terror.

The Jesuit order began working toward overthrowing Protestantism and firmly establishing the pope's power all over Europe. To enhance their power to do this, the pope started the Inquisition, a powerful office inside the Church that gave permission to search for Protestants, considered to be heretics, and kill them. Over the years, thousands were killed in many countries. These years are known as the Dark Ages.

Switzerland became a refuge for Calvin and many of the Reformers. When they came to the city of Geneva, they received a warm welcome and were accepted as if they were citizens. Eventually many returned to their own countries, including England, Scotland, Holland, and France to help spread the truth.

The Netherlands and Scandinavia
In Holland, a priest named Menno Simons, who was educated in Catholic schools, at first refused to read the Bible for fear that he would be tricked into heresy. He finally decided to read the New Testament and then progressed to Luther's writings. Soon afterward, he saw a man who had been baptized into the Reformed faith being beheaded in a neighboring village. This led him to search Scripture for information about baptism. Baby baptism, which the Catholic Church practiced, was not in the Bible. When he couldn't reconcile the Church's teachings with the Bible, he left the Catholic Church and began teaching what he found in Scripture.

Simons traveled throughout Holland and nearby Germany with his wife and children for twenty-five years preaching the truth. Many people were converted and baptized. Soon persecution broke out, and those who refused to bow before the statue of Mary and pray to her were condemned to death. Thousands perished; men were killed by the sword, and women were buried alive. Even though young men and women saw all this, they met persecution with unflinching courage.

In spite of persecutions, students at Wittenberg in Germany took the Reformed faith to countries to the north, including Denmark, Norway, and Sweden. A young man named Tausen lived with his parents in Denmark. He was a good student and went to a monastery to become a priest, but then he decided to get more education. He left the monastery and went to Cologne, where he enjoyed studying the teachings and writings of Luther before transferring to the University of Wittenberg.

When he returned home to Denmark, Tausen went back to the monastery. At first, he didn't say much about his new faith, but then he started sharing it with his friends.

> In a loathsome dungeon crowded with profligates and felons, John Bunyan breathed the very atmosphere of heaven; and there he wrote his wonderful allegory of the pilgrim's journey from the land of destruction to the celestial city. For over two hundred years that voice from Bedford jail has spoken with thrilling power to the hearts of men. Bunyan's *Pilgrim's Progress* and *Grace Abounding to the Chief of Sinners* have guided many feet into the path of life.
> —*The Great Controversy*, 252

When the prior heard what he was teaching, he sent him to another monastery and instructed that he be kept in a cell. He continued teaching those around him, and several of the young monks accepted his faith and took their stand with him. Eventually, he was kicked out of the monastery, so he preached the Word of God in the churches that welcomed him, and soon others began preaching the truth.

In Sweden, several young men who had heard the truth at Wittenberg came home and began sharing what they had learned. Two brothers, Olaf and Laurentius Petri, sons of a blacksmith, preached the truth with unflinching courage. The Catholic priests worked constantly to turn the people against them, and on several occasions, they barely escaped the attacks of the mobs. However, the king protected them because he liked the idea of a revival of faith. On one occasion, Olaf stood before the king and defended the teachings of the Bible in simple and clear language. He said that the Bible, and the Bible only, was the rule of faith. The king of Sweden accepted the Protestant faith, and soon the national assembly voted to do the same thing.

Olaf had translated the New Testament into the Swedish language, and, at the king's request, the two brothers translated the whole Bible into Swedish. The truth went everywhere, and Sweden became one of the strongholds of Protestantism.

> At a meeting of the Moravian society in London a statement was read from Luther, describing the change which the Spirit of God works in the heart of the believer. As [John] Wesley listened, faith was kindled in his soul. "I felt my heart strangely warmed," he says. "I felt I did trust in Christ, Christ alone, for salvation: and an assurance was given me, that He had taken away *my* sins, even *mine*, and saved *me* from the law of sin and death."
> —*The Great Controversy*, 256

Later English Reformers

What Luther did in Germany, Tyndale determined to do in England. He preached fearlessly, telling the people that all doctrines must be tested by Scripture. The priests claimed that only the Catholic Church could interpret the Bible correctly. Tyndale continued preaching while the priests did all they could to destroy his influence.

In a discussion with Tyndale, a Catholic professor said, "It is better to be without the Bible and God's laws than to abandon the pope's laws." Tyndale responded: "I reject the pope and his laws and stand on the Bible and God's law. If God allows me to live long enough, I will help even simple fieldworkers to know more about the Bible

THE GREAT WAR

than you do." Then he did all he could to make this come true. He printed the New Testament in English and began circulating it. When he became blocked in one place, he would move to another. This is how knowledge of the Scriptures spread throughout England.

One time, the bishop of Durham went to a bookstore to buy the whole stock of Bibles and burned them. His intention backfired, though, because with the money, the bookseller printed a new and larger edition of the Bible. Soon after, Tyndale was arrested and promised release if he would tell who helped him finance the new printing. He told them that the money had come from the bishop, who had purchased all the Bibles. He was released but soon arrested again. Tyndale spent many months in prison and was ultimately condemned to a martyr's death.

Others continued to defend the truth and to fight for people's right to read the Bible. They pointed out that God is the Author of Scripture and that no other earthly ruler has the right to say otherwise. No one has a right to control another's conscience.

Columba and his friends preached the truth in Scotland, and those visiting from England did all they could to help them. Scotland clung to its freedom for hundreds of years after England pledged itself to Rome. The writings of the Reformers quietly slipped in, lighting the fire of faith. However, when the papists realized what was happening, persecution began and many people, including nobles, were martyred. Their blood gave still greater impetus to the truth.

A man named John Knox turned away from Catholicism and joined the Reformers. He was urged by his friends to become a preacher. At first he hesitated, but after days of study and prayer, he agreed. Once he committed, he preached the truth with power. One time, when he stood before Mary, the queen of Scotland, on a charge of heresy, he bore witness to the truth. Without hesitation he said, "True religion does not get its authority from earthly rulers, but from the God of heaven through the Scriptures. What would have happened if the Israelites had adopted Pharaoh's religion or if the apostles had adopted the religion of

> The infidel Voltaire once boastingly said: "I am weary of hearing people repeat that twelve men established the Christian religion. I will prove that one man may suffice to overthrow it." Generations have passed since his death. Millions have joined in the war upon the Bible. But it is so far from being destroyed, that where there were a hundred in Voltaire's time, there are now ten thousand, yes, a hundred thousand copies of the book of God.
> —*The Great Controversy*, 288

the Roman emperors? Your Highness, study the Bible for yourself. The Bible is plain and clear, and the Holy Spirit will help you." Knox continued to fight until Scotland was rid of papal control.

In England, the pope and his teachings had been rejected, and the teachings of Protestantism became the national religion. However, the queen took the pope's role, and those who did not observe the official form of Protestantism were persecuted. Many Reformers wrote powerful books from England's dungeons, including John Bunyan, whose well-known book, *Pilgrim's Progress*, has inspired generations.

Others left England, some traveling to America, where they laid the foundations of civil and religious liberty. The two Wesley brothers, John and Charles, were sincere seekers of truth, but they struggled to accept that they could not become holy by their own efforts. Faith in Christ's sacrifice alone was a difficult concept for them to accept. The brothers were ordained to the ministry and went as missionaries to America. Aboard their ship, they met a group of Moravians who had complete peace, even during some violent storms. When the ship finally docked in Savannah, Georgia, the Wesley brothers decided to get off, too, and stay with the Moravians to learn more about their faith. When they returned to England, they studied with a Moravian preacher and fully accepted that we are saved by grace through faith in Christ alone. This led the brothers to preach more and more about Jesus. As a result, many people gave their hearts to Christ and followed the faith of the Wesleys. This group became known as Methodists, and they were persecuted by the Church of England.

> The coming of the Lord has been in all ages the hope of His true followers. The Saviour's parting promise upon Olivet, that He would come again, lighted up the future for His disciples, filling their hearts with joy and hope that sorrow could not quench nor trials dim.
> —*The Great Controversy*, 302

Antinomian theology was one of the biggest challenges to the gospel in England. Some taught that Christ did away with the Ten Commandments, and that Christians were no longer required to keep them. They also taught that the religious elect were not required to keep the law of God because nothing they did would be considered a sin. Wesley continued to preach that Christ had not destroyed the law of God, and that the law and the gospel of grace are perfectly paired.

The Bible and the French Revolution

In France, the war against the Bible by the papacy had been going on for years. The French Revolution was the result. A French army under Napoleon's command invaded

THE GREAT WAR

Italy and captured the pope, who soon died. Even though a new pope was eventually elected, the Catholic Church was never quite as powerful as it had been before.

The Bible was like two witnesses (Old and New Testaments) that continued to speak for God in spite of the Catholic Church trying to hide the truth from the people. Those who learned the truth and dared to share it with others were still enduring persecution and martyrdom. In addition to opposing the full authority of Scripture, Satan attacked the truth by coming up with all kinds of ideas and diversions of belief.

Few true Christians remained in France during the eighteenth century. Those who held to Scripture were killed or sent as slaves to work as oarsmen on ships for life like common criminals. Hundreds were killed in their churches and their bodies left there. One night, the king of France, urged by the papists, issued an edict against the Christians. Beginning in the middle of the night as everyone slept, soldiers dragged thousands of Protestants from their homes and murdered them in the streets in cold blood. This went on for a week in the city and for two months in all of the French territories under its control. When the pope learned about the massacre, all the clergy and leaders celebrated with great revelry. They even created a medal to remember what was called the St. Bartholomew Massacre.

Satan led France into atheism, the belief that there is no God. The National Assembly outlawed worshiping God, burned Bibles, and exalted human reason. At one convention, the speaker for the day brought a young woman up front and presented her to the people as the Goddess of Reason, the only acceptable object of worship in France. During this Reign of Terror, when multitudes were killed for their faith in God, the atheists turned on the Catholic clergy and killed them too. Three and a half years after it outlawed the Bible, the same assembly rescinded that law because the devastation in France made it painfully clear that faith in God is the foundation of an orderly society.

The atheist Voltaire once said that it would only take one man to overthrow the Christian religion. However, the Bible declares its own longevity (Isaiah 54:17). Many

> Unless the church will follow on in His opening providence, accepting every ray of light, performing every duty which may be revealed, religion will inevitably degenerate into the observance of forms, and the spirit of vital godliness will disappear. This truth has been repeatedly illustrated in the history of the church. God requires of His people works of faith and obedience corresponding to the blessings and privileges bestowed.
> —*The Great Controversy*, 316

have tried to squash the Word of God and His followers, but He always sustains the truth.

> The proclamation of Christ's coming should now be, as when made by the angels to the shepherds of Bethlehem, good tidings of great joy. Those who really love the Saviour cannot but hail with gladness the announcement founded upon the word of God that He in whom their hopes of eternal life are centered is coming again, not to be insulted, despised, and rejected, as at His first advent, but in power and glory, to redeem His people.
> —*The Great Controversy*, 339, 340

The Pilgrim Father

In the early seventeenth century, the new monarch in England demanded that everyone be loyal to the church in England. Rather than compromising their faith, some decided to leave and go to Holland. These Puritans left everything they had behind, so in Holland they had to develop new skills and find new jobs. These were hard times, but the Puritans were glad for the freedom to worship God as they chose. They got together and committed themselves to the principles of Protestantism. Their pastor in England, John Robinson, had not been able to go with them. In his farewell address, he said, "I'm not sure that I will see your faces again. But if God will reveal additional truth to you from Scripture, be sure to accept it."

Others fleeing religious tyranny in England decided to go to America instead of Holland. However, while they rejected Rome's intolerance, they were not always tolerant toward others. About a decade later, Roger Williams came to the American colonies and began teaching the importance of religious freedom. Though he was a beloved minister, he was finally banished and forced to flee to the forest. He later said, "For months, I had no bed or bread, but I found shelter in the hollow of a big tree, and the ravens brought me food." He eventually found and befriended a Native American tribe with whom he sheltered for some months. Finally, Williams traveled to the shore of Narragansett Bay and established Rhode Island, a state with civil and religious liberty.

Pilgrims who settled in the colonies used the Bible as the foundation of their faith. Biblical principles were taught in the home, in the school, and in the church. Its influence was clear. But eventually, as in Europe, the principles of the Reformation began dying out as people arrived who weren't interested in living Christian lives. Satan had changed his strategy from persecuting Christians back to leading them to worldliness.

Heralds of the Morning

One of the most wonderful truths in the Bible is the promise of the second coming of Christ. For centuries, believers have held on to this promise. The patriarch Job said, "I know that my Redeemer lives, that He will return, and that I will see God with my own eyes."

Isaiah said, "Wake up and sing, the time is coming when the dead will live again, and they will say, 'This is our God, we have waited for Him, and He will resurrect us and we will rejoice forever.' "

Jesus said, "Don't let your heart fret, and don't be afraid. There are many mansions in My Father's house. I am going to prepare one for you, and then I will come back to take you there with me."

As Jesus ascended, the angels said to the disciples, "Jesus will come back down the same way He went up." Paul said, "The Lord will descend from heaven." And the apostle John said, "He will come with clouds, and everyone will see Him coming."

Luther said, "God will not let this wicked world go on forever." Calvin said, "The coming of Christ is desired more than anything else." John Knox said, "We know that He will return." Ridley and Latimer and others who gave their lives for the truth looked forward to the coming of Christ.

Jesus said, "There will be signs in the sky and on earth to let you know that I'm coming soon. There will also be disasters, earthquakes, hurricanes, and huge wars just before I come. When you see these things, you'll know it's almost time." Many of these signs have already occurred.

Sadly, faith in Jesus' second coming has grown cold because people are absorbed with the things of the world. Making money, seeking pleasure, finding popularity, and securing power occupy our mental energies. Instead, we should be immersing ourselves in sharing the good news of Jesus with everyone we can so that they, too, will give Him glory.

> Men are instruments in the hand of God, employed by Him to accomplish His purposes of grace and mercy. Each has his part to act; to each is granted a measure of light, adapted to the necessities of his time, and sufficient to enable him to perform the work which God has given him to do.
> —*The Great Controversy*, 343

An American Reformer

In America, William Miller was a farmer, physically strong with exceptional intellect. His father had been an army captain during the Revolutionary war for independence.

The whole family supported freedom. William loved to learn and was a very careful student.

In his young adulthood, he associated with deists whose moral code was shaped largely by their Christian culture but who didn't take the Bible seriously. The Holy Spirit impressed Miller that he needed a closer walk with Christ. He felt no assurance of life beyond the grave. He said, "The more I thought about it, the more confused I became. I was miserable." Fortunately, he continued studying and found the answer in Christ. He gave his heart to Jesus and began to share his new faith with others. His skeptical friends brought up all the arguments that he had used against the reliability of Scripture, so he continued studying, comparing verse with verse. He was especially interested in the prophecies in Daniel and Revelation. He found that these books clearly spoke about the second coming of Christ, the resurrection of the dead, and the gift of immortality.

Miller wondered, "When will Jesus come back?" He studied the prophecies more carefully and found in Daniel 8 a prophecy that seemed to answer his question. He wanted to know when it began and when it would end. Using calculations based on prophetic time, he decided that it would end in 1844. This made him excited, because it meant Jesus would come very soon! He began sharing this news with others, and they, too, got excited about Jesus' soon return. The doors of all denominations opened to him. The Baptist church even gave him a license to preach. He could hardly keep up with the requests and demands.

Of course, there were critics who questioned Miller and refused to believe that the end of the world was near. The same thing happened in the days of Noah when he said that it would rain and flood the world. The people didn't believe it, but the flood did come.

Why was the second coming of Christ so unbelievable and so unwelcome? Ministers were saying that the prophecies of Daniel and Revelation were mysteries that no one could understand. Yet Christ Himself had told the people to study the prophecies.

Light Through Darkness

God calls men to preach the gospel, including the promise of the second coming. No one called to work for God perfectly understands the plan of redemption and his or her own part in such a calling. Even the prophets in the Old Testament did not fully understand all the purposes that God had in mind for them. And that's OK, because God knows the beginning from the end.

When Christ came, the disciples thought He would set up His kingdom. How shocked they were when they saw their Master arrested, beaten, and crucified. They could hardly believe that He was dead, even when they saw His body in the tomb. They didn't realize that God's promise of salvation through Jesus had been fulfilled.

THE GREAT WAR

After His resurrection, Jesus appeared as an ordinary man to two of His disciples as they walked from Jerusalem to the little town of Emmaus. They had not heard about His resurrection. Jesus asked why they were so sad, and they told Him about their Master's crucifixion. He explained to them that the prophecies had said He would be crucified, buried, and resurrected. Jesus wanted them to put their faith in Scripture. When they put it all together, the two disciples got so surprised and excited that they rushed back to Jerusalem and told the other disciples everything that had happened. Suddenly, Jesus appeared among them, and they saw for themselves the scars in His hands and feet.

Just like the disciples didn't really understand that Jesus would be resurrected literally, William Miller and his associates had a hard time understanding the biblical prophecy about the soon coming of Christ. Because the accepted theology in that era held that the earth was the sanctuary, Miller believed that at the end of the 1,260 day-year prophecy the earth would end and Jesus would cleanse it with fire. However, the sanctuary was actually a symbol for Christ to begin His end-time work in the heavenly sanctuary. The people didn't understand that Christ had to complete His final work in heaven before He can come to earth.

Because Miller believed that Christ would come back in 1844, there was a great disappointment when He didn't arrive. Some gave up their belief in the Second Coming, while others prayed and tried to understand where they had gone wrong in their Bible research.

> He who deliberately stifles his convictions of duty because it interferes with his inclinations will finally lose the power to distinguish between truth and error. The understanding becomes darkened, the conscience callous, the heart hardened, and the soul is separated from God.
> —*The Great Controversy*, 378

A Great Religious Awakening

Like Luther's preaching, which brought about the Reformation, Miller's preaching brought about the Advent movement, the firm belief in the second coming of Christ. People began studying the scriptures to learn more.

In Germany, a young man named Joseph Wolff belonged to a family of Jews. His father was a rabbi. When Joseph was about seven years old, he heard about Jesus and wanted to learn more about Him. A Christian neighbor suggested that he read the prophecy of Isaiah 53. When he asked his father about it, his father didn't want to discuss it. This only increased little Joseph's interest. When he was a teenager, he decided to leave home to continue his education elsewhere. Under the influence of a

Catholic professor, he accepted the Roman Catholic faith.

As Wolff continued to study, he believed that, as Miller had said, the return of the Lord was not far away. His theology ultimately led him away from the Roman Catholic Church and he accepted Protestantism. Wolff wanted to share the good news of Christ's second coming with others. When he came to the United States, he preached the Second Coming in Philadelphia, Baltimore, and Washington. On the invitation of President John Quincy Adams, he gave a lecture to the members of Congress.

He also traveled extensively throughout Africa, Asia, Syria, Egypt, and Palestine. He preached in some dangerous countries and was often attacked by robbers, starved, beaten, and once left to travel hundreds of miles through mountain snow on bare feet. Holding on to his Bible, he felt that he was prepared to face anything.

In South America, a Jesuit priest studied the Bible and accepted the truth of Christ's soon return. He wrote books about it under an assumed name to avoid agitating the papacy. In Germany, Bengel, a Lutheran minister and Bible scholar, began studying the prophecies and also accepted the truth about the soon return of Christ. His preaching attracted attention, and his messages spread to German-speaking churches in other countries.

Gaussen preached the message of the second coming of Christ in Geneva, Switzerland, and soon the truth spread to France. He focused first on evangelizing children because their interest would draw the adults. Then he decided to write out his Bible lessons and publish them, and his books were circulated everywhere.

In Norway and Sweden, the state church opposed the message of the soon coming of Christ. Those who preached were often sent to prison. However, the little children, moved by God, started preaching the second coming of Christ. Because of their age, the state churches could not use force or the threat of prison to stop them. The hearts of the people were touched, and many began searching the Scriptures for themselves. As they studied, the message of the soon coming of Christ took hold, their lives were changed, and they began sharing the good news with others.

All classes of people came to the Advent meetings eager to hear the message of the

> When the sons of God come to present themselves before the Lord, Satan comes also among them. In every revival he is ready to bring in those who are unsanctified in heart and unbalanced in mind. When these have accepted some points of truth, and gained a place with believers, he works through them to introduce theories that will deceive the unwary.
> —*The Great Controversy*, 395, 396

Second Coming. Every day more people became believers. Unfortunately, many lost friends and family and were barred from their own churches.

Those who had looked for His return with faith and deep love for their Savior were bitterly disappointed when He didn't come in 1844. The prophetic calculations had been correct, but the event they were expecting wasn't the right one.

A Warning Rejected

In his day, William Miller's purpose was to prepare men and women for the coming of Christ. He assumed that all Christians would be happy to know that Christ's return was imminent, and that they would prepare their hearts to meet Him. However, as the years went by, ministers and leaders of various churches turned against the doctrine and forbade their members to attend events on the topic. Many decided that their loyalty to God was a priority and refused to listen to their church leaders, resulting in about fifty thousand believers separating from their churches in 1844.

One purpose of the message of the soon coming of Christ was to separate people from the influence of the world, creating the togetherness and unity among believers for which Christ prayed. However, the churches were experiencing a general decline in authentic faith and an increase in worldliness, which weakened the spiritual condition in the church.

> As anciently the sins of the people were by faith placed upon the sin offering and through its blood transferred, in figure, to the earthly sanctuary, so in the new covenant the sins of the repentant are by faith placed upon Christ and transferred, in fact, to the heavenly sanctuary.
> —*The Great Controversy*, 421

In this age, professing religion is popular. Politicians, lawyers, professors, and business people join churches as a way of getting the respect and confidence of the people. However, their hearts are not converted, and the ministers' sermons do not confront the sins of the people.

The Bible says that Satan will continue to work to make people believe all kinds of wrong things and to distract them from the truth. A great number of Christ's true followers are still in other churches. They're longing and praying for Christ to come, and they will respond to God's call, "Come out of the false churches, My people."

Prophecies Fulfilled

When Christ did not come as expected, the people began searching the Scriptures again. They knew the Bible wasn't wrong, so they must have misinterpreted its meaning. They had faith that the Holy Spirit would makes the truth clear in time.

Most of the people believed God knew everything about their disappointment, so they continued to hold fast to Scripture. The parable of the ten virgins in Matthew 25 helped them. Those bridesmaids were waiting for the bridegroom to come to the marriage, but there was a delay. While they waited, they all fell asleep, some in expectant rest with plenty of oil in their lamps, others in hopeless exhaustion with no more fuel for their lights. After some hours, the bridegroom finally came. Those whose lamps still burned bright got up and followed the bridegroom to the wedding. Those whose lamps had burned out hurried to buy oil, but when they finally arrived at the wedding venue, it was too late. The door was locked.

> Had the Sabbath been universally kept, man's thoughts and affections would have been led to the Creator as the object of reverence and worship, and there would never have been an idolater, an atheist, or an infidel.
> —*The Great Controversy*, 438

The closer the time came for the Advent believers to meet their Lord, the more time they spent with God in prayer, asking for His blessings and praying for each other. Satan was busy too. He drew the believers in fanaticism and blind zeal, then zealously pointed out the defects of God's people. It was the same in Paul's day and in the days of the Reformation. To combat fanaticism, Miller spoke out against believing any doctrines that couldn't be proved in Scripture.

When Christ did not come as expected, first in the spring of 1844 and then again on the revised date that fall, the world expected the whole Advent movement to collapse. While some gave up their faith, many stood firm. They did not dare to go against what the Scriptures taught or against the power of the Holy Spirit, who attended the preaching of the Second Coming. They stood firm against the criticisms of the people and the most powerful religious teachers and preachers. Ultimately, Miller said, "If I were to live my life over again, I would believe and do as I have done."

God did not forsake His people. The only safe course was to hold on to God's promise, to continue to search the Scriptures, and to watch and wait patiently for the Lord to come.

What Is the Sanctuary?

The Scriptures have always been the focus of the Adventist faith. The name Adventist means to accept Christ's promise that He would come again. Miller and the other early Advent movement leaders expected Him to come in 1844, but that did not happen. Instead, Christ's end-time work in heaven began. When He finishes it, He will come.

In the Old Testament, perfect innocent lambs were sacrificed as a symbol and reminder that Christ would die to redeem humanity. Once a year, the high priest cleaned the blood, the sin, from the Most Holy Place in the sanctuary. So now, in heaven, Jesus, our High Priest, has begun the work of making sure that those who love Him are doing their best to obey Him. To redeem man, both love and justice are necessary. Christ proved His love when He died for our sins. Justice was served when He, who had never sinned, paid the price for us by dying a criminal's death.

In the Holy of Holies
The sanctuary doctrine shows God's hand in the Advent movement. God had told Moses how to build a sanctuary and how to administer the regular services. The daily service had to do with the forgiveness of sins and the yearly service with evaluations. This is what Christ's ministry in the heavenly sanctuary is all about.

Before Jesus comes, the wedding guests will be examined to make sure that they are ready and dressed for the wedding (see Matthew 22:11–13). In 1844, He began evaluating the heavenly records of history to determine who, by faith, had accepted the atonement of Jesus' blood, which covered humanity's sins with His righteousness. The Scriptures say He will come to pick up His bride—those who love Him and are faithfully waiting—and take her to heaven where the wedding will take place. New Jerusalem will be given to Him as a wedding present, and it will be the capital of His kingdom.

> Religion has become the sport of infidels and skeptics because so many who bear its name are ignorant of its principles. The power of godliness has well-nigh departed from many of the churches. Picnics, church theatricals, church fairs, fine houses, personal display, have banished thoughts of God. Lands and goods and worldly occupations engross the mind, and things of eternal interest receive hardly a passing notice.
>
> —*The Great Controversy*, 463, 464

God's Law Immutable
The two tablets of granite on which God had written the Ten Commandments and given to Moses were kept in the Most Holy Place of the sanctuary. They are now in the heavenly sanctuary, which demonstrates the unerring, unchanging, and unending nature of God's law.

What Daniel saw in vision reminds us that the Catholic Church changed the day of worship. He saw various animals representing different kingdoms. One kingdom that he saw had two little horns like a lamb. It was a gentle nation and provided freedom of conscience for its people. Soon it became a powerful nation and began to apply pressure on people to worship God on Sunday. This went along with the papal power in Rome, which changed the day of worship.

Eventually, all Christians and the whole world will have to decide on which day to worship God. Jesus said, "If you love Me, keep My commandments." This means all His commandments—including the fourth, which asks us to keep the Sabbath.

> The law of love being the foundation of the government of God, the happiness of all created beings depended upon their perfect accord with its great principles of righteousness. God desires from all His creatures the service of love—homage that springs from an intelligent appreciation of His character. He takes no pleasure in a forced allegiance, and to all He grants freedom of will, that they may render Him voluntary service.
> *—The Great Controversy*, 493

A Work of Reform

In the last days, the Sabbath will become an issue. People will say, "We have always kept Sunday, our parents and grandparents kept Sunday, and so have many others. To keep the Sabbath will split the family and disrupt society. Our church leaders know the Bible and don't see any reason for keeping the Sabbath. How can you be right and everyone else be wrong?"

People will say that keeping the Sabbath is not convenient. Christ never claimed that keeping the commandments would be convenient. Followers of Christ don't wait until obedience is convenient; they do what's right because it is right.

Modern Revival

Whenever the Word of God is preached faithfully, the Holy Spirit is there to help the message reach people's hearts and to bring conviction. Those who listen will repent and their lives will be changed. Of course, there will always be some whose repentance is not genuine and doesn't bring about real change. Their commitment to Christ lights up based on emotion or fear, then flickers for a little while and dies out.

There are genuine believers in all churches, and even outside the churches, and when they learn the truth, they will commit themselves to keep the Sabbath. Jesus said, "If you love Me, keep My commandments." Unfortunately, some accept the promise of salvation and join the church without uniting their hearts to Christ. True conversion brings people into harmony with God's law.

The Holy Spirit brings us to Christ and helps us to become like Him, living to please the Father. Some believers want to have an easy religion, one which requires no self-discipline and no separation from the things of this world. They say, "We are saved by grace, so we don't have to keep God's law. It was nailed to the cross." They forget that Jesus Himself said that He did not come to destroy the law but to fulfill it.

Those who have given their hearts to Christ are expected to do all they can to keep mentally and physically fit and to present their bodies as a living offering to God. Everything we do that damages our health makes us less able to serve Christ as we should. Our bodies are like a temple in which the Holy Spirit lives, and we need to take care of them.

God also wants us to remember to give Him our tithes and offerings, which is a symbolic act recognizing that everything we have comes from Him in the first place. Too often, the needs of the poor, hungry, and homeless are forgotten, or they receive our scraps and leftovers. This is not what God intends. In addition, the church must take the gospel to the world, and that mission requires support.

Facing Life's Record

Before Christ comes back, He will complete the evaluation of His people. The judgment of the wicked will take place later. He reviews the Book of Life, which has the names of all those who loved and served God. Every good deed, temptation resisted, evil overcome, and sacrifice made for Christ's sake is recorded.

Also recorded in heaven is every sin committed, lie told, and warning rejected. Next to the names of all who repented and by faith claimed Christ's sacrifice, the word "forgiven" is written. The forgiven are considered worthy of eternal life.

While Jesus is standing before God representing His people, Satan is calling them sinners, pointing to the record of their sins and the defects of their character. Jesus acknowledges their sins but points to their repentance and forgiveness. He then rebukes Satan, rejecting his accusations.

Everything has to be reviewed, including how we use our time, abilities, and money and to what extent we helped others and shared God's love. No value is attached to talk without action, and our secret motives are included in the record.

The judgment and evaluation that are now going on in the sanctuary in heaven have been going on for some time, but soon Christ's work will be done. He will come to take us home. So stay awake spiritually. Those who are half asleep, lost in worldly cares, will be caught off guard when He comes.

The Origin of Evil

To many, the origin of evil is a mystery. How can evil exist when God is in control of everything? Without the Bible, it is impossible to explain it. From the Scriptures, it is clear that God is not responsible for the entrance of sin. Before the entrance of evil in the universe, everything was peaceful and in perfect harmony.

Lucifer, the lead angel, became proud and thought, "One day, I will be as powerful as the Son of God and God Himself." The angels pleaded with him not to think that way, but he refused to change and pushed ahead.

Leaving his position by the throne of God, he went among the angels, telling them that God was not fair and had put restrictions on what they could and could not do. Lucifer told them that they were holy beings and could think for themselves, so they didn't have to listen to God. He suggested that they follow him instead, and he would give them greater freedom.

God knew everything that was going on and was very patient with Lucifer. If God had disciplined Lucifer right then, the angels would not have understood the deception. God talked with Lucifer, pointed out his problem, and offered to forgive him and let him keep his leadership position if he would repent and change. But Lucifer was convinced that he was right and accused Christ of trying to humiliate him.

Lucifer continued his work of undermining God until some of the angels decided to follow him and rebel against God. He thought that if he could get all the angels on his side, he would be able to get the worlds of the universe on his side too. At first, Lucifer's sin did not appear as wicked as it really was. At first, he made it look like his intention was to make the universe a better place. He said that changes in the laws of heaven were needed because God had created His law simply to exalt Himself.

Lucifer continued to justify himself and claimed that angels didn't need to be told what to do. They were smart enough to know what was right. One-third of the angels agreed. The other angels remained loyal to God and listened to Him, but because they had a hard time seeing what Lucifer was really up to, God had to let the situation play out. The whole universe could see it. To the very end of the controversy in heaven, Satan kept justifying himself, and together with his followers, threw the whole blame for their rebellion onto Christ. War broke out in heaven. God and his angels fought against Lucifer and his angels. Ultimately, Lucifer and the other rebellious angels were expelled from heaven.

At the end of all things, God will ask Lucifer, "Why did you rebel against Me?" He will have no answer and no excuse. As Jesus was dying on the cross, with his last breath He cried out, "It is finished!" This announced Christ's ultimate victory in Satan's war against God's character.

Enmity Between Man and Satan

After God and His Son created Adam and Eve, Satan decided to turn them against God. He began with Eve, Adam followed, and they both lost their right to live. Christ immediately stepped in and promised to take their place, giving them a chance to repent and live. And God said, "I will implant in people's hearts a hatred of evil and wickedness." When Adam and Eve sinned, their nature changed, which made them more likely to do whatever Satan suggested. That's why Jesus said that our spiritual nature has to be born again.

As he did in the beginning, Satan will try to control all who are not fully committed to Christ. He tempts them to become more like the world. Those who choose to associate with followers of Satan will soon lose their love and respect for Christ. Sin will seem less sinful, and wickedness will become more attractive. People who are refined and likable, who would never commit overtly evil deeds, can also turn others away from Christ simply by exalting what the world offers. Just because people are kind or smart doesn't mean they know Jesus.

Satan is trying to intrude in every household, on every street, in every city. And he's trying to intrude in churches, in the legal system, and through government actions. From the time of Adam, he has been doing this. So we need to be careful and not lose sight of Christ. The fact that Christ defeated Satan at Calvary should give His followers courage to stand up against evil and against Satan himself, and the Holy Spirit gives us the power to do so.

> Satan's enmity against the human race is kindled because, through Christ, they are the objects of God's love and mercy. He desires to thwart the divine plan for man's redemption, to cast dishonor upon God, by defacing and defiling His handiwork.
> —*The Great Controversy*, 506

Agency of Evil Spirits

Angels existed before the creation of man. Each follower of Christ has a guardian angel who is sent by the Father to help people. There are many such examples in the Bible. One time, Jesus pointed to some little children and explained to His disciples that each one of the little ones had a guardian angel.

Satan and his evil angels were especially active during the time of Christ. They knew that if Jesus' mission was successful, their own existence would end. Satan began to act like a roaring lion, showing the control he had over men and women. Being possessed by the devil was a real possibility and was recognized as such by Jesus. Once when Jesus and His disciples landed with their boat on the shore of Galilee, two demon-possessed men ran down the hill to attack Him. Jesus stood still, and with authority, commanded the evil spirits to come out of the men. Suddenly, the spirits left and the men calmed down and sat a Jesus' feet to listen to Him speak. Then He told them to go home and tell others what He had done for them, and they did. There are more examples like this in Scripture.

Those who deny the existence of Satan and evil angels are in greater danger of being influenced by them. Satan loves when people don't believe that he and evil angels exist because they're less likely to actively resist him. Especially as we approach the end of time, Satan will work hard to deceive people. We lock our houses and protect our property from those who might break in and steal, but we seldom think of protecting ourselves from Satan and his evil angels. There is help from Jesus, our Redeemer, Savior, and Friend.

> The discord and division which exist among the churches of Christendom are in a great measure due to the prevailing custom of wresting the Scriptures to support a favorite theory. Instead of carefully studying God's word with humility of heart to obtain a knowledge of His will, many seek only to discover something odd or original.
> —*The Great Controversy*, 520

Snares of Satan

The controversy between Christ and Satan, which has been going on for more than six thousand years, is almost over. Satan knows this, so he is making extra efforts against the gospel and the work of the Holy Spirit. Like a skillful general, he carries out his plans. When he sees men and women studying the Bible, he urges them to get involved in some kind of business transaction or something else instead—anything that totally absorbs their time. He also leads people into some form of self-gratification which dulls their desire for spiritual things. He diverts their minds with the good things of life or focuses them on the faults of others instead of on Christ. Satan knows that if people neglect prayer and Bible study, he can overcome them.

He likes when people join the church and then begin to raise doubts about what the church teaches. He loves to convince people that it doesn't really matter what they believe or don't believe. And he will lead those who read the Scriptures to grab a text, separate it from its context, and misuse or misinterpret it. We must approach Bible study with humble prayer and a teachable spirit, or any verse or message can be misunderstood.

Even the most intelligent minds can be led astray if they doubt the reliability of Scripture. Another dangerous error is to deny the divinity of Christ and His pre-existence and to simply see Him as a good, religious man.

God does not remove all opportunity for doubt. If He did, then faith would not be necessary. We also need to remember the importance of prayer, asking God for strength and courage to do what is right no matter what and to fill us with the power of the Holy Spirit.

The First Great Deception

Adam and Eve were perfectly happy obeying God, but Satan determined to turn them against God. Eve got into a discussion with Satan about God and ended up believing the lies he told about Him.

Adam and Eve were immortal as long as they were obedient. After they sinned, God did not discard them like trash. Instead, He gave them hope through Jesus. It is only through Him that immortality is made available again. Satan wants to destroy people today just like he did Adam and Eve by shaking their confidence in God's Word.

Satan likes when people think that God punishes the wicked with eternal torment. Many Christians believe this. On the other extreme, Satan leads some Christians to believe that God is love only, ignoring the fact that God is also just. The deceiver also works to make people believe that when they die, they go straight to heaven where they can watch over all that is happening here on earth, including what their family and friends are going through. If this were true, how could they enjoy heaven? The Bible says that when people die, they go to sleep until the resurrection.

Can Our Dead Speak to Us?

Satan has also created the lie that the spirits of dead people can communicate with the living. The Bible says that the dead don't know anything; death is like an unconscious sleep. However, Satan has the power to pray on people's emotions and fears by appearing as a departed loved one or friend. He can reproduce the look, the words, and the tone of family and friends with amazing accuracy, so people think what they see is real.

Satan and his angels can even impersonate the apostles and say that everything "they" wrote about Jesus in the Bible is not all true. This way, Satan can make people believe that the Bible can't be trusted.

God's people should not believe that any such appearances are real. Do not listen to what these demons have to say. We need to meet Satan as Jesus did when He confronted him with Scripture, "It is written."

Liberty of Conscience Threatened

Many today don't believe there is much difference between Catholics and Protestants. In one sense this is true, because there are real Christians in both churches. In spite of its impressive worship services and awe-inspiring churches, the Catholic religion requires that people confess their sins to a priest rather than to Christ. The pope claims to represent and speak for Christ, a concept completely contrary to Scripture. We also must never forget that in the past, during the time of papal supremacy, those who openly differed with the Catholic Church were tortured and killed. Today the Catholic Church apologizes for its history of cruelty and torture, but the teachings that justified it have not changed.

If the claim that there is very little difference between Protestants and Catholics is true, the change has been among Protestants, not Catholics. Protestants have gotten away from carefully studying Scripture and diligently seeking God's Word. Protestants have largely accepted the practice of keeping Sunday as a holy day, not realizing that there is no biblical authority for changing God's Sabbath as He established it in the Garden of Eden and later wrote it on the tablets of stone. But the time will come when the United States will enforce Sunday-keeping, which rests on the authority of Rome, and the whole world will follow her example. God's Word has warned us about this.

The Impending Conflict

Satan has been able to twist the teachings of Scripture and influence the faith of thousands who say they believe the Bible. The facts of Creation, the fall of man, the atonement made by Christ, and the importance of the law of God are rejected in part or in whole by those claiming to be Christians. They believe that it's a sign of intellectual weakness to believe the Bible.

Every country requires its citizens to obey certain laws. This is what civil government rests on, and this is also what the government of God rests on. Parents who refuse to obey the laws of the land are setting a bad example for their children, who grow up believing that laws aren't important. The same is true for parents who don't obey God.

Satan likes to destroy people's faith in the Bible, and it's more effective when he chips away at parts of it, ultimately undermining the whole Bible. This is the same with the law of God; to accept only part of it undermines all of it. Some preachers say that because Jesus died for us, keeping the whole law of God is not important. Many Christian leaders believe that making Christianity the official religion of the country and enforcing church attendance by law would make society better. They are working to align themselves with civil governments to make this a reality.

The time will come when the government will require everyone to keep Sunday holy. Those who refuse will be accused of being against God and country. Then liberty and freedom of conscience, which has cost so much, will no longer be a sacred tenet of society.

> There are real Christians in the Roman Catholic communion. Thousands in that church are serving God according to the best light they have. . . . [God] will cause rays of light to penetrate the dense darkness that surrounds them. He will reveal to them the truth as it is in Jesus, and many will yet take their position with His people.
> —*The Great Controversy*, 565

The Scriptures a Safeguard

The Bible exposes Satan's deceptions. It is the only safeguard against him and other false teachers. The end-time struggle between God and Satan is very near. Satan's counterfeits will seem so real that the difference can only be known through a careful study of the Scriptures. The Bible is the test of the preaching of pastors, the advice of bishops, and the teachings of professors of theology. Everyone should study the Bible for themselves with submission and prayer.

God's warnings are so important that in the Bible they are represented by three angels flying through the heavens, each with a message of warning. Many people choose to ignore these warnings. Many people are proud that they are "good people" and don't do anything wicked, but they forget to do what is good by helping those in need. We must apply all of the principles from God's Word to our lives, not just the ones that are convenient or popular.

Remember that the Sabbath is the test of our loyalty to God. When the laws are passed to enforce Sunday observance, the government will also pass a law against Sabbath-keeping. The faithful will respond, "Show us from the Bible that God changed His holy Sabbath to Sunday." Their obedience to God will be called stubbornness, and they will be threatened with imprisonment or worse. Those who were only half-hearted in obeying God will give up, but Christians from many churches will show their commitment to God and begin, or continue, to keep the Sabbath holy.

The Final Warning

A second angel will then be sent from heaven with a message for the world: "Christians, come out of the world and the fallen churches." This means that our focus must be on our relationship with God and serving His people here on earth. The Sabbath is, and will remain, the final test of loyalty to God.

As the civil authorities begin enforcing Sunday observance, the message of the importance of the Sabbath will be preached with great power by those empowered by the Holy Spirit. Thousands will listen to them who have never heard such powerful preaching before. As the message of the Sabbath goes around the world, Satan will stir things up by causing the enforcement of Sunday to spread around the world.

Those who are keeping the Sabbath will be threatened with fines and arrest if they don't change and start keeping Sunday. They may also be bribed and offered advantages and rewards if they switch. In every situation, the faithful will respond, "Show us from the Bible that Sunday is the day of worship." When these things are on the news, thousands will learn about the truth of the Sabbath who would not have otherwise known.

God's last messages will go to the whole world by the power and conviction of the Holy Spirit. And in spite of government actions against the truth, a large number of people will take their stand for the Lord.

The Time of Trouble

When the time of the end comes, Jesus will stop His intercession and announce: "Let the ones who have chosen wickedness stay wicked, and those that chose holiness stay holy." At this, every person's case in the heavenly record has been decided. When He stops His intercession and makes this announcement, the final troubles will begin.

Satan considers this world his, but the people who love God and keep His commandments reject this claim. Satan will blame Christians, who keep the Sabbath, for bringing the final troubles and disasters on the world, and the only solution is to kill these commandment-keepers. That's when our faith will really be tested.

Satan's crowning act of deception will be when he impersonates Christ Himself. He will look like Christ, his voice will be soft and gentle, and he will work what will appear to be miracles. When people see this, they will get excited and shout, "Christ has come! Christ has come!" This will be a powerful deception. Only those who have studied the Bible will not be deceived. They will not yield to what they see and hear and feel.

Will the Lord forget His people during this trying time? Can a mother forget her baby? Some mothers may, but Jesus said, "I have scars in My hands to show you how I love you and care for you, and I will not forget you." God will send angels to help them, and for their sake, He will cause this time to go quickly.

God's People Delivered

In various countries there will be a simultaneous movement to kill God's people. When the time comes for the decree to go into effect, groups of armed men around the world urged on by evil angels will plan to kill all the Christian commandment-keepers in one night. They rush ahead with their weapons, but God protects His people and their weapons fall useless to the ground.

Suddenly a deep blackness covers the whole earth and a glorious rainbow appears in the sky. God reveals His power and delivers His people. The mountains shake, huge ocean waves lash in fury, islands disappear, and huge hailstones begin to destroy cities. Prison doors are opened, the dead are raised, and as Jesus promised those who crucified Him, they too will be raised from the dead to see Him come. Satan and his angels tremble at the sight of Christ's power.

Then there appears in the sky a hand holding the two tablets of stone on which are written the Ten Commandments. Those who ignored God's law and did not give their hearts to Christ will be overcome with horror beyond imagination. Then God announces the coming of Christ, and Jesus comes as "King of kings and Lord of lords" with unnumbered angels. He looks on the graves of His people and calls, "Wake up, my children; come out of your graves and live!" His people come out of their graves young, healthy, and strong. Family members and friends separated by death are reunited forever.

Before taking His people into the City of God, Jesus places on each of their heads a sparkling crown, which is a sign of royalty. Then He opens the gates to let His people in, and they hear Him say, "The fight is over. Come and inherit the kingdom that My Father promised you." Then He presents the redeemed to the Father and says, "Here are those who have been redeemed."

As the redeemed are welcomed into the Holy City, they see Christ and Adam embrace each other, and a shout of praise fills the air. When Adam sees the nail marks in Jesus' hands, he falls on his knees and cries out, "Worthy, worthy is the Lamb that was slain!"

Desolation of the Earth
For six thousand years, the great controversy between good and evil raged on. At the return of Christ, the wicked die, the righteous are taken to heaven, and the earth is empty, much the way it was before Creation. Satan and his evil angels will have to live here alone for a thousand years.

Finally, it will be time for Christ to clean up the mess. Those who were not among the redeemed are still in their graves awaiting sentencing. Business people who were dishonest, pastors who did not preach the truth, people who didn't have the right relationship with God and keep His law, and every other non-repentant sinner in history will be judged.

For a thousand years, the righteous will have been in heaven, and together with Christ, reviewing the reasons that the lost are lost. Satan and his angels will be judged the same way. At the end of the thousand years, the wicked are raised from the dead to appear before God to receive their final sentence.

> Satan leads many to believe that God will overlook their unfaithfulness in the minor affairs of life; but the Lord shows in His dealings with Jacob that He will in no wise sanction or tolerate evil. All who endeavor to excuse or conceal their sins, and permit them to remain upon the books of heaven, unconfessed and unforgiven, will be overcome by Satan.
> —*The Great Controversy*, 620

The Controversy Ended
Christ and the righteous return to earth accompanied by angels. The wicked from all time are raised from the dead. It's now too late for them to repent. As the feet of Jesus touch the Mount of Olives from which He had ascended, the mountain splits and makes a place for the New Jerusalem to settle there.

When Satan sees all the wicked raised, including mighty commanders and generals with their armies, his hope for victory revives and he organizes them to attack and take the Holy City. As they advance, Christ commands the city gates to be closed. Then He appears above the city for everyone to see. The glory of the Father surrounds Jesus and floods the earth with His glory.

Next to the throne are people who were once on Satan's side but who gave their hearts to Christ and followed Him with deep devotion. Next, are those who kept the law of God and those who were martyred for their faith. Beyond that stand millions of people from all nations who gave their hearts to Christ. All of these people are dressed in white robes and singing praises to God. Then, with the redeemed and the lost all watching, the Son of God is crowned and invested with supreme authority and power.

The history of the world, beginning with the sin of Adam, is on display. The witnesses see the birth of Christ, His early life, His baptism, the temptations He had to face, His agony in Gethsemane, His condemnation by the Pharisees, His sentencing by Pilate, and His scourging and crucifixion. Satan and his angels and the wicked can't turn away. The wicked remember every sin they committed.

Satan stands frozen as he sees the glory and majesty of the Son of God. He also recognizes Gabriel, who took his place when he was expelled from heaven, and he watches him place the kingly crown on Jesus' head. The wicked realize that their case is hopeless, and with the fury of demons, they turn on Satan. Then the glory of God destroys Satan and his angels and all of the wicked. They are no more.

Free from the burdens of sin and mortality, the redeemed will spend eternity exploring all the secrets of the universe and learning more and more about the goodness of God and Christ. All of His creation will experience harmony and perfect joy forever and ever. Amen.